HYPOCRATIC
Oaths

A Doctor's Journey
of Redemption
from Broken
Promises

Gisela de Oliveira Esteves, MD

Published in 2021 by Gisela de Oliveira Esteves, MD
Copyright © 2021 Gisela de Oliveira Esteves, MD

ISBN: 978-0-620-92908-0

Photographer – Robert Harris @ Optical Noise Photography
Editor – Louise Stokes
Cover design by Monique Piscaer Bailey
www.artzoo.co.za
Typesetting by Gregg Davies Media
www.greggdavies.com

Gisela de Oliveira Esteves, MD has asserted her rights to be identified as the author of this work in accordance with the Copyright, Designs and Pattern Act 1998

All rights reserved. This book was printed in the Republic of South Africa.
No part of this publication may be reproduced, stored in a retrieval system or transmitted in any form or by any means, electronic, mechanical, photocopying, recording or otherwise without the written permission of the copyright owner.

*To my darling Lara
– may you always know your Truth and always follow your Light*

PROLOGUE
THE HIPPOCRATIC OATH

*"As a graduate of the University of the Witwatersrand, Johannesburg,
I do solemnly declare:
That I will exercise my profession to the best of my knowledge and ability for the safety and welfare of all persons entrusted to my care and for the health and well-being of the community.
That I will not knowingly or intentionally do anything or administer anything to them to their hurt or prejudice.
That I will not permit consideration of religion, nationality, race, politics, or social standing to intervene between my duty and my patient.
That I will not improperly divulge anything I have learned in my professional capacity.
That I will endeavour at all times to defend my professional independence against improper interference.
That I will not employ any secret method of treatment, nor keep secret from my colleagues any method of treatment that I may consider beneficial.
That in my relations with patients and colleagues, I will conduct myself as becomes a member of an honourable profession.
I make this declaration upon my honour."*

I swore into this Oath on 26th November 1996,
the day I became a Medical Doctor.

There has never been a greater false promise made.

CONTENTS

1. The Drop Off — 1
2. S.O.S — 9
3. God must be crazy — 27
4. Lend me a hand — 45
5. Conformation — 67
6. In the eye of the storm — 87
7. Miracles abound — 105
8. Resurrection — 129
9. Lifelines — 153
10. Cleanse and cross — 171
11. Omissions — 187
12. Breathe — 203
13. Heaven — 221
14. The Long Walk Home — 237
15. Surrender — 245
    Epilogue — 257

APPENDIX — 263
Acknowledgments — 267
About the Author — 271

1
THE DROP OFF

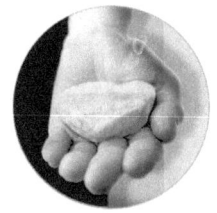

Sink or Swim

I have only ever associated "The Drop Off" with the animated movie *Finding Nemo*. It often brought precious memories of my two-year-old daughter jumping with delight in front of the CD player, insisting on watching it over and over again. Nine hundred and sixty-two times exactly. To this day, I can mutter every line in my sleep… "fish are friends, not food." This became a well-versed phrase in our house. When Nemo, the over-excited orange clownfish, went to Ocean School for the first time, his neurotic and anxious father warned him never to venture past the 'NO-GO' Drop Off zone. This was the demarcated area where the coral reef's protection ended, and the point of no return into the depths of a dark, dangerous ocean began. A single swim-stroke past the edge of the reef would lead to certain death. It was a place full of fear and monsters, where sharks lurked around every change of tide, ready to eat you alive in one single breath.

GISELA DE OLIVEIRA ESTEVES, MD

Never in a thousand years did I imagine that one day I would be the one leaning over the Drop Off, staring down at a bottomless, dark abyss. I realised another tiny step forward would throw me over the jagged, unforgiving edge to seal my fate for all of eternity. But this damnation would be worse than physical death. It would be purgatory in a hell that would forever prevent me from feeling an inkling of any joy, any pleasure, any love or, ever having any hope for anything at all. Emotional death was one of my grandest fears, second only to the thought of losing my child. Physical death would be a preferable relief. The fact that I was presently beyond suicidal ideations, catatonically numb and, wandering aimlessly through life was a sign that I was at the precipice of the Drop Off. And in serious trouble.

It is the Saturday morning of 22nd July 2017, when my husband brings his car to an idle outside Johannesburg's O.R. Tambo airport Drop Off zone. He walks around to the boot of our sedan in a perplexed state and hands over my travel duffle bag. We say our frigidly warm goodbyes, and I turn to hug the bravest teenager in the whole world, who is trying her damnedest not to let her lower lip quiver in sadness. I am boarding an aeroplane to Port Elizabeth to join a group of eleven strangers on a retreat for the next two weeks. Not the happy-clappy, fun-filled getaway variety, but rather a withdrawal into the unknown to try and find an answer, a solution, a miraculous way to walk away from that dreaded Drop Off.

As I watch an exhausted, pale-looking life partner and a very confused tearful daughter get back into the car, I walk away with a one-ton heart wrapped in a blanket of failure. The trolley carrying my bulging-at-the-seams Indlela tog bag, sleeping bag and pillow, is being pushed by autopilot but driven by utter madness. I remorsefully look back at the vehicle driving away with my most precious possessions, but it is already out of sight. By the time I reach the entrance door of the airport, I am out of breath, my heart is pounding in my ears, and the pit in my stomach is screaming, "What the fuck are you doing? You are not prepared for a 300-kilometre hike! You haven't hiked a day in your life, you idiot! You have just dumped the most important people in your life, left them confused and worried, to venture out into the wilderness, not even knowing what you are looking for!"

I am mad. Not yet psychotic, but insanely angry at the world, God, humankind, my job, myself and life in general. Here I stand in front of departure terminal B, rigid and hateful, trying to look for my boarding time through three-inch glasses of tears, but visibly blinded in every sense of the word.

I am a devoted mother to a perfect child, a catholic daughter of very loving parents, a fairly good wife, a successful medical doctor, financially stable, and living in a modest home by choice. I am the owner of two gorgeous Labradors. I have a close-knit family, a small group of wonderful friends, and I enjoy family holidays in my happy bushveld place. I have no recollection of childhood traumas. I have never been hijacked or robbed and was never involved in drugs (one dagga cookie at medical school hardly counts). I was popular at school and won the school's beauty contest twice in a row. I have never been physically abused, raped, or had any dreaded diseases, serious accidents or cancer, and I am in reasonably good health.

God almighty, what the hell went wrong?

Standing still next to my duffle bag, I can't yet see my flight registered on the departure board. Maybe it is because I can't stand to look at my profile reflecting off the screen, and I am compelled to look away. Human figures obliviously drift past in front of and behind me. I fumble for a *tissue*, mentally disconnected from the hub of activity around me. My attention is suddenly drawn to a dinky toy doll that is pirouetting on the floor next to a small airport stall. It was a cheap singing and dancing plastic miniature version of Elsa from another animated movie, *Frozen*. She was twirling round and round and round, filling my ears with the song "Let it go, let it go."

I just listened for a long, long while until the tears dried up without the need for that handkerchief. I think I wiped the snot on my sleeve. I became acutely aware that I did not care for what people thought of this lost, pathetic statue staring at this "fong-kong" Elsa. A strange feeling that. Not caring what anyone thinks of me...

I wander back outside to get some fresh urban air. I look again through the window at the departure flight board and still can't find flight FA234 flashing anywhere. Another sinking feeling. Shit! Am I departing from O.R. Tambo or Lanseria airport?! I check my flight details, and all that is printed on the online booking piece of paper is, "Leaving Johannesburg at 11.20 a.m." I rush back inside (for better cellphone reception, no doubt), thinking I still have time to call my husband to turn around, fetch me and take me to the Lanseria Drop Off instead. I stop in my tracks, realising that the man was probably ready to drop me off at the edge of the last Universal Inferno for all he cared, poor guy.

At teleportation speed, the Fly Safair counter is upon me, and I confirm with one of the polite attendants that there is indeed a flight departing from O.R. Tambo airport at 11.20 a.m. to Port Elizabeth. My indigo-breath-held face returns to its usual sallow glow. I purposefully order my ever-present panic to recede into my brand new Salomon hiking boots. Surely, I should have broken them in already? Well, now is as good a time as ever. The Salomon twins and I march off to the luggage wrapping counter with unconvincing determination. I wait my turn for one of the three efficient workers to cling wrap my tog bag. Not seeing any sign requesting a service fee, I naively assume that this is part of airport services. There was no such service last time I travelled overseas, many moons ago. How generous. As I reclaim my newly protected purple bag and turn to leave, one of the workers gestures with thumb and index finger, "Where is the money?"

I ask, "How much?" I obligingly reach for my purse, and the three gentlemen proceed to laugh and jostle with each other in their native language, muttering something along the lines of, "This stupid bitch thinks she can just walk away without paying!"

"Here is your R80," I hand over.

In my head, I also laugh rather wickedly: "Fuck you! Fuck you! And fuck you too!" The exact words with which Eddie Murphy greeted his fellow neighbours from his Queens veranda in the movie *Coming to America*. Only he was trying to be polite with a broad, genuine grin. I spat venom out my eyes.

I wondered when I had become so obscene. Where did all this tongue-spice come from? Three days ago, my sister had sent me a WhatsApp picture of a cute little girl possessively holding onto an armful of FUCK words. The caption said, "You can't have any of these. They are all mine!" I decide at this moment that I wish to relieve myself of all this vulgarity that is not me. I make a mental note that by the time I return to Johannesburg, I would limit myself to only saying the word shit.

Back at the check-in counter, my medium-sized purple Indlela bag gets weighed. Thirteen kilograms are well within the accepted limits. This was the total sum of all the food, clothes, toiletries and possessions required for my next two weeks' trailblazing. Apparently, we are to hike with a personal day pack only. All eleven participants received the same purple duffle bag a few days ago for all the items needed for this hike. Whatever belongings did not fit into these bags would not be transported from one destination to the next. There was limited space in the support vehicle.

The check-in attendant was not as rigorous in his ways. He curiously asks how one says 'travel safe' in my language. My Portuguese surname is a giveaway that I was born elsewhere. Chuffed with his newly acquired knowledge, he waves, "Boa viagem!"

My day pack makes it through the security X-ray machine without any confiscations. I would hate it if the tiny scissors in the first aid kit did not arrive in Port Elizabeth. There is a rescue pack full of blister plasters, bandages, strapping tape and Wintergreen ointment for my soon to be tortured feet. I had nothing else to cut bandages with and had never seen Bear Grylls on TV cut any bandage with his bare teeth. But never mind the feet; this backpack is already cutting into my neck.

By the time I get to the boarding gate, I am positively nauseous. A cup of coffee should cure this illness. The barista at the coffee shop says he is making my coffee with love. I believe his borderline passion. I love coffee. With three packets of sugar added to sweeten the deal, I realise I have nothing with which to stir my medicinal potion. I am issued with a wooden spatula. Irony. The exact item I use to look into patients' throats all day long, symbolic of one of the demons I am trying to escape for a while, is precisely what I am about to dip into my perfect latté. Perhaps the bran muffin will taste better. There are three banana slices on top of it. Three. My husband, my child and me. Before a wave of reflux ascends up my oesophagus, I eat the three banana slices. My family is coming with me.

Last boarding call. Shit! That's precisely what will happen if I don't get to the toilet right now. With guilt, I toss the half-eaten muffin in the wastebin before my bowels proceed to bless the ladies' bathroom plumbing system. As I get ready to wipe my arse, a message comes through on my cellphone. It's my sister. "Have a good trip, *mana*. Leave all your shit behind, so you can come back to face fresh shit."

She had seen this coming. Years ago, my sister had bought me Louise Hay's book, *You Can Heal Your Life*, as a birthday gift. It was at a time when I had been sporting a persistent cough that no amount of antibiotic, cortisone, nebulising or cough suppressant could cure. Blood tests and a chest X-ray did not reveal an obvious cause. We just called it the 100-day cough, and I eventually accepted my 'tuberculosis' as simply an occupational hazard. But my sister insisted there was a metaphysical reason for it and wanted me to read in between the lines. What did metaphysical mean? And I had never heard of this author. Spiritual teachers did not feature in our Physiology or Microbiology lecture halls. I had not come across her name in the 400th translated edition of The Bible (not that I had read all the chapters and gospels). I flipped through a few of Louise's pages. Apparently, the reason I had such a chronic cough (without fever, weight loss or bloody phlegm) was that I had a fear of taking in life fully or that I held in so many emotions they were making me sick. My body wished to release them. OMG. This is my diagnosis? What crap! The book promptly took centrepiece on a forgotten bookshelf, and there it remained for five lonely years. But my sister was patient. She knew this pretty porcelain doll would eventually crack.

Predictably, two months ago, the realisation finally came. Every fibre of my being and all of my existence was desperately pleading for time out from this world. A deep-seated instinct told me I would not physically end my life. God, in his divine cynicism, had blessed me with a beautiful, perfect daughter. An angel. My guardian. Even in my worst of all-consuming infernal despairs, I would not intentionally ruin her life by voluntarily taking my own. So the next best thing my mind and soul could beg for was some 'Free to Be Me' time. A time that did not require me to *have to* do anything.

Not have to shop, not have to make daily breakfast or dinner, not have to meet anyone's expectations, not have to pick up dog poo, not have to answer the phone or answer emails, not have to think of what to get for this one's birthday, or speak to that one's overbearing relative. I did not have to do my weekly accounts or count how many times I checked in on my parents or decide what to pack for the weekend away. I vividly remember having a panic attack in the Woolworths' tinned food aisle when I could not decide how many cans of baked beans or sweetcorn we needed for our trip to Botswana. I had abandoned the half-filled shopping trolley and sprinted away to regain control of my tachycardia, scorching tears and stop my throat from screaming in wild despair. A similar anxiety attack at a Herbalife Extravaganza function organised for four thousand people had me leaving the event before it even began, with five tranquiliser tablets on board, where I couldn't remember driving home. Even the simple act of choosing what clothes to put on my body every morning had become a mental nightmare. I did not want to have to think anymore. The constant and pestilent task of worrying about missing a diagnosis with every person I examined, how to console or comfort a patient, what words to use to deliver bad news, thinking ahead of prognoses or potential complications... thinking, thinking, thinking. I do not want to HAVE TO do anything! I just want to FEEL like doing. In fact, I just want to feel something other than hopelessness.

So, it was no coincidence that within 48-hours of deciding that I was going to escape the life of a mother, wife and doctor for a while, I came across an article in the *GO!* travel magazine. Toast Coetzer was sharing his experience of hiking the Indlela yoBuntu trail with eloquently written enticement. He had just completed the first stage of a four-part 1200 kilometre pilgrimage across the Eastern Cape Mountains, aptly called "The Crossing".

Oh, my God! This is it! I emailed the organiser and booked my place. I read further. Three hundred kilometres of walking and backpacking through sparsely inhabited rural and primarily unchartered territory. Shit! I cancelled the booking.

Mmm, free to be me...

Maybe this was my third worst fear. What will I find behind the 21-fake-smiling masks I had been wearing for so long?

Then Mrs Mary Soap seriously pissed on my battery the following day at work. Screw this! I sheepishly asked the organiser if my spot was still available. It was. Time to drop the bomb.

"My love, I am going away for a little while..."

2
S.O.S

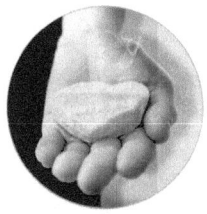

Let's take this soul for a stroll

Bloody hell. When did these aeroplane seats get so small? This is too cosy for my liking. I truly and seriously dislike people, you know. Oh, I get it. My soul-searching training begins. This must be the manual. *Free to Be Me for Dummies.*

Lesson number one: To begin the liking for human company, get crammed with three hundred other fellow Sapiens into a small plane with seats that have long ago shrunk with the volatile changes in altitude and squash up against the teenager to your left. Try not to inhale his stale exhaled carbon dioxide and look out the window to your right. At any stage of your choosing, you can start to warm up to your neighbour.

"This is cosy," I mumble out loud.

The teenager ignores me, finding his iPhone more entertaining. I agree that this is a crappy first lesson, so I mimic his action, place my earphones in position under loosely tied hair, so my face is out of sight, and open my journal. I stroke the empty pages for a moment, previously having had doubts as to whether to bring it along or not. I was not sure that I was ready to have a personal introspective experience with me, myself and I. But several reasons convinced me to lug along these extra few grams of paper.

Firstly, I never wanted to be at this unbearable crossroad ever again. Hopefully, this journal would become filled with miraculous enlightenment that I could always refer back to, should I accidentally extinguish my flame again.

Secondly, the shame and embarrassment of my thoughts and experiences put on paper may help with my psychological recovery and perhaps help another soul struggling with similar anguish. Even the best of the best are only human and can fall mercifully to their knees.

Thirdly, I secretly hoped to write a book one day. Maybe my confessional cop-out from medical practice? A girl can only dream. However, the clueless author in me would not mind if this book never reached the Amazon online shelves or the Exclusive Books front-shop window. It was interesting that all my life I liked to write notes in pencil. I could always rub out the words and change the facts or story. But this time, I had brought along a pen. There would be no further erasing. If the only purpose of this journal were to provide my family with better insight into why they saw me to the Drop Off, I would be satisfied.

Oh, Jesus! This is going to sound like another *Eat, Pray, Love* book. Worse even, Sonia Choquette is going to think I copied her *Walking Home* story. I am seriously pathetic. I am probably not even going to find myself, whatever that means. The Gods must think I am crazy and are also laughing at my expense, just like those airport cling-wrapping buffoons.

Oh, screw it! If this journal goes unnoticed and unread, may it serve as excellent fuel for an enormous camp bonfire. Along with my other scrapbook albums, photos, documents, paper piles and crap that I have accumulated over the years; none of which would be of any value to anyone else.

And please, God, the fire master must at least have a generous glass of Pinotage in hand.

Press pause. The air stewardess claims our much-divided attention to puppet out the in-flight safety rules and instructions. Thinking I was the one wearing the catatonic face, I was surprisingly irritated that she was providing stiff competition. My phone pings loudly. I am in the front row, so I receive a cold side glance.

Lesson number two: You are permitted to be a respectful rebel. Discretely ignoring the half-dead demo-doll applying her oxygen mask in case of loss of cabin pressure, my mother has replied to my earlier message of reassurance that I am all right and everything will be ok, and not to stress about me. She wished me well, but I knew she was worried sick.

Until a week ago, my parents were under the impression that I was attending a medical congress and asked if my fellow medical colleagues were on the same flight. When I gently corrected that this was actually a self-mutilating walking pilgrimage into the *bundus* in search of spiritual salvation, my mother's face dropped two inches south, and her smiley eye wrinkles instantly disappeared. Then came the disappointed stare. I hated that stare. It always made me feel guilty that I didn't measure up, even though I knew she was proud of having a doctor for a daughter. But I could never figure out why she intermittently gave me that dispirited look as if I was responsible for all of her life's shortcomings. In her defence, though, she was silently shocked. She was trying to fathom how the smiling-joking-jovial daughter she knew since the beginning of her inception could suddenly decide that life was not worth living. Clearly, she had not heard of Robin Williams and countless other comedians that have already lost this disheartening battle.

My father was stunned and then expressionless. Depression talk is mostly taboo in our culture and our home. We pretend it does not exist, and we don't talk about it. It only happens to 'other people.' So when he came past my consulting rooms yesterday for a brief good-luck kiss, he was not expecting the uncontrollable tears and desperate long hug he received in return. I never break down in front of anyone (except my husband), so he was somewhat taken aback. He too went pale, and in the instant that I awkwardly looked at his face, he was suddenly so old and defeated. It broke my heart further, the remaining few pieces that were not yet fine dust. Quickly and hopelessly, I tried to explain my reasoning for abandoning ship for a short while in the hope of finding a way back into normality (whatever that was), which was nobody's fault, of course. But his face could not lie. My darling dad, my first hero, was wondering what had happened to his baby girl. Where had he failed as a parent? I didn't know how to reassure him any further.

The noise of the revved-up engines on the runway forces me to close my journal. The air hostess had long stopped pointing to all the exit routes but cast a wannabe dirty look my way. Her Botox-gone-wrong made her face look like she was about to implode from built-up flatulence.

Ah, time for take-off. The turning turbines get louder and louder, and the sudden thrust behind the plane abruptly jets us down the runway. With a deep breath in, this flying monster pulls up off the ground. Hold it, hold it…Then, with exhilaration, I exhale.

I love flying! FREEDOM!

I see Mel Gibson in his all-revealing short Scottish quilt and blue-painted face, bolting down the battlefields on horseback, shouting to his other patriotic brothers-in-arms, "They may take away our lands, but they will never take away our freedom!" They then run into a full-scaled disastrous, bloody war with brave (or stupid) gusto and balls. I do hope to be the exception, where my ovaries make the return trip back home.

I catch sight of the fading Gauteng landscape, a brown-green entanglement of urban and rural settlements. Unexpectedly, the tears start up again. Grateful for a window seat, I turn away from the teenager on my left and gaze downwards with newfound overwhelming admiration at the reflections from below.

Dear God, it's all so beautiful from up here! Everything is beautiful – the Joburg suburbs, the busy roads and gridlocked traffic, the thousands of cars and taxis, the skyscrapers, the torn-up mine dumps, the factory dams, the open fields, the townships. It truly is all beautiful. I am in sincere appreciation. No wonder 'God' is a happy place. From up here, everything is divinely beautiful. Surely, He has no idea of the shit that lies beneath. From up here, God is permanently on holiday, or I believe, vacationing on the magical azure islands of Bazaruto or Fiji, where two-legged uprights hardly make an appearance.

The teenager's elbow is poking my left rib. I am forced to face forward again. I open the journal to begin writing the best-selling autobiography ever and notice for the first time that my daughter had, at some stage in her early life, already drawn a pink butterfly on the very first page of this journal book. A butterfly. A *bayeya*. One of my daughter's very first words, her version of the Portuguese 'borboleta'. She loved butterflies, and by the age of eighteen months, she would squeal with delight and point every time she saw one. *Bayeya, Bayeya!* My precious child. I am so sorry to have disappointed you.

The waterworks start all over again, but this time I don't care much for what the teenager thinks.

Woman, stop coughing behind me! I have been nursing another stubborn 4-week cough with the umpteenth antibiotic. My 'tuberculosis' is forcing me to piss in my panties with every respiratory spasm. I was totally out of breath just climbing the aeroplane stairs, so I don't need your added germs, silly cow. I am about to go hiking for 300 kilometres.

Oh, God. As one of my prestigious surgeon colleagues would say in the middle of a surgery going wrong: "I am so fucked."

Not even Lucy Hay or whatever her name is can save me now.

We begin our gravitational descent. Where are the peanuts? Don't we get complimentary peanuts? Jeez, times have changed. I refuse to buy a R30 small bottle of water from the prissy air hostess. She asked if I wanted to buy any food. "No thanks, I have three slices of banana in my tummy."

My goodness, when did I get to become the prized cow of them all?

I am relieved to part with the teenager's the-world-owes-me disposition, but the Port Elizabeth airport is small and again crammed with more fellow Homo Sapiens. A new wave of tangible anxiety hits my solar plexus as I notice an elderly couple walking timelessly, hand in hand, towards the exit terminal. I think of my husband and his confused frown that must be burrowing deep into his forehead by now.

Lesson number three: If you continue to be the world's No.1 sarcastic bitch, you will end up all alone. So, some positive self-talk is required at this point. Stop feeling so guilty that you are here now because at least you have chosen to try and 'fix' yourself for your sake and the good of your family. You can be a decent human being. Start noticing the nice things, no matter how small. Yes, good plan.

I was trying so hard to find another positive thing to focus on that I did not notice Johan Someone (I didn't quite catch his surname) from JC's Shuttle services, holding up my name in bold letters on a piece of cardboard paper. I walked straight past him at the exit terminal. Still, he recognised my purple tog bag, which was the same as the ones carried by Felicity and Maeve, the other two passengers that were hitching the same ride to our Indlela meeting point in Grahamstown. Johan ushered me into his oven-heated *kombie*, where I peeled off my jersey and proceeded to generously sweat during the entire 100 kilometres to Grahamstown, while the sun burnt my face through the left back window of this bus. Dammit, I can't remember having packed sunscreen.

The three female Camino trekkers make the usual idle chit chat at the back of the van, as strangers do when testing the waters. The expected weather for the next two weeks, what each one packed for snacks along the way, how much water one should carry, and the plasters of choice to prevent blistering on each reflexological part of the foot were the ice-breaker topics of choice. Oh, dear. My in-depth research on how to look after my feet for the next gazillion miles consisted of a brief WhatsApp message from a first-time hiker friend of a friend who did the Karoo's Tankwa Camino once. I was so grateful for her advice on what to buy that I now realised I had no clue where to apply what and at which point. Do you plaster your feet up like a mummy beforehand, or do you wait for the blisters to form so you know what needs plastering? And to pop a blister or not to pop a blister when it does come? That is the real question, my dear Shakespeare.

I turn my train of thought onto something more hopeful. I pray and pray (to no one in particular) that no one asks me what I do for a living. I ponder over this Doctor title of mine. What seems to be a noble and rewarding profession had become a burden and a daily hateful mission for me. I was not one of those that had dreamt of becoming a doctor since her infancy. In fact, I reached the last year of my high school career without a clue of what I wanted to do with my life. On a whim, during first break on the 31st July 1990, I thought it would be a splendid idea to enlist in medical school after my friend had informed me, whilst munching on his peanut butter sandwich, that he had done just that. I rushed to the school secretary's office and asked her if I could urgently call my mother (no cellphones at the time). I then informed her of my spur-of-the-moment decision, with the same nonchalant tone that begged her to cook my favourite dinner tonight. However, the last day for submitting application forms for the first year of doctorship was on the 31st July. That same day. I forced my very surprised mother to leave work, rush to Wits University to obtain application forms (no emails at the time), and go back the following day to beg the Faculty Dean to accept my late application. My subsequent entry interview was disastrous. I knew nothing of infectious diseases or the current medical research in progress. I had no clue about the world's affairs, as I grew up in a very contained, sheltered and oblivious Apartheid era, where the name Nelson Mandela was foreign to my ears. I remember talking about giant rats as the biggest carriers of human illness and that poor people were suffering from many problems. I did not know, to be more specific, that we were at the start of the HIV pandemic, and malaria was killing two million people in Southern Africa per year. I was, medically speaking, clueless. They must have liked my perspective, though, because when I achieved very substandard exam results at the end of Matric, they accepted my candidacy. Destiny was yet an unknown phenomenon to me. I did not give a single thought as to how my parents would afford this whim. And I had no idea what I was getting myself into.

Seven years later, I had completed my Internship at Chris Hani Baragwanath Hospital, then spent another year in the Paediatric hospital wards as a Medical Officer. I eventually declined my Paediatric Registrar training post as I could not bear to watch another baby die from AIDS (pre-antiretroviral rollout), nor could I imagine studying for another four years in that depressing setting. Wandering aimlessly for two years through locum jobs in GP rooms and at the Rosebank Casualty department, I then completed a one-year training program in the Trauma and Emergency Unit and ICUs of the Charlotte Maxeke Johannesburg Hospital. That is where I found the morbid thrill of riding in ambulances and flying in helicopters. After another year of managing an Emergency Unit as the principal doctor, I took a post with International SOS, a company proficient in worldwide rescue evacuations and medical assistance. I joined their fixed-wing flight crew and proceeded to have the most rewarding time of my medical career. I did not only see this as an operation of saving other souls; it was more of a pursuit that kept me alive through the freedom, the spontaneity, the adventure, the anticipation and the unexpected drama that had me flying at the seat of my pants in exhilaration. The EMS personnel team also became a family, and I was accepted and integrated with a part to play in their grand quest for making a clear difference in people's lives.

I also had the privilege of evacuating patients out of Mauritius, Amsterdam, Brazil and Sydney. It felt like I was cheating on the patients by enjoying many adventures as a result of their holiday heart attacks (Insurance companies find it cheaper to treat their local clients back home).

But raising a toddler through 24-hour missions, night shifts, and weekends away from family life was proving increasingly difficult. I went back to working at a private hospital's Accident and Emergency Unit for a few years to be more present at home, but my husband was still in the position of being a single father. So, when my daughter fell in love with Nemo and My Little Pony, I conformed to the dreaded role of becoming a Monday-to-Friday General Practitioner behind four prison walls while slowly falling out of love with life. Nine years later, I was on a search and rescue mission to save my own soul.

Hence, I was not ready nor willing to answer the onslaught of questions that usually followed when people caught wind that I was a medical professional. "Ooh, you are a doctor?! What do you think is this thing on my leg? What do you think this rash is? What is the cheapest medical aid that won't cost me an arm and a leg? Have you seen a lot of flu lately, because it's just terrible how many people die from Bird flu, hey? I have had stomach cramps and constipation for so long. What do you think is wrong with me?"

I would generally be tempted to say, "Well, why don't you just lie here on this *kombie* backseat and let me do a quick rectal examination, so I can tell you why you are such a pain in the arse."

Felicity brings me out of my sardonic trail of thought. She shares with Maeve and me that her husband could not come on this pilgrimage as initially planned. He had just been diagnosed with prostate cancer and was receiving radiation therapy. However, he insisted that she still go ahead with their bucket-list dream and complete it for the both of them. She avoided adding more painful details, but with Lesson number four's Humility slapped on my face, I sunk back to down to earth, as there was no need for me to offer any 'expert' medical advice.

I listened to the two of them chat about their teaching professions as I fell into an odd comfortable silence. As comfy as a 40 °Celsius heat could get inside a 1980 VW *kombie* without air-conditioning, driven by a man past his sell-by-date, on a mission to get us to our rendezvous point at the speed of light and straight into my next lifetime.

It felt good not to do the talking for a change. I tried to soak in the Eastern Cape's passing landscapes, the endless spans of cultivated fields of wheat and maize, the commercial livestock farms, the eucalyptus trees and endless green hills. I began to notice the many, many hills around this part of the country. A nauseating feeling ascended and descended in waves with each giant passing mound. Up and down. Up and down. I turned to look back, and a scream rose into my larynx. Jesus Christ! We have just driven for an hour and a half. We are heading east, but tomorrow we start WALKING west, back to where we have just come from. Holy crap! This shit just got real.

We veer off the highway onto a lonely dirt road that was so discrete; not even Surry would know it was there. Leaving a jet stream of dust behind us, Johan Someone steers his *kombie* for a few kilometres on the gravel road before passing through the gates of the Holy Cross Monastery, just outside of Grahamstown. A long row of towering 3-pronged windmills line the hillside ahead and taper off into the horizon. I marvel at these modern structures and am mesmerised by their ever so slow gyrating blades, which beckons my nerves to calm down and profess to slow down

Hypocratic Oaths

time. Tucked away amongst a cosy green valley, this Anglican St Benediction Brotherhood monastery was built on a spacious property, housing a school for the local community, offering a large guesthouse, a prayer room, dormitories, servants quarters and a dining hall to all those who visit. It is an American funded establishment, with four brothers of the Brotherhood currently living here. However, it seems that the brothers will soon be relocating, and the monastery shut down. Internal politics and disgruntlement do not escape even the holiest of intentions. I guess these boys are also not as 'N Sync' as St Benedict would have liked. A silent private chuckle.

Our welcoming hostess, Madeleine, walks towards the van to greet the first three arrivals that gratefully step out of the smoking oven-hot time-machine on wheels. We get ushered into a communal sunroom to have some refreshing hot tea and biscuits baked by the monastery cook. Another half-hour of polite chatting continued whilst still avoiding the dreaded question: "So what do you do, Gisela?"

I am relieved to hear the decibels outside being taken to another level as the rest of our fellow pilgrims arrive at our meeting point. Felicity, Maeve and I join the greeting handshakes and nods whilst Madeleine orientates us to our new surroundings. Once we had reached the end of silent smiles and mutual up and down assessments, the hostess decided it was a good time to take the weary strangers to their dormitories. George Euvrard, the Indlela organiser, had by now joined his eleven intrepid followers.

My smirk aimed at my own joke earlier on quickly vanished, as I realise that I will be sharing a two-square meter bedroom with another pilgrim. I had intended on taking the first pick of the only single-bedded room in the dormitory house, but before I had a chance to mark my turf with the smallest of farts, I was abruptly interrupted by a giant of a man that pounced upon me from behind (lucky timing for him), declaring that this room was his, as he was the only single male pilgrim present, and would respectfully not share a room with another man's wife. His exposed body parts glittered with beads of sweat, and his lungs heaved from carrying his equally enormous rucksack. As I mechanically extended my neck backwards to look up at his face, I saw that his eyes were of an angelic blue behind oversized glasses. Still, his bulky auric presence rendered me speechless, promptly directing me to the twin-bedded room next door. I later learned his name was Hank. His mother should have opted for Hulk.

I toss my purple tog bag and backpack on the bed to the left of the twin room with despondent resignation. The other bed had already been taken by a skinny Julie. Her purple bag was wide open with all its contents hurled up all over the bed. In her late fifties, Julie was a slim athletic lady who smiled through small moist eyes and sad sun-kissed wrinkles. I greet her, but I don't feel like unwrapping the 50 metres of cling wrap around my tog bag (so much for recycling plastic). With a half-smile aimed at no one in particular, I turn to go back outside as a tinge of loneliness begins to creep in.

I sit for a while on a warm solar-infused rock, listening to a myriad of birds chirping and twittering. A Double-Collard Sunbird flies past and settles on a lush branch ahead of me. Within minutes, I have spotted a White-Eye, several Robins, the iconic Loeries (or 'go-away' birds), some doves and a few other LBJs I don't recognise (Little Brown Jobs). A nostalgic quietness comes to say hello.

I breathe it in. I have only heard this quiet in the far ends of the Kalahari Game Reserve desert and deep under Bazaruto Island's sea waters. Only this time, the silence teases me with a promise of a peace that feels palpably unattainable.

As verification of this impossibility, our pilgrimage leader gathers our attention and summons us to the communal lounge to begin formal introductions.

Hypocratic Oaths

George Euvrard is a psychology professor and former Dean of the Faculty of Education at Rhodes University. He is the founder and mastermind behind The Indlela yoBuntu pilgrimage whilst enjoying the organisational and supportive assistance of his wife, Gwenda. Indlela yoBuntu is Xhosa for 'The way of Ubuntu'. Inspired by his love for hiking and trail running and his desire to assist others in journeying through life more mindfully and soulfully, he has set up an African spiritual equivalent to the Spanish Camino trail, without ascribing to any particular religion or language. As I erroneously presumed, a pilgrimage objective is not to simply have fun or rest or get away from it all. It is not necessarily an act of devotion or penance. It is more of an inward journey, where a renewed reality can take shape by unpacking mindless and soulless behaviours and releasing automated ill-serving belief systems. It is a scared road of revelation if one is willing to be open to such awareness. George wished for more people to experience this transformative journey, so whilst on sabbatical in 2011, he recced on his own through the Eastern Cape farms in what would become this 'Crossing Over' section of the Indlela. His ultimate dream is to one day complete the end of the four-stage pilgrimage at Nelson Mandela's old prison cell on Robben Island in Cape Town. Thus far, he has brought the first two stages into reality. I could entertain signing up for the second stage of this local Camino onto Knysna one day, but there would be no trail running, Mr Euvrard.

Seated in a circle on single lounge chairs and sofas, each pilgrim had a chance to introduce themselves and share their expectations and reasons for joining this pilgrimage. I guess I did expect a degree of talking about myself, but I hoped there wouldn't be too many group discussions. I was here to dictate my own therapy. It was a free-to-be-me treatment, and right now, my brain was so lost up my own arse that I did not wish to talk to anyone. Yet, it was interesting to hear George speak. He carried a lot of knowledge in general, but in particular, he was very familiar with the back route terrains that we would be traversing. He had memorised every detail of each days' hike and the names of the people we would be staying with. He spoke of our hosts as lifelong friends, even though some of them he had only met by chance a year ago on the previous Indlela pilgrimage. I felt I was in the capable hands of a very wise, organised, insightful, humble big daddy. I passed my introduction by simply saying that I was a wife and mother, currently at crossroads in my life and needing some time for myself. I was so not present that I could not recall anyone else's forewords in the moment of this day.

By 17.30, the monastery bells signalled the time for a Brotherhood mass. Most of us chose to attend the service, some out of respect, some out of compulsion and others needing as many blessings as they could get for what lay ahead. I was in the category of all three. Perhaps God was taking me by the scruff to either render absolution or issue punishment with the penance of getting lost in the desert, just as Moses had received. I did not wish to be out here for forty years, but I certainly insisted on an updated version of the Commandments at the end of these two weeks.

Molly, the purple-tongued Chow dog, stood guard at the door of the chapel. She looked as solemn as the four brothers already inside the sacred room. Even though the gorgeous smell of rosemary and frankincense filled the air, one member of the Brotherhood placed a hymn book in each of our hands with welcoming irritation. We were given the order of the hymns that were to be sung, but there was no doubt we were to be still and let them do the singing. No problem, I was not in a jiving hallelujah mood. Half an hour of medieval gothic chanting ensued, which was both soothing and scary, as I witnessed an ancient ritual rather than a spiritual service. Except for a few glimpses at a serious but comical-looking blond brother that resembled Bill Bryson, the author, I kept my eyes glued to the ground, not knowing my place in this universe at this present moment.

A visiting Tanzanian Brother said a few words of prayer, something about consolation and compensation, but I guess I must not have been listening because I lost track of the point of the story. Another two chants, and it was over. I glanced around, and no one had mutated, appeared possessed, nor disappeared into another galaxy. Partly rushing to get out of there, I also wanted to take a photo of the inside of the chapel. The view out of the large window in front of the altar was magnificent. But I didn't dare. By the time I got to the door, the brothers had disrobed from their white gowns and were ready in their civvies to meet us at the dining hall at 18.15 sharp. I almost marched Nazi-style into dinner but thought it might seem disrespectful. Instead, we stood in the dining hall in a circle again, this time for thanksgiving. The Chief Brother blessed the food, announced some house rules, and then said: "Here is the soup, here is the salad, and there is the bread. You may help yourselves."

So we did. We sat at a long table without any particular allocated arrangements, except for George seated at the head of the table. A brief vision of "The Last Supper" came to mind. Almost every Latino home has a framed picture or painting of Jesus's last meal hanging over their dining room table. I was never sure how I felt about that image – I fluctuated between a sense of peaceful comfort and the feeling of impending doom. It was the same feeling I had whilst enduring my First and Second Communions, my Confirmation ceremonies, as well the pre-marital sessions I had with Father Gerard at Bez-Valley Church of Holy Angels. Even my marriage vows carried an unspoken burden I did not know I was signing up for. Lord only knows how many of these promises I had already broken. Our religion was intent on fear-filled communal cooperation via threats of eternal damnation, desolation in hell by sinning, passing judgement and punishment to anyone who did not conform to the rules and selected ancient scripture manuals; hand-picked by a self-serving group of men intended on keeping Constantine the Great heralded as one of the 'great' Christian Roman Emperors of all time, three hundred years after Jesus' death. A fact conveniently omitted in my Catechism classes.

I had bought into this lie and had been living a life in fear of an invisible divine enemy.

Interestingly, the written words of Jesus' First Apostle, Mary Magdalene, have never featured in any Bible. Considering she was his life partner and the single most appropriate person to speak of Jesus' life and principles, one would think we should be better informed about balancing out such a divided patriarchal version of the Truth. I am convinced this is why more women are loving women, and more men are softening to their feminine, to balance out our Earth's overpopulated masculine ego.

Granted, much has been accomplished in the name of the Lord for the poor and needy, for charity and the upliftment of communities. Still, many more horrific wars and atrocities have been fought and inflicted in vain in His holy name.

I had long ago stopped worshipping this conflicting relationship. Maybe that is why I felt left for dead, and this was hell already. In which case, if these pilgrims were here with me through no fault of their own, perhaps there was hope for my resurrection; we were ready to face our demons, and we should continue to celebrate our last meal of this soon-to-be morphed stage of our lives.

I turned my attention to salivation because, by now, I was starving (my banana slices had long completed their transit time through my gut). Despite my hunger, I can honestly say this was the best Mediterranean soup I have ever eaten. It was warm and spicy, with colourful veggies, beans and chorizo, and it tasted hearty and homely. The salad was homegrown and nutritious, and the freshly baked bread was truly God sent. I ate this blessed food with a thankful glass of water and couldn't remember the last time I had such a satisfying and comforting meal.

And then it came.

"So, Gisela, what is it that you do?" asked Iris, who was seated to my left.

Hypocratic Oaths

Aarrgghhh!

"I am just a GP," I whispered, hoping no one else heard me.

"Ooh! Really? A doctor? Where do you work?" I could see George's eyes lighting up. He was seated five people down to my right, clearly not far enough for eavesdropping.

"I am in private practice, but I really need a break right now."

I must have cast such an unintentional (intentional) evil look that every human in the vicinity visibly backed down. George's one eyebrow dropped in disappointment, but the other raised in curiosity. Oh goody, he found himself a psycho patient! He was professional enough not to overstep his boundaries, so asked no further questions, but I secretly knew he valued having a doctor on board. Everybody does, regardless of the event. It seems to be one of the most reassuring things for people to know there is always a doctor around. God only knows what tricks I would pull from my small personal hiking backpack if someone plummeted down a mountain precipice to 500 metres below, landing in a heap of fractured bones. Sending a 'Get Well' card would not be appropriate, no doubt. Still, their feet would be beautifully bandaged, and a protein bar should at least make me feel better whilst attempting to manifest a rescue helicopter for the occasion. I left George in his quiet false satisfaction.

Shortly after we all had our share of dinner, the dishes were washed by the hosts under the 5-minute military efficiency mark. The Brothers were a working marvel. We retreated to the communal lounge to receive instructions and advice for the next day's hiking route. The map on my A4 piece of paper did not provide me with many directions, but I was not worried about getting lost here. I would be the last one trailing behind my fellow pilgrims in my current unfit physical state and could surely just follow their foot tracks or bread crumbs. After a long while discussing the necessary preparations, it was time to gather our thoughts back into our rooms. I took a soothing hot shower, updated my journal and went outside to phone home. There was not much to say; my family already knew I had arrived safely. No present emotion, anyway. But it was a prelude to the insomnia that was to follow. I had no expectations for tomorrow, although I was hoping for a miracle even though I had just arrived.

My roommate had already snuggled into her sleeping bag, and the overhead lights were out - time for me to do the same. I switched off my headlamp and crawled inside my brand new expensive thermal cocoon.

My last hopeless thought for the day was of an old comedy theatre pantomime I watched a long time ago about a misfit hairdresser, useless at her job, getting through her ridiculous daily follies.

The show was called "Curl up and Dye".

3
GOD MUST BE CRAZY

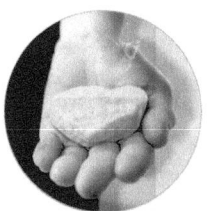

Some people get wet; others feel the rain

The monastery bells awaken their sleeping caterpillar guests at 6 a.m., precisely. I did not know that one can hear church bells in hell.

Oh, I am still on earth. I confirm this by opening one eye to check for phone messages, not knowing what to expect. No surprise, no messages. Only the realisation that my husband changed our family trio WhatsApp group profile photo. Sometime after I fell asleep, it had been replaced by a picture of a smiling me. I could not process the simultaneous thankfulness and guilt, hope and sadness.

It is time to get this circus on the road. It is still dark outside, but the slow rustling of bodies creeping out of their nocturnal swaddles gets me out of mine. I fold my sleeping bag slowly, deciding what to do next. My body was still lost in the twilight zone. The hours between 2.30 and 4.30 a.m. were spent wide-eyed, awake and in dead silence. Any slight movement within my sleeping bag mimicked a crazed cat rustling up a pile of dry leaves. So, I had lain frozen and mummified, not wishing to disturb my slumbering partner. But now, I copy her actions of strapping feet before emptying bladders. Of course, I had bought the wrong material, so I was offered some Elastoplast from a more experienced Julie. Feeling very inadequate, I graciously accepted and made a mental note to replace the strapping as soon as we came across a pharmacy.

Getting dressed required a decision of how many layers of clothing to put on. Checking my backpack for the tenth time had me doubting whether I had too little food for the day and too much water that would render the backpack impossible to carry on top of a body low on fuel. Fortunately, I did not have a panic attack. Still, I really should have walked at least two kilometres to my local shopping centre and back home a few times before deciding whether this Indlela was actually a good idea.

A strong cup of coffee downed two Myprodol anti-inflammatories, an antibiotic, a probiotic, an Altosec stomach protector, and one paracetamol, just in case. This stubborn cough of mine was going to be left behind on these healing mountains, even if it killed me. Thinking I was now ready for my miracle, I stepped outside only to be smacked in the face by a down-pour of light rain. Now, this was a wake-up call! My Lord, I have not catered for rain gear. It is now mid-winter in sunny South Africa. It does not rain in winter for goodness sake. Holy crap! Talk about a prophetic cleansing.

The mist was thick and tangible, the grey clouds folded and unfolded in an invisible wind, and the views of the escarpment were mystically beautiful. Embracing a plastic poncho that was unexpectedly rolled up at the bottom of my purple bag (the first oblivious sign that miracles do happen), I take a last walk up the embankment to the chapel. Inside, I breathe in that blessed rosemary incense, take in the peace of this sacred space and stare out of that large viewing window over the majestic green valley below. I do want to take a photograph of this view after all. How is it possible that amidst such thick grey mist and dark drizzling clouds, there can exist such beauty and magnificence? Alone and in quiet desperation, I turn to a God I have ignored for so long and say a prayer for my family to stay safe back home and another pleading one for my divine cosmic intervention that is sure to come.

The Brothers had left our cereal, toast, and fruit breakfast prepared, but they were not joining us this time. They had requested that we eat in silent contemplation, which we were glad to do, each to our own thoughts.

We then gathered in a departure circle at the monastery courtyard, holding hands like children in a playground. We were establishing a new ritual where each pilgrim would be given a turn every morning to provide their version of a prayer or set an intention or motto for the day. No surprise that today's quote had something to do with rain. I wanted to be one of those that felt the rain and didn't just get wet. Maybe it was also why only one of the friendlier Brothers came out to bid us farewell. We did not get any of their names but felt grateful for this overnight sanctuary in the middle of nowhere I never knew existed.

With meaningful blessings and good wishes bestowed upon us, we set off after taking a group photo at the entrance gate and walked away from this haven in silence. The morning drizzle gently teared my face as we walked in pre-planned solitude for the first six kilometres. Every morning we would be initiating the first hour of our walk in silence. We would then break the quiet at a designated landmark pit stop.

I was unsure if my fellow pilgrims were giving me a false sense of hope, but my legs set the pace, and I just followed. I had nothing to prove, but the initial six kilometres did not seem distant, and I was the first to arrive at the radio tower landmark two hours later. Surprising myself, I had to make a mental note to take it slower, to allow my thoughts to come and go, to be open to whatever arose, to remember the smells of the pine and eucalyptus trees, to take in the sounds of the birds, sheep, cows, and of that one Border Collie.

One kilometre into the hike, I did become aware of a crow that flew from tree to tree for almost the entire first leg, as if showing us the way or just enjoying our company. "Hello, Mimi. I knew you would be with me on this journey."

My beautiful mother-in-law defied every sarcastic version of that word. She was the kind of woman I aspired to be, even though I have just as much adoration for my own precious mother. Irene dos Anjos (of the angels) was affectionately known as Mimi and loved by every human that fell under the spell of her smile. She was a devoted mother and wife, a child-minder and caregiver adopted by every toddler that had the privilege of her hugs. She loved all things pretty and beautiful. Her house was spotless and adorned with gorgeous decorations and creations. She loved gardening and animals, and she sang when she was happy and sang when her sorrows were too heavy to bear. She did not only get wet in the rain; she kept getting handed thunderstorms. But in all the years I knew her, I admired her genuine kindness and simplistic love the most.

She was a God-fearing devotee but was never allowed to exercise her beliefs in front of her husband, as much as my father-in-law is a wonderful father-in-law. On the other hand, I had free access to the throat-stuffing religion she was deprived of. But the God-loving aspect of the gospels was what kept her hopeful and resilient. So she worshipped in secret, seeking pleasure and feeling great gratitude in the simple things life offered her – her home, her children, her family. She was always as content as one could possibly seem and so did not even have a bucket list when she died.

For years, it remained a tragic mystery how such a loving woman could have a rare cancerous tumour grow like a wild creeper around her heart, the very thing she gave so freely to all who knew her. I wondered if she bore hidden conditional suffering and sacrifice so deep-rooted in her beliefs that it ultimately consumed a love she tried so hard to hold onto. But five days of chemotherapy was all it took to shut down the rest of her organs, and she spent the last 24 hours of her precious life in a coma on life support. Now I know about divine timings. When life's dash has been fulfilled in a pre-conceived soul's contract, we will each expire at that time, regardless if we exit this lifetime via an accident, a stroke, pneumonia or cancer. I was not fully appreciative of this fact at the time. So even though I believed Mimi was no longer in pain when she crossed over, we were nevertheless left shocked and in utter disbelief with tightly strangled hearts.

I spoke her Eulogy. On the morning of her funeral, I was woken up at 5 a.m. with a deafening silence that I had not experienced in a long while. There was no humming of electrical appliances, cars driving past, crickets chirping, nor the soft rhythmic breathing of my husband that lay sleeping next to me. There was no sound other than the sudden and distinct melody of a single bird's song that reverberated through my bedroom window and sang the light of dawn into being. Whenever I hear that unique chorus, I know Mimi is at peace, still happily singing, and very close by.

I am brought back to consciousness when the Indlela pilgrims stand up and are ready to get going again. The designated twenty-minute break at the first stop was over. The rain had also stopped, but I do a quick calculation and realise that I will be walking for the next seven hours to complete the remaining 500 miles, or so it seemed, to our next overnight stop. God help me.

But so far, so good. Just keep going. At your own pace. Faster or slower. Stop, don't stop. Talk, don't talk. Don't care. Just keep walking. Just keep swimming, just keep swimming, Nemo.

An hour later, in the hope of relieving more weight off my backpack, I chomp on two holy bananas with the further hope that I won't vomit from indigestion and sudden gastric arrest. As a doctor, I should know better not to do strenuous exercise after eating. The vivid image of regurgitated bananas while doing mouth to mouth CPR hit me from nowhere. Really!? I could not believe this is what now entered my thoughts.

At the peak of my cycling 'career', I entered my first 94.7 Cycle challenge race. It is a well-frequented annual cycling race along 94.7 kilometres of Johannesburg's urban roads, when most of the city comes to a standstill (except for the 30 000 riders), as half the highways are closed off for the day to allow safe transit for these frenzied sportsmen and women. Some riders do it for professional and personal competition, some people do it for fundraising purposes, others as a work team-building exercise, and some do it just for fun. Ferociously pedalling a two-wheel mode of transport without a motor, in 35 °Celsius African heat for almost 100 kilometres of crowded roads with inaptly dangerous cyclists, I included myself in the last group. However, it was still elusive as to what got me to sign up for this event in the first place.

The 94.7 Cycle challenge of 2008 brought me to a dead halt halfway through the race. I jumped off my bicycle at the sight of a bystander hunched over a male cyclist that lay limp and motionless on the hot tarmac. The bystander was scooping out a half-digested banana from the rider's mouth with her bare hands in order to blow some oxygen down his throat. She had no barrier mouth device. There was no one helping her, but no matter how much air she tried to get past those bananas, it was not going to reach the rest of the man's body, if his heart was not pumping the oxygen around. There was nothing wrong with my pumping adrenaline, as I confirmed this man had no pulse, was not breathing, was deathly grey, and already halfway down the tunnel of light.

I heard someone say, "An ambulance is on the way", and thought, "Yes, that will only take a whole day to get past these hordes of racing fanatics and blocked off roads."

The bystander did not seem to know how to do chest compressions, and I did not give her a chance to prove otherwise. I was not about to eat recycled bananas, so I took charge and ordered her to stay at the mouth-end and breathe out life if her own life depended upon it. I knelt on the ground and began the laborious, repetitive chest compressions on this very large, lifeless body. My knees started grating and chaffing against the boiling road surface. My hands kept sweating and slipping under my riding gloves (I was so used to working gloved up, I did not think these half-fingered leather gloves were so useless), and cascades of perspiration poured down my face from under my riding helmet. I knew I was doing good CPR when I felt one of the man's ribs crack under my chest compressions. Then a second rib gave way. The man did not flinch an inch nor show any signs of responding to our *'pomp 'n blaas'* efforts.

Where was the damn ambulance? My own heart was beating for both of us, and I thought my temples might explode. It was so bloody hot. An eternity passed, or so it seemed, the man still without reaction. Without a defibrillator and IV adrenaline, this was hopeless. I was finally too exhausted to continue and accepted that this man's divine timing was up (for all Triathlon ironmen and women out there, you don't know exercise until you have done CPR). As I rested back onto my numb haunches in defeat, the mouth-breathing bystander whispered, "Don't stop. His wife is right over there."

Oh, fuck! I turned to stare at a heap of a weeping woman, eyes focused in horror on her partner's motionless body, hands clasped over her mouth, suppressing the scream that was dying to be released. There was no point in going to speak to her now. If I did, she would know it was the end. As long as someone was trying to revive him, her hope was alive, and I wouldn't be the one to break the news amidst this chaos. So I resumed the chest compressions and ignored my bleeding knees, which paled in comparison to what this woman was going through.

She had been riding with her husband on a tandem bike when he suddenly collapsed without warning. At a time gone by, when I had managed to desensitise myself against all normal human emotion to survive on scorn, I would have probably made a sick mental joke about how he finally got tired of lugging his wife around and decided to croak instead.

But right now, I was just grateful to hear the ambulance sirens and see two paramedics dressed in bright red overalls, head in my direction. I leave the poor bystander doing her good Samaritan deed for a moment and brief the senior paramedic that we have been doing CPR for over twenty minutes without a response. We need to evacuate him a.s.a.p. The bold red pepper behind arrogant sunglasses announces that the patient is dead then and will not be transported by ambulance. I must call the mortuary van.

I turn my back to the wife and stand in front of this bright buffoon so that the wife cannot lip-read any other nonsense coming from his mouth. I reply through gritted teeth, "I know he is dead," adding under my breath, "you idiot!"

"This man's wife is standing over there, and if you declare him dead now, I am leaving you to deal with her melt-down and the hoards of spectators that will rain down on this parade whilst I get back on my bike before the road gets backed up."

He did not need further convincing. Men don't know what to do with hysterical women. I was close to demonstrating my own femme fatal mania. Still, I decided to calmly drive home my point under five seconds, "If you continue with CPR to the hospital, the E.R. doctor takes over, declares a DOA (dead on arrival); and you prevent thousands of people from cycling past a corpse on the road, that will rot in the heat before the mortuary van decides to come. The wife will be in a more private place with the hospital chaplain when she receives the bad news, and you avoid making headlines by not being the EMS company that refused to transport a collapsed patient to the hospital on such a worldwide viewed event."

I cannot remember my exact words, but I know I have never spoken to anyone with such cheek. I usually just shut my mouth. Clearly, I must have been slightly agitated with this unexpected turn of events. I left the paramedics to intubate, drip, and load the man into the ambulance.

I felt bad for the E.R. doctor on duty at the nearest hospital. I hated receiving DOAs when I was on duty. The paperwork was a nightmare when Casualty was usually bursting with screaming and wailing patients, some of them too alive for my liking. And dealing with bereaved families was the worst.

We were in a suburban area with several houses lining the street, and I asked which one of the spectators had a bathroom I could use. I was ushered into a domestic helper's room at the back of a house, into a toilet that had never seen sight of a cleaning agent or cloth. I reluctantly rinsed my face with tap water, emptied my bladder, hovering over but not touching the seat, then wiped my hands. I could not suppress the bile that rose up my throat. I felt dirty and bitterly ill. Not because of this bathroom's hygiene status (or lack of it), but for my intentional, cowardly avoidance of the wife. I had allowed her to climb in the back of an ambulance with her dead husband without giving some explanation or offering a meagre consolation. I did not even make eye contact. The terrified and abandoned look on her face I will never forget and would always regret.

At some point, I got tired of my haunted thoughts and the sound of crunching boots on the gravel. I reached for my iPod's welcome distraction, and the upbeat music that came through on Shuffle mode reminded me of a time when I once did enjoy exercising. It seemed that every decade of my existence came with a flavour. Childhood had me climbing trees and jungle gyms, running, cartwheeling and rolly-pollying on the grass. My teenage years had me involved in every high school sport on offer: gymnastics, volleyball, hockey, swimming. I hit my twenties in the era where Jane Fonda aerobics and Arnold Schwarzenegger gymming was in fashion. I owned a road bicycle and a mountain bike by my 35th birthday, and cycling was then the name of the game. It was pedalling for hours on a tar road to high-energy tunes that made dance music a mental motivator for me. That doof-doof beat matched every forceful down-stroke of my pedals in resistance to the uphills. It was this music that got me to the finish line on the day of the 94.7-race-CPR ordeal. I would not have reached the finish line without it. I wished for this sound energiser to help me get to the Indlela finish line too.

I have always loved dancing to any music that got my blood flowing, my body jiving, and my mood grooving into laugh mode. But by the time I reached the forties, my arse made friends with a swivelling office chair in a general medical practice room, and there it had remained sedentary for the last five years.

It was no wonder that by lunchtime, two toes on my right foot had announced their surrender. So relieved was I when George called us to a stop on the side of the road to refuel and rehydrate. I had no idea how far we had walked or where we were on the land GPS, but I promptly sat down and removed my now dusty brand new Salomon hiking shoes to examine my feet. I could not tell if there was a blister on its way yet, so I cleverly concluded that my shoelaces were tied too tight around my midfoot and strangling the nerve sensation to the fourth and fifth toes. I could deal with neuropraxia. I let them breathe for a while and started munching on my daily allowance of allocated cracker biscuits and Melrose cheese triangles. Brenda shared some of her avocado in exchange for some crackers. A protein bar and peanuts followed. A glimmer of confidence began to creep in as my tummy graciously accepted this nutrition. My mind acknowledged the moist earthly smells of the forests, the lulling cows mowing the green fields, the sight of zebra and hartebeest antelope on neighbourly farms, and the random secretary bird and warthog going about their business of pecking and shovelling.

As we pushed on further, we walked by a few settlements that had long been abandoned. Without fence demarcations, some plots comprised only one or two farmhouses, but all stood crumbling at the mercy of erosion and conquered by wild bushveld, insects and rodents. The snakes were sure to follow. A lonely railway station mirrored the surrounding evasiveness, its railway tracks rusted, having long forgotten the exciting steel speed that made them glitter in the sun.

Nineteen kilometres into our walk, only six cars had driven past, leaving us in a path of dust to follow. We were seriously off the beaten track now and pretty much in no man's land. Except for the scattered trailing pilgrims, there was no other human soul to be seen. That inkling of confidence quickly turned to foreboding. But I did not indulge it further. I revelled in the feeling that I was alone but not exactly lonely. And I had survived the first day's hike.

At the time of writing these words, I did not appreciate that our first night of shelter following our rendezvous point was at the St Cyprian's Anglican Church. A small medieval stone building tucked away amidst ancient pine trees at the bottom of a valley. It, too, stood alone and isolated from any evidence of civilisation or any other man-made structure in the mid-afternoon. I did not remember a signboard pointing us towards its location. It did not have a definitive address. It's simply off the Highlands Road, down the hill, 21.5 kilometres from the N2 highway Grahamstown turn-off, in the direction of Alicedale.

Yet, St Cyprian's Church was far from neglected. The surrounding farming community travels for miles to congregate under its refurbished zinc roof for various celebrations, ceremonies, and Almighty worships. Stepping inside this welcoming haven confirmed the doting attention and communal care it receives on a regular basis, even though no priest or pastor lives on the premises. It stood firm and embracing, clean and accepting.

I sat my rucksack down on one of the middle pews and stretched my inflatable hiking mattress on the floor. Sitting on the mattress, I place my sun hat and cell phone on the longest bedside table I have ever had. Shoes off. Minimal foot and body damage on this first day. Yes, I am blessed, I thought with mild sarcasm, as I lay on my 'bed' in between the pews, our resting place for the night. I was almost expecting to see some sheep, three wise men and a manger with a baby gurgling in its centre. But instead, George surprised us by playing the organ that was perched in one corner of the church.

I had no idea this particular wise man could create such a beautiful song. The first sound that infused the still space was the 'Hallelujah' melody. Staring at the heavenly ceiling above, there was a moment of quiet appreciation and paralysis of time. It was the best I could master just then. I had not yet learnt to breathe correctly, nor reflect or focus on the inner self, nor had I ever meditated, so I was unsure how to take it all in. Meditation was not done in my religious upbringing; that is for Buddhists only. I had long ago stopped praying and long ago forsaken my God, so I had no words.

Early on in my life, I was made to believe in a God that 'allowed' misery, crime, poverty, violence and destruction. After years of witnessing atrocities committed by man towards each other, against earth's creatures and the planet, I had lost all faith in a God that had created such a species as the human race. At the same time, self-resentment was ever-present. I was a human too, and I did not need a God to point out how atrociously I had behaved toward my own kind. I had enough self-loathing to subconsciously believe I did not deserve to enjoy all the blessings and riches that were evident in my life.

In walking away from everything God-given to me, in my quest for deep, meaningful answers, I was now forced to sleep under His roof! I was not able to admire the irony. I just lay on the floor of this church sanctuary and watched the fine specs of dust hovering in the sunlight that beamed through the overhead multi-coloured glass windows. I could not see past my inertia.

The organ gently came to its finale, and the silence opened my eyes. This was George's unique way of announcing that there were no shower facilities at the church. There was only one toilet to share amongst us, no electricity or cell phone coverage. No problem, I shall be wearing the same stinky underpants tomorrow, and I hope my family don't think I have bailed down a mountain on the first official hiking day, given the lack of communication.

I needed a cup of coffee. It was getting chilly. Thoughtless of me not to pack the vodka. Or rest shoes, for that matter, another oversight when I saw all the other eleven pairs of feet in soft fluffy slippers. I slipped my cold toes into my only other personal footwear, a pair of beach plastic flip-flops, and took my cup of coffee for a stroll down a narrow path away from the church for some more alone time.

Actually, I desperately needed to degasify. I was not yet that comfortable with my fellow pilgrims to openly sound my rectal trumpet. Whilst I was at it, I also marked my territory with a familiar urinary bush squat, glad to have found a *tissue* in my pocket. Comforted by the surrounding pure air breezing softly through the trees, I sat on a rock for a long while, blowing puffs of smoke from my Dunhill menthol cigarette.

I had earned this sucker today. Nobody really knew I smoked. A few friends had seen me take a few drags when we had socialized in the rebellious years before my daughter was born. My husband had seen me smoke plenty in those days. But never my parents. As far as I knew, they did not suspect it, or so I would like to think. I always felt ashamed and disrespectful if I had to pull a drag in front of them. I could not taint the perfect image they had of their youngest born. And I could not decide if it was because I feared their judgement more or feared not being accepted as I was a smoking failure.

A thousand years ago, if a human was not accepted by their tribe or had violated a rule or social regulation, they were forced to sleep outside the protective communal *boma* and risk being eaten by lion and wild animals. This ancestral survival instinct is still embedded in our DNA, and we will do almost anything and pretend to be almost anyone just to be accepted into our various tribes. We are all so desperate for approval and recognition that we will, at times, sacrifice our own soul. And we learn these false habits from an early age.

I remember a helicopter call-out to a head-on collision between two cars on the treacherous road to Heidelberg. The sun was setting, and we were rushing to get back to base before nightfall. Of the six motor vehicle accident victims, a young boy aged seven was the only person who survived the impact, miraculously only sustaining two broken legs. We had to airlift him to the Charlotte Maxeke Hospital (the old Joburg General) for fear of other internal injuries, given the massacre sprawled on the road.

In one instant of an undesirable sealed fate, this gorgeous blue-eyed blond boy had lost both his parents and both his older sisters in this one singular freak accident. There was no way of blocking his sight from the wreckage, as he had already witnessed the dismembered bodies of his family ejected out of their mangled car before EMS could arrive on the scene.

We scooped him off the road, inserted intravenous lines, splinted his fractures and loaded him into a noisy helicopter away from the chaos of police, sirens and darkness. Not once did he whimper, squirm, or utter a single sound. He did not speak nor ask about his family. He was a statue in shock.

Once we arrived at the hospital, we handed him over to the receiving Casualty Officer for urgent care and further investigation and stabilizing of his injuries. The young boy suddenly grasped my pants and signalled for me to come closer. The only words he spoke to me in Afrikaans were,

"*Tannie*, you must go tell my grandfather that I did not cry. I was a good boy."

How tragic that we are not allowed to be scared or sad, or vulnerable. Our will to please is so much more valued by others that we have to pretend to be such brave and 'good' boys and girls to prove ourselves worthy of living. But who is judging, for God's sake? We are taught to deny our natural feelings, instincts and emotions, believing that it is unnatural or ungodly to have any 'negative' emotion. It will later leave us paralyzed without joy or purpose. This I know, and this is where I currently find myself at. Because how can we know joy if we can't acknowledge sadness? How do we know compassion if we do not experience indifference? The emotions that don't feel good allow us the opportunity and awareness to learn what does feel good. None of them are wrong or right; they are simply all part of our whole.

The church bell calls the Indlela pilgrims at 5 p.m. to assemble outside the church lawn under the giant pine trees. It was reflection time, which meant we were all having a turn to share our experience and thoughts for the day. This was to become another routine end-of-day ritual. I somehow don't remember seeing this written in our memo.

We sat on scatter cushions spread upon recently erected cement benches. These were part of a new garden, designed and built around a *braai* area by a nearby farmer Peter Rose, in honour of his ailing wife. She still witnessed its completion before her passing six months ago.

Peter had somehow arrived to unlock the front church gate earlier in the afternoon, as Ronelle could not drive the support vehicle into the grounds before our arrival. Ronelle was one of the disciples who were meant to have hiked the entire 300 kilometres with us, but she sustained a leg injury a few days before starting. She was thereby upgraded to driving our support vehicle to chart our overnight sleeping bags and purple tog bags from one destination to the next.

In a comedy of errors, the church gate was not meant to be locked. No one ever locked it. Ronelle spoke something about 'Divine Intervention'. Peter had coincidentally arrived when Ronelle was struggling to get into the church property. Once the vehicle was parked next to the church, he made sure Ronelle was settled in. They both then relaxed for a while in the rose garden drinking coffee, quietly enjoying the sun.

They reflected on the fact that Ronelle had also lost her life partner just four months prior to Peter becoming a widower. They shared how each was getting along with their lonely lives. They offered each other comfort, compassion and sympathy. It seemed that this unexpected encounter deeply touched both at the sacred rose garden.

Reflection time conversation flowed from people and places in general to histories and legacies we leave to our children and appreciation of nature. Someone mentioned that perhaps she viewed her husband in a better light after today's contemplations. Another spoke of her divorce and the hope that this pilgrimage would help heal some residual wounds.

When the spotlight came my way, my gaze shifted from the mesmerizing pine tree branches that grew and pointed in a northerly direction to my hands resting on my lap. I expressed genuine gratitude for the opportunity to be here, present in this moment (the wise old tortoise from the Kung Fu Panda movie had mentioned something about yesterday being history, tomorrow being a mystery, but today being a gift. That is why it is called the present). I admired the organizer for putting together such a unique and passionately planned spiritual pilgrimage. It had brought my awareness back to the purifying sights and smells of Mother Nature and into the cleansing morning rain. It provided a safe space for walking openly in our homeland, without the fear of getting lost and with the reassurance that there was always a presence nearby, should I feel the need for conversation. I voiced my surprise at completing 19 kilometres at a similar pace to my expert hiking mates, but most of all, I was satisfied that no one needed, wanted or asked anything of me.

No further enquiry came my way, so we proceeded to discuss the next day's 27-kilometre route. A remarkable dinner followed. The church's warden, Rob Wilmot and his wife had left a large pot of delicious chilli con carne, rice and homemade bread in the kitchenette, which just required serving onto each of our paper plates. Rob is a well-known farmer in the area and one of George's new friends. I was sorry not to personally thank him and his wife for the comforting meal and hospitality. The meat chilli was just right for a cold winters' night.

By now, I was simultaneously wearing the only four layers of upper body clothing that came along on the trip. I was cold. Nevertheless, I savoured every forkful of spiced rice in a most unusual setting. We all sat inside the unlit church on our bedside bench pews, each with our headlamps intermittently bobbing some illumination into the darkness with every mouthful. We looked like giant fireflies munching in silence. A simply divine supper.

Washing up dishes at an outside tap involved cleaning a fork and rinsing a coffee mug. It was 6.30 p.m., and there was nothing left to do. It felt odd but so pleasing not to hear a TV, phone, car or radio in the background. The onyx sky was packed with every twinkling constellation visible on a clear Southern African winters' night. Even Scorpio's red heart was salient. Some pilgrims stayed on to contemplate the cosmos, others settled indoors to read their novels, and others struggled to stuff their overdressed bodies into tight sleeping bags.

I wrote in my journal whilst George tenderly filled the void with several more organ notes. It left me floating in a celestial twilight zone. Just a week ago, I could not possibly imagine that I would be sleeping in the dark on a church floor, amongst strangers, in the middle of nowhere and at the mercy of something unknown. I had not read the T's and C's of this journey correctly and felt a bit pitiful and abandoned by myself. But I was at least *feeling*, and I allowed myself to just sit with it and be with it without judging it or myself. Is this what it means to feel the rain?

Years of catechism, communions, priestly sermons and sacramental confessions had not prepared me for this ceremonial evening. I was used to the occasional congregational fidget, cough, yawn, shuffle or even ruffle of windbreaker jackets. It was the first time in my Catholic memory that I lay in darkness, inside a cocoon designed to withstand minus 5 °Celsius freezing conditions, on holy wooden floors, listening to strangers grunt, snore, burp and fart. The ultimate ice-breaker.

A period of silence followed once we had all settled indoors for the night. A moment of déjà vu. I recall sitting at Sunday Mass after parishioners had all received the Holy Communion and feeling the awkward five minutes of silent anticipation before the priest got up to bless the service to a close. I wouldn't be leaving the church tonight, but sure enough, Hank finally concluded, "*Julle*, when was the last time you slept in a church?"

Christy promptly retorted, "Every Sunday."

4
LEND ME A HAND

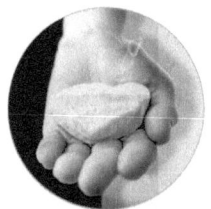

Your whole life has prepared you for today

I was not prepared for the snot that froze over my upper lip as I stepped outside of St. Cyprian's Church at 5.30 a.m. the following day. Jim Carrey had nothing on my Dumb and Dumbness. Here we were in the middle of winter in the Eastern Cape mountains, and I did not think to pack thermal underwear, a snow jacket or even a beanie. Jimmy was at least wearing gloves on his motorcycle, and his hands were no doubt warmer than mine. In my favour, I had the discretion to wipe the frozen mucus on something other than my sleeve. I hoped this would not become a common practice.

I did, however, wish to set a new daily routine of wake up, strap feet, put on pants and shoes, empty bladder (not necessarily behind a bush), brush teeth, fold sleeping bag, and pack snacks, fruit and water for the day. Breakfast would be last but always rewarding. Today, it consisted of muesli, plain yoghurt, bread with peanut butter, and coffee. I was pretty chuffed with myself for bringing a small thermos flask along. It was a good enough incentive to warm the hands again at our first tea-break stop.

I walked back into the church, where my purple tog bag still rested and pulled out the flask to fill it with hot water. It was the smallest one we owned but given to me as a gift for Mother's Day by the Primary School, where my daughter was attending grade seven. It had the school emblem with the motto "Respice Stellam" engraved on it. Reach for the stars.

My child was certainly reaching for the stars and the heavens. She is an exemplary student with consistently outstanding academic achievements. She is this year's Primary School Head Girl and elected as Management Executive for the Johannesburg Mini Council group. She is a team player; she is funny and quirky but stands her ground for what she believes in. She is healthy, beautiful, confident, considerate, a joy to be around, and constantly tells me how much she loves me. In her mother's eyes, she is the perfect child and always has been. And for the first time, I am not at home to make her breakfast and pack her school lunch on a Monday morning.

I slumped back into the church pew next to my tog bag. The tears just flowed again at the realisation that I was the one who let my daughter down. As parents, we can subconsciously expect to see a time when our children will be disappointing us. We can become disappointed if their school grades are not adequate, if they don't make the first team on the sports' ground, dress inappropriately or curse in front of others. Or if they pick the wrong crowd to hang around, the wrong career or marry the wrong partner. Or maybe they turn to an addiction or become chronically anxious or depressed, or they rebel with a dozen body piercings and tattoos, or God-forbid, change their sexuality, we can become so disillusioned.

None of these was yet part of my reality, and none of the above would ever make me turn my back on her until now.

Only this exception was not of her creation. *I* was the real disappointment here, the moment I turned my back on her for these two weeks. There was no greater travesty in my current state of mind than to feel like you have failed as a parent.

I returned the empty flask into the tog bag; there would be no hand-warming today. I hauled my very full rucksack onto my back. The weight of it was not punishment enough. A flagellation would be more in order. I wiped the tears and was consoled by the fact that I had only walked 20 kilometres thus far. Plenty of opportunities lay ahead for more deserving self-castigation.

As we re-grouped on the lawn outside, a dark-green Robin chirped and called from a tree above, begging me to look up. I could not identify its genus name from my limited knowledge of the Roberts' Bird Book of Southern Africa, but I knew who it was.

"Good morning, Mimi. I know you are with me. I really am trying..."

George provided this morning's reflections and motto for the day. My whole life has apparently prepared me for today. I can't wait.

Now in customary silence, we bid last night's blessed shelter farewell and walked away onto the gravel road in a single file. Sure enough, everything just felt so much heavier today: my rucksack, my legs, my lungs, my heart.

"Alright, girl, we are doing this shit. One step at a time. One kilometre at a time. One day at a time." This self-talk kept me going for the first 500 metres before we came to a stop under a small arched tunnel. It supported an extension of the abandoned railway line and stood alone and pleading, waiting for some sort of attention, even though the rising sun had all of its golden light upon it.

Lenny and Iris curiously caressed the inside walls of the stone tunnel, their fingers probing and prodding the natural stony bricks and cement.

This lovely, dear-looking couple from Durban in their late 60s, possibly 70s, quietly searched and fondled above and below the sides of the tunnel. What the heck were they doing? I thought I was the only fruit-cake on this team. It's a pretty tunnel, alright, but if we were going to stop to hug every tree and rock, we were going to take a damn long time to get to the next overnight destination. The rest of the clan watched, perplexed as Lenny eventually retrieved a small plastic box from behind one of the wall stones that magically came loose. Iris kneeled and opened the box to reveal several random and cheap trinkets, which she laid out on the ground. She chose one for herself and replaced it with one of their own – a crystal stone. They wrote their names on a piece of paper that was already scribbled with previous explorers' signatures and put the lot back in its secret hiding place. Our vow to remain silent for the first hour of every day's walk did not permit me to ask questions. It also prevented them from shouting with glee at their discovery, which they were desperate to do. Their smiles of triumph and satisfaction said it all.

I realised this is what they meant when they spoke of Geocaching earlier at breakfast. I had never heard of it before and had looked at them with a dumbfounded stare.

Geocaching is an outdoor recreational activity in which participants use a GPS (Global Positioning System) receiver or mobile device and other navigational techniques to hide and seek containers, called 'geocaches' or 'caches', at specific locations marked by coordinates all over the world. That is Wikipedia's definition. My definition that sparked a twinkle in my eye is that they were treasure hunting!

Was this a tingle of excitement I sensed within me or just plain curiosity?

We continued our steady gravel crunching in silence, and as we ascended above the valley, my pocket began to vibrate furiously. A dozen messages were coming through as we acquired cell phone coverage again. I restrained myself not to check those messages, as the group was still walking in 'quiet time.' It meant staying disconnected from the outside world in order to respectfully get to know oneself again. God knows how I longed to detach from that which no longer served me, but I had no idea what to plug myself into either.

The first three hours took us alongside a mountain ridge, a wild forest, numerous farm fields and beautiful escarpment views. We would exit a farm gate and enter another adjacent farm gate without ever encountering a single person, repeatedly trespassing with pre-granted permission. We passed a lonely man-height monolith, an 1800s Settlers monument that was left to tell a short tale in someone's backyard, long after that someone moved on. In fact, it was quite a few people that had moved on. A humble metal board was the only evidence of their passing existence. "Highland Nek – over which the 1820 Settlers travelled to Grahamstown and beyond." But the beauty of the surrounding landscape overshadowed any nostalgia held within that historic structure.

It was lovely to smell freshness and purity in the breeze that cooled my now perspiring face. It was satisfying to take in the natural sounds of rustling trees, busy birds, and mooing cows in the distance. I began to feel the presence of being in the moment, and it felt good for a little while.

The climb to the higher ridges soon had me huffing and puffing like the big bad wolf. The pilgrim piggies could hear me coming from a mile away. The first two kilometres of the day to the Vodacom cellular tower definitely felt more distant than the first six kilometres of yesterday. I kept my restrain not to look at my phone messages until we got to our first rest point. We spotted the renowned Cockscomb mountain peak from this distance, a landmark which we were heading towards and soon due to cross over, as the official hallmark of "The Crossing" pilgrimage. Interestingly, the mind corrects our spatial perception of distant objects to suit our desire. The distant misty speck of the quaint town of Alicedale was equally and deceptively within reach. We were destined to rest here for the night, but I was not to know this little town would be undesirably etched in my memory forever.

Farm gates were becoming regular and familiar occurrences. One particular massive gate opened onto a gravel path lined with tall pine trees on either side, which lead us up a hill towards a most magnificent ancient tree. We mercifully plonked our rucksacks and our weary selves under its embracing shade to refuel the body and break our silence. We had not seen another human being all morning. There were cows, horses and sheep milling around on the property with free access to a fair-sized pond, but there was no sight of their owners. A windmill moved the still air at snail's pace, and a pair of ducks waddled past, seemingly oblivious to our presence. The overhanging branches were comforting enough to welcome us into the invisible Johan Doe's back yard, although I half-expected to hear sudden shouting being bellowed from the main house, telling us all to sod off his farm.

No such obscenities came as I gulped down my meal replacement milkshake. I munched on the protein bar at a gentler pace, reassured by the soft whispering wind that encouraged the swaying trees to hush us back into silent contemplation. There appeared to be great wisdom in the beckoning of its branches, and vocalized words were not necessary. I noticed two sheepherders in a far corner of the fenced fields, ambling along but not paying us much attention, and almost felt the mother-tree smile at me in an I-told-you-so fashion, "It is okay for you to be here, and everything is going to be alright."

I presumed we were not the first or last strangers to take refuge under this wise-old arboreal friend.

Looking back now, I neglected to appreciate that a surreal or supernatural presence was trying to calm my spirit somehow, for it knew the challenges that lay ahead. It was as if 'IT' was trying to give me a giant-sized energetic and encouraging hug from above. Still, I was so focused on inspecting my feet for incoming blisters that I failed to acknowledge the magic and peace of that moment.

The punishing God that was my faith at this time in my life made sure I paid for this oversight. The walk away from the farm was downhill. My toes slammed against my shoe caps with every step as I tried to refrain from gaining too much momentum down the steep and stony descent. This Jill did not want to come tumbling after, to ten-pin bowl her fellow pilgrims into the bushes. Even though I managed to remain upright, I inadvertently overtook all the others who were slowly and cautiously finding sure-footed grounding, thus preventing twisted ankles. I did not mean to get ahead, for when I arrived miraculously unscathed at a T-junction at the bottom of the hill, I had to look up behind me for George to point me in the correct direction with his waving hiking stick. Go right.

Immediately, I was on the flat and very, very long gravel road to Alicedale. For the remainder of the day and the last kilometres of the day, we were to march on this straight, unending, relentless and desert road. The foreboding scarcity of trees, farms, houses, and animals for miles on end should have made me suspicious.

When the first truck came past and left me behind in a trail of thick grey dust, my brain decided I needed a mantra to set my pace. My feet were sore, but I had my legs marching to the mental tune of 'One step at a time, one day at a time'. Over and over and over. Without real intent, I remained in front of the pack hour after hour of tedious foot-slogging. The repetitive motto and eyesore of one foot in front of the next led me to the next train of thought, "Leave your past behind and take it easy— one day at a time. Retrain your brain. Reprogram your brain. Don't ever look back, move forward, and just keep walking; just keep walking. Over and over."

All the while and for thousands of steps, the legs and feet slapped on the hard compacted gravel.

At some point in the space of lost time, I became aware of my hands on either side of my body, ambitiously swinging to and fro, in rhythm to my beating feet. They were swollen and very red. The weight of the rucksack on my shoulders and nature's gravity had allowed venous blood to pool at the ends of my upper limbs so that my fingertips were now a tad purple. Despite finding a tube of sunscreen cream (another miracle found in a hidden pocket of my rucksack) and having applied a generous amount this morning, the sun was adding a deep crimson colour to my face. The morning's icy chill had long vanished, and the heat that had pent up under my jerseys was now throbbing through my hands. I was so absorbed in my mental reprogramming that I had not peeled some cotton layers that were adding to my discomfort.

Nevertheless, I focused on my pulsating hands and realized that they were not cold for a change! During winter, the only time my hands are warm is during the five minutes that I am in a scorching shower in the evenings. I spend six months of every year touching patients with icicles.

My hands were now hot in plain daylight! In the magic of the moment, I began thinking of all the wondrous things my hands can actually do for me. I began to speak out loud to them, fully aware that I was alone and at least one kilometre ahead of the 2nd place. I announced to these amazing features, "Thank you for what you can touch and stroke and feel. Thank you hands that I can hold my child's face, kiss it, comb her hair, hug her, and tuck her into bed. Thank you that I can hold hands with my husband, I can write, bake, cook, paint, draw, type, clean, wash, wipe, sew, rub and wave with you. Thank you that I can hold, grip and put make-up on. Thank you hands that I can examine patients, stitch, dress wounds, drip, intubate, resuscitate. Thank you that I can garden and pull out weeds, I can drive, I can push a trolley at the store, and I can feed myself, wipe myself and dress with you." The list went on and on (including a few intimate functions) until I could no longer think of anything else I could do with my hands. Still ahead of the pack, my voice got louder and louder whilst I desperately forced this gratitude into my heart. The road was so bleak, flat and disregarding that my words surely dropped to the ground as soon as they were uttered. No echo reverberated back to my ears, just my feet that crunched on.

I had no idea how far I had walked, but the feeling of heatstroke began to play on my mind. I had better shut up, take some clothes off and drink some water. It is too early in the trip for a stupor. My left knee was starting to hurt a bit, though. I shouldn't have marched like a naïve young soldier eager for war. When is George going to call for a break? Maybe they have all had a break, and I just plodded on without noticing?

I take the weight off my shoulders onto the ground and dare to look back. I don't see anyone behind me. Shit. I can't be lost as there have been no turn-offs or any other sign of life, except for three trucks that have whizzed past. Surely, there is no other road to Alicedale? I calmed myself to a gentle panic and took out a snack. Food always makes me feel better. Not sure if it's a Mediterranean thing, a woman thing or a basic survival instinct, but I find it the ultimate dopamine enhancer. As if on cue, or maybe she too smelled food, Christy's figure rose up from the horizon behind me. Accepting it was not a mirage, I lift my rucksack onto my back again and in one second of horror, my left knee buckles up in agony under the sudden weight placed upon it.

The pain catches me so off guard that a wave of nausea raises the bile-coated snack back up to my throat. WTF? This can't be happening. I steady myself with the right leg, hoping Christy was still too far away to have noticed. I hold onto the air and tame my heaving breath, giving my left knee a chance to get its act together. My earlier bravado comes shattering to pieces. I take small steps testing the knee function, furiously trying to establish what kind of injury I have brought upon myself. Stupid woman. It can't be a ligament sprain as I didn't slip, and it can't be a cartilage tear as I didn't fall. And I am too young for fucking arthritis. My slow pace is evident because Christy is soon by my side, asking if

I am alright. My false smile came across as a grimace, I am sure, but I insisted she must carry on ahead.

It was not long before Hank was beside me, asking the same question. My limping is obvious, and he commented on the inadequate bandage I had just placed, found in my very ill-prepared first aid kit. I did not need advice at this point, and I did not wish to talk to anyone. Every step I took required a surmountable effort not to cry. I was angry, scared, in pain, and in denial as I could not comprehend what was happening. Again I thought, I have never injured my knee before, and I did not twist it or bump it today. I am relatively young and have no chronic conditions. How is this possible? My mind was spinning, and there was no end to this damned Alicedale road. I also had no idea how much further I could walk. Hank sensed my despair, and after a few encouraging words, decided to be quiet but did not walk ahead. This further aggravated me. His intention was good, but an over-bearing shape of a He-man taking slow, small steps alongside me made me want to scream.

I fish out my iPod for some salvation and play some blaring music into my earpieces. It was not so much for my distraction but also the boldest and rudest hint that I have ever given anyone showing a kind heart.

I needed time to wallow. Axel Rose was quick to pick up on the cue and screeched loudly in my ears, "Welcome to the jungle honey, we got your disease…it's gonna bring you to your shun knees…and I wanna watch you bleed…it's the price to pay."

Arrgghhh. My imagination grabbed his guitar and smashed it on the backside of this cursed road to Alicedale. And screw Alice, whoever she is.

Another concerned mate soon caught up and went through the same line of questioning, "Are you alright? Have you taken something for pain?"

I felt like replying, "No, I am one of those that prefers her colonoscopy performed with barbed wire." I stopped the raging music and conceded in taking two anti-inflammatory tablets, but I did not accept Maeve's offer to wear her knee-guard. Even though my bandage kept rolling off my throbbing knee, I could not take something that she needed for herself (she was in her 50s, and I presumed she did have arthritis). Also, I could not accept my seething stupidity for not thinking to bring one along on this mission. She eventually gave up trying to convince me. It was unbearably hot, and she, too, felt the need to see the end of this road to hell.

It was no surprise that I was soon trailing behind everyone else, including the team leader. Hank became my silent shuffling shadow, and I eventually put the iPod away when I grasped that he would not leave me hobbling along on my own. Each person had passed by with concern, advice, encouragement, and some with worry. Some walked with us for a while, but with my visible anguish, curt answers, and frustrating slow pace, they continued on to cover more ground. The only thing coming to an end was the afternoon, and George was politely urging us to make haste. Not a good idea to hike in the dark, no doubt. Indeed, that did not add any pressure when I knew that I was now the only one holding everyone back.

Finally, shameful tears exploded out of my eyes when I could no longer hold the barricade. This further highlighted my self-pity when Hank considerately walked a few metres ahead to allow me to be with my painful misery in peace.

Following a trail of people, I had never felt so lost. And so abandoned. I had put myself in this position, so I had no one else to blame but myself. Nevertheless, I felt deserted by man and God and did not know how to find the meaningful existence or purpose of either one.

All my life, I had followed the rules. I had obeyed the expectations of a church, a culture, a job, society, my family. I had obliged to the needs and demands of patients and colleagues. I had always said yes, even when I felt like saying no. I had said no when I should have probably been saying yes. A sure way to get lost; you take a left when your heart says right. Repeatedly.

The irony of this pitiful, limping mess was that I had always thought I was in control of most situations in my life. I guess an addict has the same illusion. I had worked in emergency rooms, trauma units and ICUs for seven years. I made life and death decisions every single day without batting an eyelid (although my heart raced on a regular basis). I was the Doctor in charge of running a busy Casualty Unit for over a year. I hired and fired fellow locum doctors in the moral standing of the practice. I was a flight doctor with an international medical rescue and evacuation service for three years. I determined whether you flew to the heavens or the hospital after the mine explosion, regardless of whether you could voice your preference or not. Modestly speaking, I am always in charge. I manage, I fix, I treat, I direct, I order, I persevere. I am the doctor.

But I have never been the patient. I am terrified of being one. I have not found a definition of being-at-the-mercy-of-doctors phobia. It is far worse than the white-coat syndrome. I am absolutely petrified of being subject to the control other physicians may have over me. Because I know what can go wrong. I know what does go wrong.

If I could have delivered my own child into this world, I would have done so myself. For one surrendering day, in the acceptance that I could not send a nine-month-old foetus back to wherever she came from; I allowed an esteemed professor to cut open my abdomen on a planned date and time, to bring my child into the world, with the shortest possible hospital stay, so my daughter and I could be discharged home at the speed of light. From the first moment she wailed, I did not take my eyes off her and forbade any staff member to handle her. When the sister-in-charge requested the baby's first bath, I ordered my husband to follow the nurse and not take his hawk eyes off of her either. My legs were still dead from the spinal anaesthetic, and I still had the urinary catheter in place. Otherwise, I would have bathed her myself.

But this is where it all went wrong. It was a one-sided affair. I later realised that I was almost exclusively on the giving end. It was safer and more secure there, or so I thought. And so I gave plenty. Of my expertise, my time and my energy. Weekdays, weekends, public holidays, birthdays, Christmas, day after day, night after night, year after year, over and over again. I could not see that I had chosen and created my own downfall. The victim in me just regretted that somewhere along the way, I had given away my joy.

There have been times when I have felt quite helpless, but this moment now on this road to damnation was my ultimate powerlessness. Here I was, lonely amidst strangers, in a forgotten devil's desert, with the weight of a world on my shoulders, an agonizing injury I did not know how to diagnose, let alone treat, and far away from civilization or from any self-respecting orthopaedic surgeon. The incapacity was more than my soul could bear. The intense vulnerability of being at the sacrificial altar of a far more powerful Dr Deo had me on my knees. No pun intended. The stinging tears seared ragged streams down my dust-powdered face, and I had never felt so afraid in all my life.

A massive brown boulder on the right side of the road marked the single entrance to the settlement of Alicedale, where the punitive gravel became a more lenient tar track. Sitting on top of and around the monolith waited ten exhausted and politely impatient fellow pilgrims. Hank intentionally reached the resting crew one minute before I did. They all gave me a moment to catch my breath and casually looked the other way when my eyes became ablaze with shameful tears once more.

I perched my rucksack and buttocks on an unoccupied edge of the rock, without the energy to loosen the waist or shoulder straps nor the motivation to reach for a last booster snack. The only movement I could master was the wiping of my pouring snotty nose with my long sleeve.

I became aware of my body's rebellion. Rapid shallow breathing did not allow air to reach the bottom half of my lungs. My heart pulsated through every sweat gland. Each muscle unanimously seized in objection to the unprepared onslaught I had just put them through. Every scalp hair follicle throbbed and swelled under my prissy blue vice of a hat. The whole weight of my corpse rested on the only good leg as the fierce ache in the left knee took over all of my reason and all of my senses. Newfound tinnitus settled in my ears, and my multi-functional magnificent hands were now completely numb. The begrimed Salomon pair constricted a duo of red hot blisters, one on each baby toe. The lukewarm rehydration fluid from my water bottle fueled the persistent nausea. I forced the last few sips past my burning throat and found it intriguing that my dead hand could even grasp the now empty container. I look up into the blind horizon, deflated and broken, with the yielding realisation that my daily water ration was finished. And so was I.

When it appeared to Christy that I was somewhat composed, she offered me her hiking sticks for ongoing support, and I said, "No, thanks." Another well-meaning member suggested the support vehicle should come to pick me up, to spare me the last four-kilometre cripple-walk to Bushman Sands Lodge. Again, I vehemently declined. With dwindled determination, I summoned every ounce of will to stand up and face the Green Mile, but the left knee buckled again under the order. Eleven pairs of eyes waited for my next step.

All I could do was surrender to the fact that I did need help. The embarrassment was minuscule compared to the sense of defeat as I lifted my arms in acceptance of the walking sticks offered to me once more. They were not crutches, but as I started to take a few steps, I was surprised by the slight relief and appreciated the lessened pressure taken off my left leg. The eleven faces were equally relieved to get going again, albeit at a slower pace.

I had no idea at the time, but this was my first lesson in learning to receive, which is not the same acceptance as earning a salary, moving into a home that you pay monthly instalments for, or receiving a gift on your birthday. For as long as I remember, I was always in a fortunate position to be able to give. Whether it was giving advice, professional abilities, or financial assistance, or giving attention to family commitments and societies' demands, or giving of my time, resources, love and friendship, I was, for the most part, happy to be doing the giving.

Oblivious to me, I had a subconscious fear of ever owing or feeling indebted to anyone. I had an even bigger aversion to ever being the one in need. I could not fathom why I would rather be needed but had developed a hatred for being needed. It made no sense to me. I couldn't think that I had been let down by life so badly that I preferred to take ownership and control of everything around me. But perhaps I did believe so because I had become the sarcastic version of Britney Spears, snarling her way through, "So you want a piece of me?" Sod off and leave me the hell alone.

Yet, whenever my family or friends wanted to return a favour, or not let me cook for an occasion, or run an errand for me, or offer to pay for a restaurant lunch, I could never accept it. My rigid thinking constantly left my family irritated with me. I was so stubborn and adamant that I once left a patient emotionally wounded for not wanting to accept her flowers of gratitude. Years later, I realized the Martyr of my many ego archetypes was completely out of balance and leading me to the gallows.

Dr. Deo was now forcing me to accept walking sticks.

The last four kilometres through the supposed quiet streets of Alicedale lasted a lifetime, but they were mostly a blur to me. I do not remember the houses, the shops, the residents, or the route. I can't recall who said what, who was in the lead, walked beside me or offered me what. I had no sight into the peripheries of my visual field. All my awareness could master was placing one foot in front of the other. Looking back on my journal to recount this tale, the remainder of the day was a blank page. I made no further entries after we had stopped for lunch today. What I have written about this day is what remains ingrained in my memory.

I recall that by the time I saw the entrance to Bushman Sands, I was vividly hallucinating from the pain. My double vision distorted the shapes of the stationary cars and the reception building that was inconveniently placed on the far side of the parking lot. The fellow pilgrims had no faces; they each just melted into human-shaped holograms. Someone was trying to herd us into the reception area, but my body's condition of shock presented me with an even bigger dilemma. I was about to shit my pants.

I clearly remember wishing for instant teleportation to the nearest toilet. The problem was that the nearest bathroom was in the reception area, and I was not so advanced into my delusional state to know I didn't want the entire entourage to hear or smell the imminent explosion. My God, I am going to shit myself! Please help me! I know what happens next – many times, I have witnessed seriously sick or injured patients asking for a bedpan, then two minutes later, they slump over or backwards, stone dead. Was this my final moment? Is this what my whole life had prepared me for? Death by Diarrhoea?

This is the precise reason I have not done myself in yet. I had the *modus operandi* all figured out to abandon this life-boat, but the thought of some stranger finding me dead in a pool of my own faeces was not at all appealing, even to my out-of-body self.

Ignoring the well-meaning receptionist, I turned the other way toward what I later learned to be a housing hostel for young boys. In a frenzied cockroach scuttle, I barged into the first door that had a human figurine glued onto it, not caring who would now witness my shit show. My lame hands threw walking sticks to one corner of the bathroom and the rucksack to the other. My lungs were heaving, my mouth desiccated, and the odour of my body sweat was unbearable, as was the throbbing in my knee and my head. Spastic fingers urgently scrambled to undo my trouser buttons as I skidded onto the toilet. One split second before the first squirt, I squatted down in desperation, realizing there was no time to first layer the porcelain bowl with toilet paper. The horror of an absent toilet seat cover and a filthy toilet bowl festering with remnants of a thousand excrements was, for me, far worse than the faecal deluge that followed.

For anyone that knows me, I had a serious toilet seat phobia, which extended far beyond germaphobia. I had anxiety attacks using aeroplane bathrooms and those horrid portable toilets at the cycling races. I once had a full-on panic attack at one of Kruger National Park's rustic long drops. I had only ventured into that particular bathroom at night because we were in an unfenced wild park campsite. Any other time, I would usually squat behind the car or a bush if we were overlanding or camping without public ablutions. And even when ablutions were available, I would prefer the comfort of the bush squat. There was no danger or fear there.

From the time my daughter was potty-trained, she was indoctrinated in the art of layering any public toilet seat with three layers of paper before she sat her little bottom down. She would balance herself diligently with her princess hands on her lap, as she knew the verbal backlashing that would hurtle out my mouth if she dared hold onto the toilet seat, with her fingers touching the unprotected underside of the plastic seat-cover.

One year after this crappy incident, I was given some insight into where this phobia may have originated during my second consultation with a dear psychologist. My visit to the shrink was not intended to be a past life regression experience (I didn't even know this was possible at the time). Still, during my first EMDR (Eye Movement Desensitizing Reprocessing) session meant to deal with another traumatic event, my body began to tremble uncontrollably, and my voice whimpered in terrifying fear.

"I want to get out of here," I said. "Get me out of here!" I repeated.

I can't describe it as a memory per se or a vivid dream. It was simply a knowing that at some stage of childhood in my eternal soul's memory bank, I had once been hiding from someone or gotten stuck in a pool of faecal excrement for a prolonged period of time.

I did not know the circumstances around this, but of all the hundreds of movies I have watched in this lifetime, two scenes are vividly prominent in my mind. The one is of Sylvester Stallone in the first Rambo movie, where he is being tortured and hung out to dry like Jesus Christ, only Rambo was dipped waist-high in pig shit. The other scene in Schindler's List is of the young boy in one of the concentration camps that hides inside the pit latrines to avoid being caught and taken to the gas chambers. Very little else stands out for me in this emotionally epic movie, but for this moment, when the boy's petrified face is covered in crap, and he is bathing in a hundred thousand people's ordure. This is how he survived the war.

I did not complete that EMDR session. I sat up from the couch, ripped the earphones, and handed the rest of the wired contraption back to the psychologist, wiping my tears in embarrassment. This was not what I signed up for. I had dealt with that shit in Alicedale on the 24th July 2017 and had had instant forced healing. I thought my toilet phobia was cured when my bowels opened up and released what felt like a whole life's pent up manure. The relief that followed with the realisation that I was not yet dead was even more satisfying. Surprisingly.

As I gathered my breath, unaware of the foul odour and explosion that lay splattered beneath my butt, I sobbed in silence, grateful to still be alive and so thankful that I had made it in time to this toilet.

At no point during this experience did I even look around for toilet paper.

There was none. I shall not divulge how I managed to clean myself on that particular eventful afternoon. Some things are best left unsaid, as I have indeed detailed too much already. Finally, I am ashamed to say there was no toilet brush, so I don't plan on showing my face at that boys' hostel ever again.

Once my vital signs seemed stable, I gathered my belongings and sheepishly wandered in the general direction of the guest motel area. A search party was already out for me. I can't remember who showed me to my room or brought my purple tog bag from the support vehicle. My sleeping arrangements had been selected for me. I was to share the room with three other ladies. At this stage, I was still oblivious that there is usually a pecking order in the designation of any hikers' club's sleeping arrangements. On the first night of every communal slumber, the expert hikers suss out their fellow friends' nocturnal habits regarding the late-night reading habits, the snorers, the farters, the hyperactive shufflers, the incessant chatterboxes, the sleep-talkers, the twilight morning risers, etc. Then follows an undercover strategic plan for every night's order. Who sleeps with who, who gets the first pick of the best beds and hot shower, and who is the fastest walker in the favoured team to reach the next destination first. This secretive selection occurs during the day when one expert hiker casually walks along with another favourite hiker, pretending to talk about the Eastern Cape fynbos and the current prices of acrylic gel nails.

I guess I considered myself lucky tonight to be sleeping with the winning team.

Sitting on the clean white sheets of my gracious single bed, I assessed the state of my very dirty body, the damage to the now fully blistered baby toes and stuffed up left knee - what a sorry-assed sight.

Sipping in a slow stupor on rehydration electrolytes, I had no idea how to walk another 250 kilometres in this condition.

An added disbelief settled in when I came out of a cleansing hot shower and could not find the standard bath towel supposed to be hanging from the hotel towel rack. I had not thought to pack one either. Jesus Christ, what next? Standing naked, staring at the mirror above the sink, dripping water on the floor mat, I did not know that I had to learn the vulnerability lesson today as well. Total exposure is clearly required before any redemption.

I looked around for a Candid Camera in the en-suite bathroom, but I was the bare reflection of the only joke in the room. I dried myself off with the day's sweaty T-shirt. I had thrown away my underpants earlier on.

The evening supper and mandatory reflection conversations were another haze. My now apathetic demeanour did not allow anything significant to sink within. Maybe I was so high on painkillers that I zoned out of all dialogue (I had taken a handful of analgesia with the rehydration fluid so that I could stand in the shower). And tomorrow's route was for tomorrow. Whatever.

Before I shut my eyes for the night, my last thought was of the foot massage I allowed Julie to give me after I had showered. The ultimate tutorial in learning to receive. Never before had I permitted a stranger to care for or tend to my visible wounds. Never had I granted an unfamiliar person such access past my Fort Knox wall of disguise and defence. This was the ultimate surrender, as I granted her permission into my newly unguarded space. She gently rubbed and massaged endearments into my left leg and foot with her warm hands, casually whispering out of earshot that this was a sign. My body's left side reflected the female in me that was having trouble moving forward, and the knee joint signalled my resistance to flexibility or change.

What was she talking about? I am double-jointed, for goodness sake! I can put my legs behind my shoulders and pretend to talk on the phone with my feet next to my ears.

But at this point, I did not care if she was another Louise Hay fan or not. I gratefully received her gift. This kind gesture was given to me unconditionally, albeit from a place of deep hurt too.

Many people have since tried to teach me that the natural balance of anything in life always has an ebb and flow. It is the nature of energy - it is in constant motion, and it is cyclical. And everything that exists is only energy, including us - trillions and gazillions of atoms packed together in different densities, vibrating at different frequencies to produce an image or a figurative hologram. We are a giant walking battery, and the world is equally an illusion. As a doctor, I was astounded that this concept had remained elusive to me until the age of forty-six. But that is another story.

Being a practical person, I later understood how one-way deals can never feel comfortable and can ultimately leave me gasping for air if I don't learn to give and receive in equal balance. If I take in a breath and hold it, how long can I hold it in before I need to exhale? If I breathe out and hold it, how long before I am desperate to take in the next breath? Breathing in is the same as *receiving* pure life force, the energy that sustains me, the things that recharge the body, mind and soul. Exhaling is what I am letting go of and freely giving to others. Both need to co-exist in balance. Hoarding onto things or uncomfortable emotions for too long feels like drowning under them. Taking from life and not giving something back is forever ungratifying. And giving to others only without giving to yourself equally, will eventually feel like suffocation.

We have been brought up in a society that demands you to give of yourself and give to others first so that the rest of the world can be happy before you can be happy. If you don't, it is perceived as selfishness. The problem is that doing this will eventually leave you depleted of all that feels good within. When you have given away all the kindness, tolerance, patience, compassion and joy, all that will remain at the bottom of the cup is usually anger, resentment, frustration, guilt and shame that you are snapping at the kids and wishing that everybody leave you the fuck alone. This is what selfless actually means – you become depleted with nothing good left to give, with a soul or a self that has disappeared.

And so this should be the First Commandment - Love Thyself.

Fill your cup first. Breathe in all the thoughts and things that genuinely nourish and replenish your higher self, your body, and your mind. Breathe in what feels natural and good to you so that when you give, that is all that overflows from your cup.

Dr Wayne Dyer explains it simply that if you squeeze an orange, all you will get is orange juice. Whatever is filled up from within is what will come out when it is squeezed. When the drama of people and the world trigger you and squeeze your buttons, what will come out of you?

If you can love yourself first in a self-nurturing and self-preserving way, without harming others, you are naturally able to love your neighbour too.

No other Commandments are then necessary.

All my life has been preparing me for this. To accept the gift of the divine life force that is naturally mine as a birthright and freely available to me. And be *willing* or *choosing* to fill my cup first with what feels good to me.

Ask, and you shall receive.

5
CONFORMATION

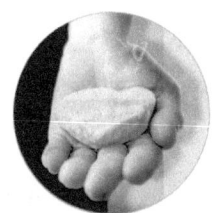

In the game of Tetris, once you fit in, you will disappear

The previous night's overdose on analgesics only allowed for one hour of insomnia, most likely from the high dose cortisone that attempted to fight the sedating pharmacopoeia. I was grateful, nevertheless, to have rested without any nightmarish entertainment. Yesterday's well-intended routine plan for the morning went out the window, as my immediate idea was to place a strong anti-inflammatory suppository up where the sun did not shine the day before.

My compact and very basic first aid kit had been raided (surely by me), and there were already eighteen various tablets missing. It dawned on me that I may need a liver booster too, but in the Gaelic words of Mel Gibson in Braveheart: "I canna worry 'bout that noe."

Still seated with sleep-coated eyes, I packed the sleeping bag and rucksack first. Petrified to get up and determine what kind of state the knee was in this morning, I found the two blisters on my toes to pop, then mummified the feet with Elastoplast tape. I did a better job of strapping the only bandage I possessed around the left knee. Hiking pants on. Feet squeezed back into the Salomons that certainly shrank during the night. Moment of truth.

A tentative erection of my body saw me stand on both legs with relative ease. Inconceivable. No pain! Lord Almighty, a miracle! I could hardly suppress the nervous smile and steadily walked to the bathroom with suppository and toothbrush in hand.

We gathered at the lodge's restaurant for scrambled eggs, bacon and toast. I made sure my tummy was sufficiently satisfied to tolerate another handful of tablets with two cups of soothing hot coffee. I was not going to take a chance today and thought to be better prepared. The 32 kilometres that lay ahead ensured my rucksack was much heavier than the day before. Extra water, fruit and snacks were necessary, but I was confident that today would be a better day. It could not possibly get any worse.

Another chilly morning, but it felt more refreshing than uncomfortable. The pre-departure reflection time was brief. By now, everyone had already enquired on how I was holding up. I may have looked braver than I felt, but I was certainly full of hope. Their kindness fueled my desire to see the end of this day with far less drama. I walked out of Bushman Lodge's main gate with mixed feelings; very grateful to have had a cosy and safe oasis to lick my wounds and gather composure, but adamant that Alicedale would not see my face or ass ever again.

The road out of this town was as straight and long as the one that brought us into it; only we headed in the opposite direction. Once the clusters of houses and buildings were out of sight, the town's secondary route led onto a busier National main road. We were to walk in single file on the emergency lane of the oncoming traffic side for better safety. The leisurely follow-the-leader pace allowed me an appreciation of the steady ease of walking on firm tar. The first hour's obligatory silence settled a welcoming calmness within me. It was too early for traffic, so we only had the soft treading of rubber shoes on a concrete surface and the chirping of an array of birds for company.

We were soon walking alongside a small river veined into a valley on our right and a towering cliff wall to our left. This majestic mountain pass was vertically and neatly sliced to make way for a road built to provide one town road access to the next. The completion of the pass was not visibly dated, so I dared to hope it was not raw manual labour that hauled away tons of rock rubble two centuries ago to make way for civilized progress. But Africa is not for sissies, and this is most likely what happened. My unsettling pondering quickly turned to jaw-dropping mesmerisation.

The exposed inner rock surface revealed slab upon slab of ancient geometric lamination. Several earth eras were fossilized between multiple layers of prehistoric soil, surmounting millions and millions of years of existence. This rock face absorbed and drowned out any peripheral noise, and we seemed to be walking through a silent portal where time and space did not exist.

This mountainous structure has been around for aeons. No matter how many times humans may try to redesign, reshape, or vandalize the earth and its natural resources and wild inhabitants in the name of progress, Mother Nature will forever outlast the hominid race, long after its self-destructive extinction.

Once we passed the empyreal gateway, the excited call of the many birds that flitted from tree to tree was once again loud in my ears. They echoed my silent satisfaction that our beautiful earth would ultimately prevail. These flying angels affirmed that no matter what atrocities were inflicted upon our planet, it would all be alright, and everything is as it should be. It does not validate our behaviour; it simply means we are just meagre mortals and non-entities at the end of the day.

This gave me great comfort.

Cars began to drive past us at various speeds. The majority of their drivers hooted or waved in encouragement. I am sure a few thought: "Who are these crazy people?" But their genuine smiles never showed anything but kindness.

I had no idea that my tear glands contained so much fluid. They started welling up again as I swallowed the deep-seated hatred I held for people of our human race. When and how had all this loathing accumulated? And how could I generalize this feeling when everyone I had met these last four days was a complete contradiction to my indoctrinated idea of such a dislike?

Several kilometres later, the hillside to our left had completely receded, and we veered off the tar road to our right to walk alongside a narrow river. Unruly bush lay tangled over the parched ground, as the river bed had dried up a long time ago. Another derelict railway line travelled alongside the other margin of the scarred river bank. We were to follow the railway landmark for a while but first had to jump one of many fences of the morning. This particular one was embroidered with barbed wire, and I hoped it was not symbolic of another cutting-edge day. George held down the bottom strand of wire with his hiking trainers and lifted the top layer with careful fingers, so we could each crouch down like rabbits through a hole.

The following two kilometres were dotted with scat, animal footprints, wildflowers, and a myriad of shrubs I could not identify. Another modest mountain embraced us from the right whilst we plodded along its valley. The obligatory silence was unanimously prolonged for these first few hours, as we all took the time to soak in the tranquility, the caress of a gentle breeze and the devoted bird-singing.

I may not know what an epiphany will look like, but I was quite content and grateful to be walking quietly at an even, leisurely pace and with minimal pain. I tried to focus on the serenity of the landscape. For now, this must be my Serengeti.

By late morning, the sun had risen over the mountains and cast flints of sun rays through the trees, growing tall at their feet. As a young child, I would sometimes look up at the rays of sun splayed through grey clouds in the sky and wonder if those were God's fingers touching the earth and healing its people. Perhaps my mother told me that they were God's fingers, as I had always believed them to be. This sight always brought a sense of calm to my soul, and now it had the same soothing effect, as God seemed to be happy to connect with the People this morning.

Once upon a time, a farmhouse had been built at the edge of this once flowing river, at the base of this fertile mountain, and it had no doubt flourished for years whilst supporting its resident family. There could not have been much traffic passing through here, though. We had been walking along a narrow sandy pathway for a long while. This same track lead us past this stand-alone building, even though it could hardly accommodate the width of a horse cart. The house was now abandoned for whatever reason, leaving its windows and doors missing in action, its crumbling walls witness to a sunbaked and desiccated vegetable garden, and with no one to adore this beautiful piece of Eden.

We took our tea break on the property's outskirts and rested our feet and shoulders but did not have much conversation to go around. It was a gathering of idle mumblings of lovely scenery, soft munching on fruit and snack bars, stretching of muscles and gentle clicking of joints. It was not yet too hot, so the warmth of the sun on our backs was energizing. A few pilgrims closed their eyes for a moment, faces hidden under their hats. It was only the soft breathing of the air and the plentiful feathery friends that shared our daydreaming.

It was a bit surprising to me when my bowels gave a sign they needed to move. I thought I might have been pissed off at this unexpected inconvenience, but today I was relatively at ease with the natural call of my body's necessities. As we all gathered our belongings to continue our way, I indicated that I would catch up with the flock shortly. I was just staying behind to adjust my rucksack straps and take off a layer of clothing under my jersey. As the last person moved off from our makeshift picnic site, I ventured behind a large obscuring bush, dropped my pants, and with an unabashed squat, proceeded to release what was toxic to my body into the ground. My fits of giggles were amusing when the valley echoed back pa-ra-pa-pa-ta.

I sure hoped the others were way ahead of me and out of earshot. With relieving pleasure that I had enough toilet paper on me this time, I covered the evidence with my Salomon shoe. Satisfied that I had pulled up my zip and had all my worldly goods with me, I circled my bushy ablution and instantly came face to face with Hank.

This dutiful soldier had stood twenty feet from me, on silent guard, and had not walked away without me. Because undoubtedly, when we are at war, we never leave a comrade behind.

His eyes did not meet mine. He respectfully gazed out onto the road ahead, the oblivious pretence evident in his demeanour. I was not Will Smith or a Man-in-Black, so there was nothing I could do to erase his memory. I casually walked on past him and smiled, *"Dit was nou 'n lekker boskak!"*

The flat sandy trail became an uphill gravel trek from here on forward to our planned lunch stop. The uninhabited indigenous bushveld gave way to farmland after farmland. Only these were game farms with impala, springbok and a variety of other antelope. We did not see any of them. I suspect they were hiding and terrified of humans since our intent was to hunt them, and they had no means of fleeing past contained fencing. Not exactly fair game.

George opened one farm gate after the next. This time, no fence jumping or hurdling was required as one property was open onto the next owner's property. It did not make my uphill climbing any easier, though. I had hoped my left knee would not be giving me any more hassles, but alas. It complained with a crescendo of throbbing every time we entered another farmer's dwelling. We had walked for another two and a half hours across tended lands in this trespassing fashion. Upon arrival at a farm gate, we stopped in our tracks at a sign that was boldly marked in warning: "BEWARE OF BUFFALO".

George had arranged for Ronelle to meet us at this specific GPS location, and we waited for her to arrive through the back roads in our support vehicle. She was to be the peloton in leading the trailing pilgrims through this section of wilder acreage. If an eminent buffalo herd stampeded, I am sure we would easily fit twelve adult humans, with freshly soiled underwear, into the front seats of a Mitsubishi Pajero SUV; considering the back seats were occupied with a wagon-load of bags and spares-boxes. After all, this is South Africa, and most local taxis manage to transport regular passengers in this manner on a typical working weekday.

We were indeed grateful to have this backup facility available, as no sane and knowledgeable African citizen wants to come face to face with a grumpy old *dagga boy* on foot. They can be far more dangerous than crossing paths with a wild lion. And so, we all snuggled up behind the Pajero as a seemingly unified mammalian creature intent on tricking and intimidating the local fauna. Our trepid walking continued behind the fumes of a revving motor's exhaust pipe, leaving us with a distinct offensive scent to follow.

Of course, it was not long before I began to trail behind the herd. The drugs were wearing off, and this stubborn knee would not allow for faster heeding. Having noticed the panic beginning to set in, George reassured me we had more than enough time to reach our destination today. To keep me encouraged, dear old Lenny ambled alongside me and began with idle chat. Perhaps he needed the distraction more than I did. His feet had begun to blister, too, and I noticed his subtle limp starting to show. Hank took the last place behind these two side-by-side stragglers.

We were both attentive to the story Lenny was recounting when he broke his leg whilst hiking the Tsitsikamma trail in the Western Cape. He somehow had lost his footing and had tumbled down an incline, landing awkwardly and very painfully with his one lower leg facing in the wrong direction. His team had no means of carrying him back up the hill, so he had to be evacuated by helicopter to the nearest medical facility. However, the ordeal lasted all of ten hours from the time of the fall to eventually landing at the hospital. I couldn't imagine the pain and fear this man must have been in, so much so that I did not wish to complain again about my silly aching knee. I sympathized with his unpleasant experience and secretly rejoiced that at least that specific scenario had already been played out. What were the chances of a second helicopter rescue? I thanked Lenny for putting my mind at ease that at least I would not be making that particular phone call on this trail.

Eventually, the peloton was way ahead of our trio, though fortunately, we had not had a single African bison in sight. Be that as it may, Lenny eventually called out loud: "Hey guys, wait for us! You are leaving the testicles and tail of the big buffalo behind!"

That was a first for me. I had always hoped to be the Belle of the ball, but today I was promoted to a scrotal ball. I laughed nevertheless, hoping that a tiny bit of dopamine release would aid my failing joint.

The buffalos' homestead was another several metres up a steep hill. Hank had the idea of holding out his walking sticks behind him, which I gratefully grabbed as he half-dragged me up to the farmhouse. Definitely not enough dopamine. As good as his intention was, not even the rhythmic whooshing of his firm butt cheeks rubbing against each other could sidetrack me of the fact that I now wished to amputate this agonizing screwed-up knee of mine. To add to the insult, just when I had the farmhouse in view, I was told it was not the designated pit stop. It was another mile to the next farmhouse, where we were to stop for lunch. What was wrong with this house?

Jesus, I don't think I can do this…

Someone suggested I just hop into the rescue vehicle for the couple of kilometres to our rest-break. This was not on my program. I was adamant about walking every inch of ground. A little more nudging from concerned friends still had me wondering if riding in a car for one kilometre was considered a mission failure. There seems to be an invisible but well-indoctrinated law that you don't take shortcuts by climbing in vehicles if you hike. This is 'illegal' and considered cheating.

Before I could decide, Ronelle had made a U-turn and had brought the car to my side. She stopped and rolled down the passenger window. She read my mind and suggested I jump on the outside ledge of the passenger's door and hold onto the rooftop of the car. The look of reassurance on her face said this is not throwing in the towel and not even a compromise. It's just a little push to get you to the top so that you can gather your strength. I gratefully obliged and did as she advised.

Jeanette du Preez was the owner of the pretty homestead on the farm where we were to have tea and scones and where I was to find a miracle for this hindrance that had me crying again from the moment my eyes were lost in the horizon above the SUV's rooftop. Fortunately, our host had to go to Port Elizabeth unexpectedly, so I was glad not to have to make polite conversation in exchange for delicious homemade pastries. But with no one home, there was only the welcoming shade of her veranda to quench our thirst and a few benches and steps to rest our aching backs.

Whilst we waited for the real diehard hikers to catch up, Ronelle gently tried to soothe my broken ego, but my head hung sheepishly low, mostly to hide the tears that I hoped were unseen.

My daughter had once mentioned that she had never seen me cry. Ever. She was probably right. For her sake, I had always kept the façade that I could handle everything and anything without batting an eyelid. I had always wanted to seem like I had it all figured out and could be invincible and as resilient as titanium, believing this to be the ideal role model for her. It is known as the Superwoman Syndrome that is yet to be catalogued into the Medical textbooks of psychiatric conditions. But this fraud of a heroine did not expect a sore knee to break her invisible shield.

A handful of anti-inflammatories, pain killers and cheese with dry crackers did not bring the expected salve I needed. Sitting on a wooden bench, I was left to revive the knee with repeated and aggressive massaging with Wintergreen ointment. The local folk call it the Rub-Rub. It is the magic one-dollar balm that cures all muscle, bone and joint diseases known to man. I would not be a respectable doctor if I did not issue at least one small container to each patient at Soweto's rural community clinics all those student years ago. However, I seemed to be resistant to its magic. It was doing jack-shit for me even though I genuinely believed in it.

We were to start walking again at one o'clock, having a further 16 kilometres to cover with the hopeful expectation of reaching Kromrivier Farm by 17.00. I was at a dead-end crossroad. My sleeves wiped more tears which poured out my nose. I dreaded delaying the team and prolonging their exhaustion for the day, but I could not bring myself to admit defeat. The indecision was maddening, and I just wished I had taken my chances with a crazy buffalo. Mulling pointlessly with my bandage, the voice of reason arrived from the heavens to decide for me.

Warm merciful hands cupped my pleading knee. George's tender and steady face looked up at me from a crouched curtsy. With hypnotic blue eyes, he advised firmly: "Part of any pilgrimage is also to know when to stop. It is better to rest your knee so that you can continue with the rest of the journey. You will be far more disappointed for not reaching the destination at all." His wise and fatherly eyes sealed my surrender.

The drive to Jenny and CP Meyer's Kromrivier farm and guesthouse was far more solemn than the walk of shame after an all-night's raunchy party. I had very few words to offer in the comfort of the SUV's passenger seat in reply to Ronelle's sympathetic conversation. Of course, we completed the last 16 kilometres of country road for the day in less than forty minutes.

A larger than life Jenny awaited our arrival and pointed our car up to another little hill to the guesthouse, accommodating us all for the night. She would drive up shortly to bring some provisions. I instantly liked her welcoming vibrancy and knew this lady was about to smother us in abundant nourishment and motherly spoils.

Her guesthouse was a free-standing renovated building at the far end of her massive property, divided into a small kitchen, two bathrooms, a communal dining room and four bedrooms with sleeping space for fourteen people. She had personally overseen its revamping, and there was an immediate sense that we had arrived home. A home does not need to have your address marked on the front door, but simply the feeling of a safe and loving haven as you enter its doors. The walls were freshly painted, the rooms tiny and quaint, all decorated with a clutter of rich family heirlooms, beautiful antiques, and refurbished old furniture.

Ronelle and I had the first pick of which room we would like to sleep in. I did not want to be presumptuous and decide for everyone else. I simply selected the bedroom with two single beds as I had no wish to share a double bed with anyone just yet. My purple tog bag was duly unpacked over the single bed closest to the window, and my territory was thus marked. We proceeded to offload the rest of the bags from the SUV and placed them in a neat row outside the front door for each respective owner to claim on their arrival. Even though I could hardly walk, I offered to hang up everyone's laundry that had not dried the night before

– another first for me. I had never had so many strangers' undergarments pass through my hands. It is a perfect icebreaker amongst strangers to guess which jockstrap belongs to which groin and which brassiere belonged to which bosom. But it did bring me some consolation, considering it was the least I could do for leaving their proprietors to walk out sixteen thousand metres without me. The martyrdom belief was deep-seated in my subconscious, and I was oblivious to it.

My blessings kept pouring in when I was the first one to get to shower with piping hot water. I did not know one had to switch on the cold water at the outside geyser first, so it was a tad too late when scalding water hit my naked body like a lightning bolt. I jumped out of the shower and stood frozen like a deer staring at oncoming headlights. I was now wet and too cold to go outside and too irritated to put my clothes back on to go and open the geyser knob. So I got back into the liquid hell to wash my body and sport a red-hot ass in the shortest possible time. The Universe was really laying on the lessons fast and furious. What exactly was the purpose of this back burn, pray, tell?

Unbeknownst to me at the time, the divine Universe *always says YES*. If you say, "I am worthy," the Universe brings you more abundance. If you say, "I am sick and tired," the Universe says yes, have more discomfort and work. If you say, "I am deserving of joy," the Universe brings forth opportunities to create and grow in love. If you say, "I have to be a martyr," the Universe says yes. And then you break your knee and burn your ass.

It is simply the undeniable energetic Law of Attraction and nothing to do with religion, voodoo, karma or superstition. Our thoughts create our reality.

A pacifying fresh cup of coffee downed a few more cortisone and analgesic tablets. If I was not going to have any epiphanies, I could at least enjoy psychedelic hallucinations. Freshly scented and sweating, I walked outside and found Ronelle sitting on the veranda at the back of the house, reading in private contemplation. She, too, had a cup of tea in hand. I sat opposite her on a cushioned lounge chair with the intent of updating my journal amidst a bit of peace and quiet. It is fascinating to me that there are exceptional instances or places where one will be in complete and utter silence. There will always be a bird, a cricket, a bleating sheep that will sound the air around you. The leaves on a tree will rustle, the air-conditioner will hum, or your tummy will grumble.

I have only ever experienced the awakened and complete silence of the Divine Universe on two occasions in my life. That morning of my mother-in-law's funeral and another time when a moment of insomnia had me awake at 3 a.m. on a random week night in the middle of the Central Kalahari Game Reserve in a place called Deception pan. I think God comes to extraordinary locations like this to gather His strength before going back to answering the masses. My daughter was nine years old at the time, and our family were the only three human souls camped out in this isolated desert for several miles in any direction. The only movement I became aware of was my eyelids' opening and my brain's calculation of where I was in time and space. There was nothing else. No sound, no noise, no palpable vibration. Just a few moments of sublime inertia with a billion twinkling stars staring back at me through the tent window, but in the absolute awe of *knowing* you are not alone. In the stillness of that suspended moment comes the *knowing* and the peace that there is indeed an invisible, Divine and powerful Source that has your back, and for a split second, you *know* All is perfect as it is. An instant of mystical awareness.

I may have had many epiphanies in my life already, only I didn't understand them fully, or they lasted for just a split second that I could not grasp any single one for long enough. Perhaps, because it did not come with a flash of white light, nor a jolt of electrical current up my spine, I did not think them to be relevant or significant. This particular moment had been interrupted by the sudden swoosh of owl wings bearing down on a scurrying field mouse, I imagined. The pitch black of the night did not allow me to see the rodent's sacrifice, but the fright of the sudden sound was enough to bring me back to earth.

Peace can, however, come without the presence of silence. The woeful bellowing of cows in the distant field can be tranquilising. The music of birds whistling can be calming, and the whispers of the chilly afternoon wind through the leaves of a large backyard eucalyptus can bring stillness to a turbulent mind. And peace can be found in the presence of someone who does not want anything from me, doesn't feel the need to offer advice, nor have the compulsion to 'fix' me. Ronelle brought just that kind of peace by simply being.

The desire for a second cup of tea initiated a bit of casual chat, which lead to Ronelle sharing with me a glimpse of the journey she was on after she had unexpectedly lost her husband and life partner the year before. He suffered for three weeks with acute pancreatitis, and his body could not survive the inflammation. Dealing with his passing was just as difficult as dealing with the regret that they never got to enjoy a long list of retirement plans which had suddenly come to an abrupt end. This Indlela pilgrimage was intended to help her process and perhaps mend some of the broken pieces of her heart and life. But she had not planned on sustaining a calf injury a few days before starting this journey and almost cancelled her trip. She was very disappointed about not being able to walk with us but had decided to come along anyway. Personally, I thought she had the most crucial role of the team - carrying our precious belongings from one post to the next, being in the driver's seat of our race, and our support rock at the end of every day. She was my spirit's solace on this day. I couldn't be more pleased that she had joined us. I hoped she would still have an opportunity to find a few of those missing pieces that had left her heart open but still bleeding. It may not necessarily come with endless walking and self-punishment. Still, I hoped it would come with the understanding that, amongst many gifts, she had great value and purpose in the simple act of being compassionately supportive and a stronghold for others.

Hypocratic Oaths

After all, Ram Dass did say: "We are all walking each other home."

The conversation flowed onto talk of a precious seven-year-old autistic artist that was Ronelle's grandson. Her face smiled with a glow of pride, detailing the many accomplished drawings and paintings that this young man had already created. He was a source of joy and light in her life, and she adored the time spent with him. My eyes may have widened a bit because I could not understand this part of her story. I clearly remember feeling sorry for her and her family. I wished I had far more admiration than pity for families raising special needs children. I had only seen the heart-wrenching challenges that parents have endured when they desperately call on every doctor and specialist to help them overcome many social, physical, mental and emotional tribulations they have with these children.

At the time of journaling this thought, I was so lost in a world of misery and my own mental suffering that I failed to understand the true blessing that these children are and the extraordinary life they can provide if you can see through the undertaking of looking at the glass half full, instead of half empty. But I was so bottomless in my cup that I confess here for the first time; I thought severely disabled people were a waste of oxygen. I am ashamed to write this on paper now, but I saw no purpose in their suffering or the suffering of their relatives. Some children and adults are so trapped in a useless bed-ridden body, mentally incapacitated without the ability to blow their nose or ask for water, that this was, in my limited perception, simply a curse. Not so much the affected person, but the parents that very often carried the guilt for being in some way responsible for this genetic misfortune. When the guilt or lack of resources or support is too much to bear, some children are left in a home for the disabled to be looked after by strangers. Of course, it can be a saving grace for both parent and child. Still, I wondered how conscious these debilitated bodies were of any pain or disappointment, or was it simply a matter of the rest of us not being able to handle our own suffering and resentment objectively? Much like a person who dies, their spirit leaves the body and finds itself back in the unified divine quantum field of unconditional love and at peace; the only problem is that their loved ones are left behind to grieve in despair.

But to be so narrow-minded was, in fact, a bigger curse.

Eighteen months had passed after this journal entry when again, my sister placed another book of wisdom into my hands. This one had Rupert Isaacs sharing his extraordinary journey of healing and courage of "The Horse Boy", who was and is his autistic son. As an independent film-maker, journalist and writer, his search for answers to help his non-verbal and seemingly disconnected child make sense of his surroundings had them on a quest to seek out the ancient wisdom of the bushmen of Namibia, the shaman of Australia's coastal rainforests and reach out to the spirit-guides of America's Navajo people. This very moving and incredible account of a father's yearning to unlock his son from a perceived lost world had him deep in realising that these beautiful and exceptional children are perhaps showing us that we are the ones living in a lost world. If we don't unlock ourselves from our own antiquated and dangerous limited beliefs and ego-driven actions, we are the ones at risk of losing our minds and purpose. It is no longer appropriate (it has never been) to force any human being to fit into an ill-indoctrinated mould. This mould cannot accommodate a unique, energetic form with unlimited possibilities and boundaries and a potential that stretches far beyond the glorious unknown.

Rupert wrote at the end of his book: "It seems very clear that our species is on the brink of an environmental crisis. An environmental crisis that the human ego has largely caused: greed gone wild. But is it possible that this very crisis is bringing our species its own antidote? Are we starting to breed a new generation of egoless, or let's say much *less* egotistical, humans? Do we, as autism parents, have a front-row seat at the accelerated evolution of our species? Individuals with the same intellect as our own, or possibly greater because it is unhampered by the ego's negative effects: individuals who can create technologies without greed, who will bring us back to a post-industrial version of the more authentic human way to live? Is autism going to save our planet? Or, rather, is autism going to be part of what saves *us*?"

I now believe this extends to every child labelled (or mislabelled) as having ADHD (Attention deficit hyperactivity disorder) or a Spectrum disorder, a Sensory Processing disorder and perhaps even Bipolar disorder. We have become so dysfunctional and indoctrinated in the confined rules of antiquated social, cultural and religious beliefs and behaviours. Moving towards the possibility of something more liberating, magical, fulfilling, albeit facing many unknown outcomes, and creating new progressive milestones opposite to the mainstream, become our biggest stumbling block in life.

I was not yet on this yellow-brick road, but Ronelle was definitely onto something grander than I could imagine. She had found the pot of gold at the end of a colour-filled rainbow.

Our intimate conversation ended when Jenny brought a homemade cauldron of her hearty vegetable soup into the kitchen. It was 17.00, and she had spotted the first of our tenacious pilgrims appear on the horizon. They must be utterly exhausted, and she was making sure they had enough welcoming consolation with an extra supply of butter cookies and rusks on the coffee table. I curbed the urge to clap upon their arrival, even though I was so sheepishly impressed by their endurance. I still felt very guilty for bailing out halfway through today's parade, so I simply gave them the space to pass through the front door's finishing line. Even though they were visibly tired, dusty, sore and hungry, there was still a distinctive scramble for the claim on the beds for the night. Only a handful were unfazed as to where they would have tonight's sweet dreams. The relief of arriving at this cosy and delightful oasis was ample reward.

The warm homecoming of hot soup, life-giving tea and biscuits, and release of claustrophobic shoes and heavy bags had everyone's general disposition perk up a notch. Hank seemed to be agitated, and I thought he was not pleased with his sleeping arrangements. Later at reflection time, he voiced his anger at the Rwandan genocide, which had him almost spitting bile at the senseless madness when he visited the country three weeks before this Indlela. The others had merely allowed him to be with his depressing rage at this stage, but when he was given the first option to speak after supper-time, I fought very hard to suppress agitating my inner anger.

I could relate to his hatred. I had seen on countless occasions the aftermath of the complete disregard and disrespect for human life: men shooting, hacking and stabbing other men, people throwing each other off high balconies, communities 'necklacing' a man with a rubber tyre and watching him helplessly burn to death, children being neglected, abused or raped, a drunken husband kicking his 8-month pregnant wife until she bled and delivered a stillborn baby, countless drinking and driving poly-traumas and preventable loss of life. This is not counting the dead bodies that have never reached the hospitals from suicides, murders, hijackings, self-inflicted accidents or serial raping. Or the atrocities inflicted on a myriad of animals and earth's creatures and the destruction of our planet's pristine eco-systems. And I am not counting the knock-on devastation inflicted on the families or communities of all of the above by a handful of politicians, ministers, religious leaders and corporate moguls.

In my everyday struggle of trying to help people, I saw no hope for the human race, and at times I felt like I was wasting my time and my life. The funny thing was I had become so discouraged and internally galled by such cruelties. However, when I attended to head colds, ingrown toenails and ear wax build-up in my GP practice, I was intolerant of people's complete lack of resilience. When they came to see me for a headache from work stress or a project deadline, I wanted to visibly eye-

Hypocratic Oaths

roll instead of only doing it in my head. I then thought they were wasting my time with menial complaints!

I was angry that I had chosen this seemingly unrewarding profession. I was mad at myself for not knowing how to do anything else. I was enraged at feeling trapped in this life. And therein lay the absolute truth. It was revealed to me months after this admission.

I hated myself the most.

Now there were turns to drink, eat, sit at the tiny kitchen table, shower, and get settled for the evening. George was the last one to shower. He had spent some time catching up with Jenny and enquiring about her well-being amidst the drought that had adversely affected their sheep stock's upkeep. He showed much gratitude for all the effort and kind hospitality she was indulging us with, knowing full well the financial and emotional strain all the farmers were currently experiencing. He was the last to join at the supper table, arriving with a sore knee, a sunburnt face, and a smile of genuine contentment.

If I hadn't known better, I would have thought Jenny was of Italian descent. The spaghetti bolognese that we all voraciously dug into could have easily been delivered from Naples. Coupled with a delicious crunchy green salad and home preserves on fresh bread, I, too, felt admittedly satisfied. A glass of boxed wine was the cherry on the cake before we relaxed into our chairs for reflection time.

I was the last one to speak. I expressed that my day was filled with much contrast from the comfort of knowing Mother Earth will forever prevail any harm inflicted upon her to the other spectrum of grave cynicism. It is only a matter of time before the human race self-destructs and becomes extinct (I did not elaborate further on my disdain for my fellow man). Later in the day, I was faced with a more critical dilemma to resolve; whether to incur further physical damage, run the risk of inconveniencing others and not completing my journey, or guiltily throw in the towel for the day. I thanked George for deciding for me. I appreciated the lesson that Superwoman also needs a little help from time to time from her fellow avengers. Taking time out to rest is not necessarily an admission of defeat. Giving myself the time to catch my breath allows sustainable stamina in the long haul, both for self-preservation and in the vested interest of others.

I thanked everyone for their support, encouragement and understanding today and voiced sincere gratitude for Ronelle's counsel and a lovely afternoon spent in her company. This was a great and precious contrast for me - to receive such compassion and kindness from strangers that knew nothing of me.

I later appreciated that the most remarkable contrast of all was from this human that through her own deep grief and suffering, she unknowingly challenged my very restricted and blinded beliefs about the special people of this world, giving me much-needed insight. Each of us is individual, and we all have something unique to offer each other and the world.

When I forgot to think for myself when I neglected to question the bounded rules, obligations and judgements placed upon me from a young age (often with good adult intention), I disappeared. When I stopped listening to my intuition and gut feeling when I conformed to the expectations and the confined boxes of a sick society, medieval culture and a segregated religion, I had lost who I am.

6
IN THE EYE OF THE STORM

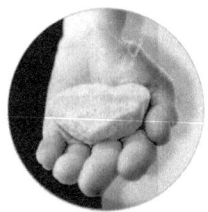

Be in touch with your inner senses

I suppose it is expected for life to make more sense once we have accumulated a wealth of experiences over a long period. Whether they are good or bad experiences, it is the hopeful wisdom gained after a plethora of life's eventualities, which often makes many elders the sensible patrons and advisors for a better version of the meaning of life. A long life of raising children and grandchildren, surpassing wars, holding various jobs, immigrating to different continents, financial strife and a continuum of the loss of loved ones can certainly provide enough opportunities to reflect on the actual value and purpose of this living journey. But wisdom is not age-dependent. Wisdom can be attained at any stage of a person's life.

I spent the better part of a century believing that only the 'good' is good and taught to reject the 'bad' or not to be 'bad', whatever that may mean. Most of us wish to negate the experiences that leave us feeling angry, betrayed, ashamed, abused or rejected. But we often hold onto those resentments and raw deals, thinking that someone or something out there must somehow make it up to us or that by clinging onto that anger or hatred, it can somehow vindicate us.

Yes, I have heard: "What does not kill you makes you stronger." However, I have never really appreciated how these painful situations hold equal weight in moulding and shaping us into the person we wish we could be. I have discovered they help us create a different reality for ourselves if we accept their teachings and choose to overcome the pain. How do we become stronger through the hurt? By accepting that these 'lessons' are not punishments, they are not inherited karmas that we are stuck with and are certainly not curses (these can just be part of what we believe in). These not-so-good experiences and emotions are simply a contrast or a reference point for us to know what we don't want to move towards and what we do wish for ourselves instead. Once we realise that hardships, broken hearts and distressing life circumstances allow for personal growth and are necessary for our evolution as a human being; we start to accept that we must embrace the Ying and the Yang in this plane of Duality, as they are part of the Whole and the fundamental truth of this Physical plane and planet. Then we have hit another pot of gold.

Some people are relatively slow at learning this or are ignorant of this idea for most of their lives. I was one of them. In fact, the above concept was simply something that had not entered my mind. I thought I was a lousy person having all of these 'negative' or 'bad' feelings. Having studied science for a good few years, I was never truly appreciative that nothing can exist in this physical dimension without having polarity, including human emotions. Perhaps I wasn't paying attention because I got myself lost in a world of overthinking and second-guessing. Constantly. Incessantly. Over time, they occupied every nook, cranny and fibre of my being. And when they are not pleasant thoughts, then trouble lies ahead if we don't learn to use them as reference points and

Hypocratic Oaths

guides as to where we are in our journey. Ironically, we cannot ever get lost on our journey because the Universe sends out constant reminders. They get louder and louder if we don't listen until there is a bang that finally catches our attention and brings us to our senses.

Hank was very determined this morning to get us to stop thinking and instead get us in touch with our senses before we headed out to Village Inn, twenty-something kilometres away. This man had clearly mutated overnight. He had gone to bed a raging Hulk and woke up a sweet Dr Robert Banner.

He now wanted to play Biodanza. I had just finished a very sensual breakfast of egg frittata with *boerewors*, heavenly muffins with homemade fig jam and a large mug of hot drugged up coffee (self-prescribed of course). My chronic mystery cough had surprisingly disappeared from all the chemicals I was consuming, or so I thought, and I was not in the mood to get it started up again by playing silly games.

What on earth was Biodanza? For the last four days, this persistent bulk of a man had been begging George for an opportunity to share his passion for this "Dance of Life" experience. We had to stand together with music and move in some rhythmic manner to promote feelings of positivity and deep self-awareness. Or something like that. I could not quite grasp the idea, and we certainly did not have a jukebox, so what exactly did he want us to do? It was a voluntary suggestion, and two or three pilgrims had clearly indicated they did not wish to participate and remained indoors. This oasis of a farmhouse had just provided me with such quiet consolation and gentle mending of my wounded spirit, and I did not wish to get overly excited again by entertaining the musings of this strange mammoth, bearing the blue eyes that missed nothing.

But I did it anyway.

Those brave enough to face the silent music and icy cold breeze went outside to gather in a circle on the white-frosted grass. The sun had not yet peeped from behind the mountains, and our mouths smoked out condensed air with every uttered word. We were all a bit apprehensive but were gently briefed as to what was required of us – to hold each other's hands, close our eyes, slowly breathe, then relax and hear the silence, which included listening to the birds. These were the only sentient creatures providing sound for a while. If we were to hear a dog bark in the distance, the soft voices coming from the kitchen or the jingle of a sheep's bell, we were to breathe that in too. Relax and just observe through closed eyes.

We were to feel the energy flowing through our bodies on three levels. The energy flowing around our legs and through our feet grounded us and connected us to the earth. The energy circularly flowing through our hearts connected us to each other as human beings, and the energy circulating above our heads joined us to the heavens beyond.

We remained in this suspended state for a long while; then Hank told us to open our eyes and to look at and see the person standing directly opposite, perhaps in a different light now. We all smiled with newfound amusement and uncomfortable ease.

The next instruction he called the 'opening of the heart' exercise invited us to take turns to hold out our hands and connect with any person in the circle. They could refuse the invitation or not. Without speaking, we each picked the first partner to connect tête-à-tête and hear what their eyes had to say.

The famous cliché, 'the eyes are the windows to the soul', was about to resonate its truth with me for the first time in a very long while, as I truly *saw* and appreciated what was voicelessly being spoken from their hearts.

Christy was the first to hold my hands. Her eyes seemed cold at first glance, but in the next instant, all there was, was hidden kindness and incredible generosity. We smiled at one another.

George then touched my hands, his deep blue gaze solely saying, "I am so glad you are here."

Hank was next to connect with my hands. His entire body emanated ADHD (talk about not labelling people), but his soft celestial eyes just embraced me with an angelic giant-bear hug and much-needed reassurance. My tears could not refrain from joining the fun and games at this point. I felt very defenceless as this stranger read deep into my soul, but at the same time, was astounded at the surreal wonder of this experiment.

The next person to make contact with my tear-filled baby browns simply smiled in a manner of: "No need to take life so seriously, my dear." Lenny was one of those wise elders that had certainly experienced much in his life and had reached a point of not paying further attention to pettiness nor conflict. I really did wish to see the lighter side of life.

Jenny then mimicked my sentiments, "I know it's hard..."

It was one thing to let my guard down by allowing someone to touch my feet, but it was something quite extraordinary to allow someone into my soul.

A few strangers had just cracked through a very dense layer of steel armour that I had been wearing for at least two decades in self-defence. It was an invisible shield that had protected me (or so I thought) by desensitizing me to the horrors of human nature, but it prevented me from feeling most of life's simple pleasures.

This was uncharted territory, and I did not know what to make of it.

An awkward but comfortable quiet settled in as we ended our visual conversations and broke the circle. No one spoke further, and we understood the game was over.

I turned to collect my rucksack with the strange feeling we had all just participated in an initiation ritual, or made a secret tribal pact of sorts, only I was unsure of the deal. It was all too new to me.

The rest of our crew tentatively joined us to bid Jenny farewell and thank her for her blessed hospitality. We hoped for rain to come soon to relieve her and the many neighbouring farmers from this dreadful drought and strain. I wished to return here one day with my family to show them that there are still beautiful people in this world, and even the harsh contrasting beauty of these landscapes, are indeed captivating.

I was the first to walk away from Kromrivier in the now customary morning silence. I had not intended to be ahead of the group, nor did I notice what discomfort I was in from my knee. The tears had just flowed as fast as my feet were taking me, and the desire to clear myself of this deep resentment I had for most of humankind was just as shameful and determined.

The better part of the morning took us from one expansive farmland to the next. Despite the scarcity of water, the ground was still coated with several shades of olive-green grass, peppered with myriads of scrubs and trees. We scaled one fence after the next, one farm after the other. Today was fence hurdling day. And it was another day of climbing. Talk about overcoming obstacles. Each hill was steeper than the next, and the next one even steeper. I still had one of Christy's walking sticks, and at some point, I was holding it in front of me with both hands as I pierced the ground to haul me up the 90-degree inclines. It also offered much anchoring when loose rocks and pebbles threatened to launch my body into an avalanche down the hill. It was very slow going with a great deal of huffing and puffing, such that the little piggie's house could hardly withstand all the heaving and wheezing that went along with it.

At some point, we had climbed so high up that we could not help but stop to look at the magnificent sun illuminating the earth and the spectacular views of the infinite horizons and velvet valleys below. Far from taking my breath away, it was effortlessly steadying and calming the pumping of blood in my ears and the flow of air into my lungs.

There must be a God. This Creation did not just make itself. Just three days into this journey, looking back at my life with hopeless eyes had become taboo as I could sense the inkling of a shift. To look back with appreciation at what is pleasing and wonderful, reflecting on all the precious moments life has offered me already, holds the reaffirmation that there is still much magnificence and joy to be had in this lifetime. I stood facing the sun, hoping its delicious warm rays would imprint this message into new neural pathways in my brain and deliver this feeling of wonder to every single cell in my body. After all, we can delete old software and download new and updated mental Apps if we choose to.

We had reached one of the Zuurberge's peaks after six kilometres of climbing. It had taken almost three hours of tugging up against gravity. The climb was made worthwhile when George put his gear to one side and sat down on a rocky outcrop, overseeing what must have looked like Karen Blixen's farm at the foot of the Ngong hills.

I was not sure if my elation was from the go-ahead to relish a much-needed tea break, or if it was from the realization that even though my left knee was aching, it was apparent that it would be able to carry me for the rest of the day.

I found my rest spot overlooking the grandeur and splendour of a divine creation, and another long-forgotten feeling came to visit.

This is what it feels like to be on top of the world.

I grabbed an energy drink that had the label CR7 on it. I smiled as I sipped its raspberry-flavoured contents and thought, "Ronaldo, you have got nothing on me. I am the queen of the game today!" A mischievous grin munched through a protein bar and a meal replacement milkshake. I was not sure if it was the nourishment or the pure untainted oxygen that flowed through my body, but I genuinely began to feel I could conquer another two mountains today, at least. My newfound jubilation was equally humbled by much appreciation for this single metal stick that made it possible for me to keep up with my fellow climbers. I had considered, very briefly, buying a pair for this trek but thought it a redundant item that would add unnecessary weight to my baggage. It was, in fact, the other way around. One simple walking stick can determine the quality of your survival, or the absence of it can prolong your dying. To have this narrow-minded determination to wrangle my way through life without the help or assistance of others is short-sighted and stupid. We are certainly not alone in this love-and-war playing field. Yet, it would be another few months before I completely surrendered to this gift of learning to receive.

I was more taken aback by how I am constantly judging the book by its cover. I should know better and hated myself for doing it all the time. I had relied on my external five senses for so long to determine my reaction and opinion of any given situation that I had long forgotten to read people and circumstances with my sixth sense (the direct connection to my true inner self). In my defence, it was a learnt habit I developed over the years to brace myself for what was coming my way in the Trauma Unit. Here comes another drunk driver; brace yourself for the vile alcohol odour, blood and obscene slurred language. Here comes another psychotic or drugged up fruitcake; brace yourself for violent rantings and forceful restraining. Here comes the same purple-battered woman; brace yourself for the bullshit lies and refrain from punching the offender or slapping the woman for still being in this pathetic marriage. And so it went every single day, with every single patient that walked in or was carried into the E.R., for years on end. There was always an instant of judgement and critique before suddenly jumping into action. There was never time to get to know the person hidden behind the lacerations, the congealed blood, or the broken bones. Over time, all you get to see with the eyes are drama, death and disappointment. The survival mechanism to keep up with this insensible functioning is to detach, desensitize and become a cold hard bitch so that you can wade through this sick spectacle.

This process of desensitization did little to serve my family. After a long day of treating emergencies, the last thing I wanted to hear when I got home to my haven-cave was that my husband had a headache or my child had a sore stomach. God forbid they waited for me all day to get home to give them a paracetamol tablet which lay at arm's reach in the pantry cupboard. Because on my awful days, I had to fight the urge to slap either or both of them. I wanted to come home to some sort of normality and wellbeing to remind myself that life was not just disease, blood and tears.

Thus, my family's ailments got minimal sympathy from me. I remember ignoring my daughter's fever and cough for three days until I exasperatedly examined her and realized she had pneumonia, which had gone unnoticed by her medical mother. Of course, that guilt impaled me further into the ground.

My own mother had a habit of waiting for the last minute before telling anyone she had been getting chest pains for a month, and only when I was called to her bedside at 2 a.m. when she could no longer breathe, did she tell me she had been unwell for quite a while. I would silently seethe in frustration and interrogate her through gritted teeth. I could not handle self-pity and self-neglect, and my sternness was perceived as not caring. The apple does not fall far from the tree. It took me 12 years to do my gynaecological check-up and Pap smear after Lara was born.

Retrospectively, I now understand where my mother's fear of burdening others came from. Being an only child, she lost her mother at the age of five and was left to wander snot-nosed, barefoot and alone through her rural village in Portugal whilst her father was at work all day. She was seen as a nuisance by the neighbours as she was always hungry and kept asking for food or pestered them to run errands to receive an Escudo or two to buy a pair of shoes one day. After three years of neglected and ragged vagrancy, she developed Scrofula (a form of tuberculosis of the lymph glands that caused these massively swollen and painful lumps all over her body to ooze with foul-smelling pus). She was taken to a hospital far from home for further medical care, which entailed waiting for her to die without any visitors or last rights, and there she stayed alone again for a full nine months.

My grandfather had since scouted a new wife for himself, mainly to have a female presence to look after his child. My step-grandmother was the one who brought my mother back home and painstakingly nursed her to health again.

But my mother grew up subconsciously believing she was a burden to others.

I love my mother dearly. She is the one human being that wraps her arms around me in warm, sincere unconditional love and adoration. I now allow her to have her moments of fear, which are becoming few and far between, and I do what I can to help her feel better. But I wasn't always like that.

I searched for where Christy was resting, back straight, confident and focused. From the first day of introductions, my immediate judgement told me this was the person that I least expected to connect with or with whom I'd have any meaningful conversations.

I was so wrong. She, too, had a thick metal armour protecting her from her demons, but she was adamant about loaning me one of her walking aids, unconditionally. I repentantly and silently sent her my sincere gratitude for her kindness and genuine care.

In fact, since my arrival in the Eastern Cape, I had only encountered kind-hearted and well-meaning people. If I were not so lost in my own misery and blind ambling, I would be able to see that this quality lies within almost every human and that I had already witnessed it and have been the recipient of it on many occasions. But my stubbornness and layers of self-defence attitudes prevented me from appreciating such generosity, and I had deluded myself into believing people were incapable of such goodwill.

It has taken me long to realise that it is up to me to open my eyes and see through these illusionary veils. If I allow myself to move to a different viewing point, perhaps every encounter I have with another member of my species can bring a sense of hope and a new belief that we are inherent beings of light and grace. If I don't see this light in someone else, either or both of us are hiding behind a great deal of hurt. It is up to me to see the infinite ways in which an individual's richness may present itself.

Just this morning, at the breakfast table, George gingerly came to sit next to me. He placed his hand on my left knee in a discrete manner and asked me to put my hand on his sore right knee. Out of general earshot, he whispered a recovery blessing over my knee, and I did the same for his. A moment of quiet serenity and beautiful bliss followed. Then a minute later, he stood up to affectionately gather up the rest of his brood, leaving me staring at his back, open-mouthed and in awe by what had just happened.

George had now brought us to one of the northern boundary fences of the Addo Elephant National Park. When we got up from our resting rocky perches, he pointed to the vast, untamed bushveld that stretched as far south as the eye could see. This time, we were not allowed to jump over the fence. Not only was it illegal, but we would stand a good chance of coming face to face with any one of the Big Five beauties. The park's southern-most section bordered along a wide stretch of the Indian Ocean, and it was actually considered Big Six territory. Still, I would not expect us to spot a great white shark resting under a Marula tree from this vantage point.

Nevertheless, I was super stoked to be so close to a wildlife conservation reserve. Technically speaking, I was an arm's length away from touching its soil, so this could count as living on the edge, walking on foot alongside a wild game reserve.

It brought much nostalgia for our family holidays usually spent in the bush, far away from people and noise, and as close to nature as possible. We have ventured into Mozambique, Botswana, Namibia, Zambia, Zimbabwe, Malawi and Tanzania. We are always seeking peace, large amounts of solitude, and much sought after interaction with the magic of African landscapes and their primordial inhabitants. There is incredible beauty and serenity found in the savannah plains of the Kalahari, the marshlands of Savuti and the true Garden of Eden that is the Okavango Delta. Everything makes perfect sense and has its destined purpose in the natural cycle of the wild, from the Honeyguide bird's flight path to the continuous migrations of the wildebeest and zebra. The only language spoken here is the cacophony of the barking geckos, the howling of the jackal, and the hooting of yellow-billed hornbills. Every creature understands the natural seasons and cycles of life, the ebb and flow of the winds, the moon, the oceans, and they wait patiently for their season of plenty. The smell of the wild sage and the soaked earth after a thunderstorm, or the sounds of content elephant grumbling as the glorious orange sun dips behind the acacias, arouse the senses to such intense climaxing, it can leave you thirsty and begging for more.

My husband calls this his Church. And I feel he may be right. There are very few places on this planet where one can feel so in touch with this resplendent energy and Divinity that feeds the soul. It brings freedom and an escape from everyday reality. It brings childlike excitement at the prospect of a new adventure. To have to wait with an insatiable longing to visit these holy sanctuaries only once or twice a year feels like daily deprivation.

An inkling of anticipation sets in as my eyes naturally focused to my left beyond Addo's enclosed mesh wiring and darted from one tree to the next in game-spotting fashion. But it seemed that the only things that caught my attention were a variety of animal spoor on the sandy parts of the track and a lot of scat and *poop drolletjies* (animal droppings). I could not spot the owners of these wilderness trails, but the distraction and suspense made the next few kilometres easier to navigate. Ironically, the only game that watched these trekkers wrangling their way through indigenous fynbos was a herd of impala residing on a neighbouring farm to our right. It was nevertheless comforting to know that a group of gentle pachyderms or a few rhinos could be watching me from a distance. I felt like I was doing a bush-walk anyway, even though I was protected from a sneaky leopard by a three-metre tall double-layered electric fence wall.

Massive powerlines eventually guided us away from the National Park border, and we began our fence jumping and hurdling again. Here, the farm property gates were almost all understandably padlocked; it is South Africa, after all. So over one fence, we climbed, and under the next one, we crawled. Herds of brown cows were the only welcoming committees that we encountered. Every time we came to a gate that we could permissibly trespass over, George would fix a screw onto its wooden pole on the right as a landmark for the next Indlela group of pilgrims that were doing the same trek, only a day behind ours and hot on our trail. This was Hansel leaving them some breadcrumbs to let them know they were on the right path.

Later, we followed a single track that ran alongside the powerlines and left no room to walk side by side for chattering purposes. At this stage, I thought these beacons were an eye-sore and so very out of place in the wilderness, but when I think of all the electrical appliances and conveniences that they fuel in my life and facilitate my day, I am grateful. This man-made powerhouse marvel had us bobbing up and down mounds of beautiful shrublands speckled with massive cycads and cacti, and I couldn't resist stopping on several occasions to take dozens of photographs. Cycads were one of my mother-in-law's favourite plants. She was everywhere I looked.

By the time we stopped for lunch, I was relaxed, near-oblivious to my bothersome knee and close to feeling some kind of contentment. Again, it could be that filling my tummy once more was the culprit of my near-joy, but I relished the half an hour break with quiet ruminating. Once we got going again, it was easy to chat with almost every companion without provoking thought or opinion. We were still bush-bashing up and down the hills, and I was chuffed my legs could carry me the entire distance today, even if it were with stick in hand.

At some point, the shrubs and hedges got so tall and condensed that our male heroes took to chopping and scything, intertwining branches and towering grass with their walking sticks, which allowed safe passage through a jungle of overgrowth. The afternoon rolled on, and by 14.30, we had reached the gravel road that would lead us onto Zuurberg Village Inn.

It was not long before Iris and Lenny stopped at a massive rock-face that shot up to the heavens, shaped by the dynamite that mined a passageway through this section of the Zuurberge in 1855. The words 'Woodfields Krantz' were boldly carved high-up on the rock-face surface. One could only look up in awe of this incredible feat created so many years ago before the giant bulldozers and earthmoving machinery era. The width of the gravel road only allowed for the passing of one vehicle at a time. It was intended to transport stock and goods by horse and donkey carts and perhaps a few ox wagons still in working mode. Once the admiration was done, I was the only one who stayed behind on the mountain pass to provide moral support and be entertained whilst Lenny and Iris searched for the next Geocache treasure.

This was an arduous discovery to make, as it was buried somewhere along a fifty-metre wall built below the perpendicular cliff, behind a thick layer of green hedging. Every so often, Iris disappeared and reappeared from the bushes like an excited fox on a hunt. They kept checking the GPS coordinates on their phones and for further clues on the App comments. The thornbush marked her legs with tiny red scratches every time she ventured through the scrub, and her clothes kept getting hooked on thorns. As she was about to give up, she came out with a square Tupperware filled with a fortune of bits and bobs, excitedly sporting a hat speckled with leaves and cobwebs.

Plastic bangles, a peg, stickers, a seashell, a fake ladybird, a medal, and a plastic 'heart-of-the-ocean' necklace that got lost as the Titanic sunk, were some of the valuables retrieved from this very well-hidden trove. Lenny handed me a fair-sized rose quartz stone to place into the box and allowed me to choose something else to take in its place. I picked a tiny porcelain figurine of a mouse peeping through a hole in a cheese wedge. It was the cutest thing I had found from this selection, and he let me have this little treasure, even though I was not entitled to it. To this day, Mister Mousey lives on top of my study lamp, ogling at me whilst these words are being typed.

I think I have forgotten how to play.

Yes, I love fancy dress-up parties, but they only happen every ten years. I enjoyed Easter Egg hunting and Halloween trick-or-treating when my daughter was little, more for the joy gleaming from her face than for the love of candy. But lately, I avoided the board games and card games that I had indulged her in for years, as my head and body had become so tired, I could not think of anything worse than playing UNO on a Friday night after a long, taxing week at work. Life had turned into one big responsibility and duty.

But children do know the secret. They are born with the ability to love and live their life to the fullest because they only know the present moment (they can't fathom five 'sleeps' from today). They love unadulterated play. They know to use their imagination to stay in a state of wonder and get excited about the simple things surrounding them on a minute to minute basis. It is fascinating how a toddler can marvel at crinkled paper and plastic bowls. This is the ultimate way of living. Unfiltered, honestly, innocently, not yet falsely indoctrinated and persistently in a state of youthful amusement. They have no problem with pointing with excitement at the lady with pink and purple hair and cannot fathom why we slap their hand away and shoosh them into guilt for stating the obvious – they have just seen a fairy or a unicorn.

We then force them to sit still in boring classrooms for hours on end, reciting mundane facts from 1693. We force them to follow restrictions made compulsory by antiquated institutions. We force them to pursue career paths they have no interest in, and we find many other ways of brainwashing and killing their creativity, their self-worth and all their magical fairy-tale dreams.

This is when we, too, lose our inner joy, our sense of fun, adventure and wonder - when we are forced into 'growing up' and stop thinking like children. We stop imagining that something more splendid, better and more extraordinary is even possible.

The view of the Village Inn (now called Zuurberg Mountain Village) soon came into sight of these animated soon-to-be guests. Iris had just commented that I am starting to 'loosen up'. Perhaps she overheard my comment to Hank earlier on when I told him I was desperately trying not to fart in his face as he helped me climb over one of the farm gates by thrusting my buttocks beyond the fence. This seemed to amuse her, but I was presently far more entertained by this exquisite four-star oasis standing in front of me, with pastel-painted motel cottages neatly lined up on top of the mountain, overlooking magnificent views of the Addo Elephant Park down below. We had circumvented a section of the park and ended up on the gravel road that cut through another portion of the park. I was clueless with my bearings but so privileged to have arrived at such luxurious accommodation.

The grand reception area had similar antique furnishings to Kromrivier, but the walls were adorned with historical black and white photographs and colourful scenic paintings collected over the last 150 years. My tog bag and sleeping bag had already been taken to room 24 by a porter whom I did not get a chance to thank. Julie was again my roommate for the night, but she was already on the phone with her son when I walked into a spacious room with a fluffy white duvet covering one double bed. I guess I could easily sleep in a bed with another woman if it meant scoring a palatial hot shower, unlimited access to the mini-bar, and sweet dreams on a feather-down pillow.

Julie's son was studying and working at Addo. He had come to visit his mother as soon as she notified him of her arrival, bearing precious gifts in the form of sugar-free and gluten-free food, scanty in these parts of the woods. After a brief introduction, they left the room and headed to the bar for a cup of tea and much-needed private conversation. I was left to do some laundry, pack for the next day, soothe my aching muscles under a supersized showerhead and treat another large blister that had developed under the right pinkie toe. I had no idea such a small digit could flourish with so many blisters.

I sent a few photos and messages to my family; only the Lord knows what they must be thinking. I sensed they were somewhat unsettled by their short replies today, and I had no significant comforting words to offer. The daily journal was updated on the back porch bench, with a Dunhill in hand and the warm afternoon sun super-charging my every sinew to the envy of every other lizard in the vicinity.

We convened at 17.00 in the main reception lounge, where several couches and comforter chairs were poised around a blazing fireplace. The welcoming orange flames took centre stage from the sun that was near setting outside. A bottle of red wine was already resting on ice on top of the centre coffee table. We did our day's reflections and discussed the next day's route after ordering a round of drinks. I could not remember the last time I had a good glass of wine, but I sipped it with the same gratitude that I had for every pilgrim's support thus far.

I shared with my fellow friends that I was so thankful for my legs that walked the whole day, and I thanked Hank for this morning's Biodanza session. I knew the game was intended to get us to connect to our intuitive sixth sense, with the view to looking into our inner soul. I knew I was so disconnected from other souls too, so I was grateful for the reminder that as much as we derive great pleasure from the activation of our five senses, it is this intuitive feeling that helps us navigate through our own ebb and flows, only that we have forgotten about it or have not been taught to use it to our advantage.

I could also feel my mood lift somewhat, although I had no other adequate words to express it. I was just thankful. Everyone had their turn to voice their thoughts and day's revelations.

It was well into the evening when we moved into the dining room to enjoy a royal 5-course meal consisting of soup and fresh bread, roast pork, potatoes and veggies, salads, desserts, fruits, and coffee.

By the time I got back to the hotel room, I had eased into a feeling of personal satisfaction and considered if this was what true contentment felt like. The walk from the dining area to our cottages was slow and mesmerizing, as a million stars cast up against a black night canvas glittered with spellbinding smiles. The winter cold that robbed the day of its warmth did not disrupt my sense of calm, and time did slow its heartbeat for a while here in this haven close to Addo.

I should have left it there.

But I remained outside on the motel room porch to call home before going to bed. And the magic of the day disappeared at the speed of light into the dark night when my daughter asked with tentative innocence and desperate expectation, "Mamma, have you found what you are looking for?"

7

MIRACLES ABOUND

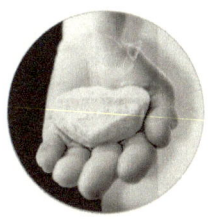

Once you get to the top, keep walking

I slept like the dead enveloped in white celestial sheets. But as my eyes opened to the flashing light of my cellphone alarm, I did not feel like I was wrapped in angel wings or deserving of any heavenly miracle. My heavy heart had once more dropped to the bottom of the ocean, and not even the deep-sea Anglerfish could retrieve it. A torrent of guilt had flooded every sensory pleasure from the day before, and my body felt like it had walked backwards for the entire distance of this journey during the night.

On the odd occasion when I did cry, it was usually done in the quiet of my own company and at night. If I happened to be in bed, there was immense control in preventing any noise or movement so as not to awaken my husband. My daughter has, on more than one occasion, commented that she has never seen me cry. Being a child, she may have thought there was something wrong with me already because she knew it is a perfectly normal human emotion to cry when you are hurt or sad (until adults teach children that it is not). I had no problem with my daughter crying, but I erroneously assumed that if I cried as an adult, it meant I did not have my shit together, and it was a sign of weakness. I did not want her to think that I was not strong enough or couldn't handle whatever curveballs life threw my way. We girls need to have our big-girl panties on at all times and never let our guard down. Not so?

How foolish of me. I was unknowingly teaching my child to become an unemotional robot or freak alien that must not cry if a loved one died or if her heart felt broken.

Still stuck in so many ways, I hoped to have succeeded this morning, hiding my tears from Julie. I thought I was done with the crying by now, but the amount of water produced by such tiny tear glands was infuriating. I could not understand how I could feel so hopeful one moment, sensing the promise of a mystery about to unravel, then come crashing down to despair with one simple trigger sentence. Was this a waste of mine and everyone else's time? I felt so ridiculous and such a fraud. If I didn't know what I was looking for, how would I know when I found it?

Of course, I didn't have an answer. I just sat catatonically at the edge of the bed, waiting for the porter to come to collect our bags. Julie and I had groomed, dressed, and packed mostly in silence. Whether she sensed my despondence or felt sorrowful herself, this morning brought in a sombre misty chill through the open hotel room door.

Back in the reception lounge, the now-faded fire hearth still resonated with the warm camaraderie from the night before. The others were already gathered, waiting for our breakfast cue. Another five-star feast was spread across a sizeable buffet counter. The smells of early morning baked pastries and bread, bacon and eggs, and a whole banquet of delectable cuisine enticed us into the dining area once more. This time, the ambience had transformed from drawn curtains and low-lit candles to window-filtered sunshine and freshly picked wildflowers propped into

Hypocratic Oaths

pretty centre-table vases. Most of us took extra helpings of fruit, boiled eggs, and peanut butter bread as take-away snacks for the way.

We were to have one of the longest days yet, as we had 35 kilometres to walk to Enon, where Livia and Tyrone Claasen were going to open their home to eleven strangers and a familiar George.

With stomachs loaded with fuel for the morning, I was pleased when Marcelle went around to all of us on a monetary collection mission for a combined tip to offer to all the waiters and porters. Just before bidding our farewells, we took turns to make use of the one guest bathroom to ensure that at least the bladder tank was empty before heading out. On my way out of the toilet, I noticed an enormous decorative pot in the corridor filled with at least twenty different kinds and shapes of walking sticks. The proverbial 'my heart skipped a beat' really did happen. I looked around for someone in charge and found another gentle giant of a man, this time a well-rounded-at-the-waist Xhosa manager, with the label 'Colin' printed on his name badge. I politely asked if I could buy one of their walking sticks, and he politely advised no. They were reserved exclusively for the lodge guests, and their booked game walks. More urgently, I pleaded if there was any way that I could come to possess such a walking stick. Without a single breath of hesitation, he offered me his own. With an imperceptible flick of his head, I followed him to his office, where he retrieved a locally made wooden-carved *knobkerrie* from the cupboard behind his desk. He was happy to just give it to me, but the only way I knew to show my sincerest thanksgiving for this life-saving gift was to leave some money for him on the table. The resistance to receiving was still at the forefront.

I could not believe my luck. I was dumbfounded and ecstatic in one single moment. I had not considered *synchronicity* at this stage of my life. Again, I was oblivious to the fact that many lessons had already begun. But, the student was not yet paying full attention.

I returned the borrowed half of Christy's pair of walking sticks and hugged her with quiet, genuine gratitude. We subsequently thanked our hosts and their hospitable staff for their marvellous homely haven of a hotel, their gorgeous food, and their smiling kindness. The support vehicle was then loaded with our overnight bags, and we re-grouped for the morning's meditation and intention for the day. I wanted to tell Brenda that I thought I was close to reaching the top of the hill last night, but after putting the phone down last night and as we proceeded onto our compulsory silent morning march, I figured I would have to start all over again and just keep on walking.

The winding road out of Village Inn had us rising and dipping again, up one mount and down the next. Despite having a new wooden walking aid (now named Colin, in honour of its previous owner), it was soon apparent that I was not the only one struggling to carry my weariness and angst. Julie lagged for a while, periodically pausing to wipe her tears and gather composure. She did not offer explanations, and by now, we all had respect for each other's roller-coaster rides of emotion. I suppose her son's visit was good for her soul, but left her heart further exposed or void when he left? It was also clear that she was struggling to come to terms with the end of her marriage.

I thought of my own relationship and wondered how long it could withstand the merry-go-rounds and ghost trains of the last thirty years. My husband and I had started dating when I was fifteen. Just two years older than my daughter is now. Thinking of her and her desperate worry over me brought me to a halt. I heard the concerned aching in her voice last night. She just needed to know that I would be alright, but I could not offer any certainty because I had no idea what I wanted. I had stopped dreaming and hoping a long time ago and had been on auto-pilot without direction or knowing the destination.

Still, in our hour of morning silence, a bird suddenly and distinctively chanted. It flew overhead and landed with a loud chirp on a dry shrub a few metres from me. I knew it was telling me all would be well, but it may as well have torn open a huge scab; my heart felt like it would bleed out once and for all.

All bleeding stops, eventually. Even if it means filling out a death certificate, this is what we were taught by the sarcastic surgeons who were also struggling to survive life's torrents. But I knew my time was not up; I just did not know how to operate on this dismal prognosis.

The involuntary shoulder-trembling that followed, and the under-sized hands that failed to cover my sobbing face, caught George's attention.

Within a few strides of trail sneakers crunching on gravel, his arms were wrapped around my shoulders, and several 'it's alright' cues whispered reassurance in my ears. It was not a prolonged affair, as I did not like anyone to watch me cry. As soon as he saw that I would not turn into a convulsing mess, George decided to end the morning's silence prematurely and simply said, "Try not to worry so much. Just be in the moment of what is."

I had no idea what that meant or how to achieve that. All I could muster was just to walk some more.

One foot in front of the next…one breath inhaled after the next.

I hoped that this exercise qualified as being present in the moment. Ah, hope.

This was another concept to which I had not given much thought. I wondered if hoping and dreaming were the same thing. I suppose that hoping meant there remained a longing that something better was in the pipeline, but it held the expectation that this wish would almost be dependent on someone or something else fulfilling it for you, so the odds were 50/50. Whereas dreaming meant you were the one to imagine how your wishes would be fulfilled, trusting that an invisible force would bring it to fruition and that sooner or later, it was simply a given. That's how my mind processed it anyway. Regardless of the semantics, I had done very little hoping in these last few years and virtually no dreaming. I had just accepted this was my life. Work, pay bills, sleep, clean, work some more, and pay more bills. Retirement was inconceivable at this stage.

So, was taking a dreamy holiday twice a year enough to make me so thankful to stop complaining? I did not think so, because my mind complained a lot.

The ground began to turn orange. Just when I was on a roll berating myself for sounding like a spoilt ungrateful brat, the pebbles, and brown gravel that were the background wallpaper in front of my eyes, turned into a dozen round yellow-orange patterns that broke the monotony. The smell of beautiful citrus flooded my nostrils, and I paused to look up and notice an endless procession of orange citrus trees had replaced the surrounding wild bushland. We had strolled through a series of vast citrus farmlands, this time without jumping any fences. Hence my oblivion to the number of kilometres one foot had already done in front of the other.

It was indeed a welcoming distraction and a spectacular sight. Rows and rows of plump green leaf tops were loaded with balls of fruit, prettier than any Christmas tree I had ever seen. There seemed to be equal amounts of over-ripened oranges that had already fallen to the ground. And the cows were having a field day. Gorgeous fluffy brown cows appeared to be the only guardians of this piece of Eden. We walked past two placid brown horses that seemed to be the sentries, albeit not doing a very good job by allowing us free passage into their territory. Their big polished black eyes followed these strangers' every footstep while the cows' mouths continued ruminating their juicy fruits. I had no idea cows ate oranges, with peel and all. But I did have a desire to sit with them for a while and feed them these delectable treats (as if they were not managing this feat on their own). And I so wished to pat one of them.

As if reading my intention, Lenny had wisely taken stride next to mine and offered me an orange instead. I was not sure that we were allowed to take a farmer's produce without permission. But in our defence, there was not another human in sight to ask (except for the usual twelve overlanding trespassers), and it appeared that two oranges would not be missed amongst a million ones lying on the ground. I accepted the precious offering that had its sweet juicy nectar running down my fingers and into my long sleeves. A few others did the same, and we walked and mainly ate in communal silence. Perhaps it was so as not to disturb the cows or the peace of the place; perhaps it was that a general melancholy weighed heavier on the group today.

It would have been impossible for George to have predicted in advance the sombre mood of this day. But he seemed to have selected the perfect opportunity with which to indulge us in a bit of morning luxury. Our first tea break was at the five-star Fig Tree Lodge, nestled secretly up on a hill with magnificent views of another green valley below. The lodge hosts had not been instructed to cater for our group. Still, they had willingly agreed to allow us to catch our breath on their colonial veranda couches, use their restrooms and refill our water bottles with spring water. We breathed in the purest air with the faint smell of wild sage and snacked on our own *padkos* (road food) while admiring this lavish oasis seemingly geared up to cater for a select few elites. Dressed in our dusty casual hiking outfits and lugging around our baggage, we appeared a little out of place where one would expect a British 20th century colonel to stride in after his hunting safari, rifle in hand, wearing a proud smirk on his face. However, our group bore the sentiments of the wounded animal instead.

Two and a half hours later, we had walked a further eight kilometres and were welcomed into Boy and Boetie's farmhouse for a home-baked lunch. A massive grumpy old Boerboel first signalled our arrival before getting his owner's reassurance that we meant his human parents no harm. Once inside the property, we were greeted with the same embracing warmth that a soul brother or sister gives their childhood best friend after years of being apart. Boy's sturdy handshake led us into one of the cosiest blue kitchens I have ever visited, and Boetie's kind motherly smile enquired how we were all doing. She seemed to acknowledge our faces one by one. Her genuine affectionate look had a bunch of strangers huddled around her centre kitchen table, with eyes revealing the contentment and love of knowing her prodigal children were home. Even if it was just for an hour, and even if it was just to devour her mouth-watering food and depart, knowing she would probably not hear from us again.

Boetie did not waste time bringing out savoury *roulades* from the oven and traditional hot *roosterkoek* (a type of bread), baked from scratch an hour ago. She had local farm cheese, jam and butter that melted into the *roosterkoek* on contact. A bottle of homemade dessert wine or syrup was on the table, and she showed us how to pour some of it into a hole made at the top of a *roosterkoek* and enjoy a novelty treat. She then served sundried rooibos leaf tea into white mugs, each one with a single word printed on it. My mug read "Rejoice".

Even though I was starving for these homely gifts, it took me a while to bite into one of my favourite breads. My mind was struggling to comprehend and make sense of the waves of mixed emotion felt. It was a constant hopscotch from sadness to gratitude, from guilt to awe, from lacking to feeling cared for. My stomach could not digest it all, so I swallowed the food slowly with sips of soothing tea, remembering George's words to be in the moment.

It still baffled me how George had stumbled upon such humble and open-hearted people whilst hiking alone to plot and plan a feasible Indlela route before embarking on this pilgrimage and leading his sheep into the plains, hills and farms of the Eastern Cape. George hugged Boy and Boetie as if they had been his best friends since high school. They had last seen each other the year before when George had brought through another group of fellow adventurers to receive the same hospitality.

At the end of this heartfelt camaraderie and tea break, there was a definite lifting of spirits that shifted my mood. And I could not pinpoint it to one individual thing.

There was patting of oversized dogs, there was bottle-feeding of Boetie's baby calf, there was petting of purring cats, there was that peaceful presence of ruminating cows again, there was soul food, and there were newfound angels that had bestowed their grace and love upon us.

There was an element of calm reassurance that came over me. Perhaps I would get my answer and eventually find what I was looking for. I just hoped to have an awareness of it when it came.

We were sent on our way with the same celebratory fondness as when we arrived. Mama Boetie ensured we had leftovers to munch on along the way, and Boy gave us all the same encouraging firm handshake. Somehow, the weight of my backpack was lighter, even though I had just refilled both my water bottles. Colin, the walking stick, appeared to take all the pressure from my knees. There seemed to be a renewed energy rippling through my muscles, and I wondered if Mama Boetie had spiced up our *roulade* with extra medicinal herbs. I turned to look back for the last wave goodbye, but they had already gone back to their farming affairs. I smiled whilst trying to put a name to what I was feeling. It seemed foreign, although I caught a sense of it this morning when Colin, the stick, joined our pack. I would describe it as a sincere appreciation, augmented by wonder and with a sprinkle of tranquillity that quietened the mind for a while. Is this what it feels like to rejoice?

The rest of the day's walk was long, eventful and beautiful. Most of the afternoon was spent going downhill. Despite continuous caution whilst treading on loose gravel and stones to avoid slipping or twisting an ankle, Brenda was the first to go down. One second had her looking at the ground and chatting nonchalantly, the next second had her sliding off her feet and landing acutely on her buttocks.

Elize followed the same roller-blading routine just a few kilometres later. Fortunately, neither of them were seriously hurt. Elize repositioned her posture and both her walking sticks with the silent affirmation that this would not happen again. The gentleman in George gave his walking sticks to Brenda to steady her descent down the rugged terrain.

I did not expect to see George copy the undignified acrobatics. Soon after, and totally unguarded, he went down with a hard thud, except that he landed rather awkwardly and lay dead still in a puff of dust. I watched it happen, not in slow motion, but with the speed of a defibrillator shock. Almost everyone had witnessed it, as we had been walking rather slowly and had ended up bundled together. An audible group exclamation preceded half the team stopping in their tracks and the other half rushing to his aid. I remember walking at a normal pace towards him, although it felt like I had just zoomed to his side. I was surprisingly calm. There was no adrenaline rush and no scurrying around for medical equipment (there was none). Nor was I irritated or annoyed that he had jinxed my 'holiday' by predicting my services might be needed that first night at the Brotherhood dinner table. However, I am sure he had not expected the patient to be him.

I eased the rucksack off my back, set Colin aside and simply sat down next to him with my legs stretched out next to his. He was at least breathing and scrunching his eyes in pain - a good sign. Then a conservative moan with eyes open, trying to focus. *Compos mentis*. No blood anywhere. Another good sign. Before I could ask if he could move, he gently eased himself into a sitting position and settled a hand on his right knee. He indicated this was the only body part that hurt and began his self-examination with tentative flexing and extending movements. He was not sure he could walk but needed a moment to let the possible magnitude of this event sink in. We both knew he had not broken any bones, but if he had torn a cruciate ligament, he could not continue with the pilgrimage, and we would not have a leader to guide us through lands that did not seem to be located on any GPS. The hand-drawn maps he had provided us with looked Mandarin to me, and most of our route was recorded in his memory.

George had previously completed hard-core Ironman trail runs in the desert in 40 °Celsius heat with little water whilst he was already well into his andropause. He was not one to give up. He wanted to attempt to stand, so I offered him Maeve's knee guard that I had been wearing since we had left Alicedale. It was the only thing he accepted besides a bit of help getting up. He declined painkillers and anti-inflammatories. He wanted to know the pain he was in so he could gauge his condition. A stark contrast to my 8-tablet cocktail gulped down at breakfast this morning.

He seemed to be able to bear some weight on his right leg and take a few steps. The panicked anticipation of the group's faces visibly turned to gradual relief. I imagined there was plenty of breath-holding going on until George finally declared he would attempt to walk for a while and see how far he could get this afternoon. He had accepted his walking sticks back, which Brenda felt so poorly about, but it was not her fault nor her doing. We had another ten kilometres or so to go, and George hoped not to make the phone call to Ronelle for the rescue Mitsubishi.

I realized later that I did not have to do one single thing or make any medical decision. It was odd that I didn't go into the automatic *3Hs* or the vital *ABC* check. Hazards, Hello, Help. Airway, Breathing, Circulation. I have no idea what possessed me to sit down next to a prospective trauma patient and wait. It went against all instinct. Perhaps I recognized that this was not a life-threatening situation, or maybe I did not know what else to do in this unprepared alien environment, out of my comfort zone. Whatever the reason, all that was required of me was just to be there. I just needed to be present for that moment.

This experience was foreign to me. Maybe as a student, I stood back several times whilst a qualified doctor took over a procedure or the unfolding drama. But from the moment that Bachelor of Medicine & Surgery diploma landed in my hand, every patient since then has needed some kind of action, counsel, decision, cure or miracle from me. In twenty years of tending to thousands of patients, this was the second time I felt that my mere presence was enough.

The only other time I sensed that simply being present in the moment was enough was during one of my visits with my mother-in-law whilst she was still in the hospital. I regret not fully appreciating the preciousness of that moment, but just before she started her chemotherapy, I happened to be alone with her one afternoon. I was sitting on the edge of her clinical bed with my idle chit-chat when she randomly reached for my hand and held it in hers. Without further ado, she began to cry and could not stop. I did not have the appropriate words of comfort as I tried to hide my fluster. But she did not need my words or counsel. She solely said in Portuguese, "Please, just let me cry." And so I did. We sat in quiet sadness with the unspoken notion that she already knew these were her final days. For a long while, she had tried to keep up with the bravado. The heroine within her did not want her family to see her breakdown nor think she had given up the fight. All she needed now was for me not to say or do a single thing. She did not need reassurance or empty promises. She just needed me to be with her as she came into the acceptance that her time was almost up.

I dusted myself off the ground and gathered my backpack. As I waited for George to get a few more steps ahead, Maeve approached and was quick to offer me her second knee guard. I did not wish to accept it as her knees had more mileage on them than mine. But she insisted that these knee guards were simply prophylactic, and she was fine. I believed her, as I had not heard her complain about a single thing since the start of this journey. I gratefully sat down again to untie my shoe and slip the guard over my left knee. This was turning out to be a game of musical

Hypocratic Oaths

knee guards. We then took a slow following behind our headman, continually gauging his discomfort and limp.

After an hour or so, George declared a tea break to rest our feet and his knee. He was not the only one tending to his injuries. By now, everyone had some sort of sensitivity, discomfort or raging blisters on their pedal extremities. It seemed that despite the beautiful pit stops and culinary indulgences, the day had taken its toll on quite a few comrades.

Julie crumpled in a heap of tears when she took her shoes off and saw a new cluster of painful red-hot blisters. All that she could muster for the day was finally depleted in that one single moment. Even as a proficient hiker, the physical and emotional hurt endured since she began this pilgrimage, had just reached its summit. The possibility of not completing the final miles of the day brought further tears when she could not get her shoes back on.

At the same time, Marcelle desperately tried to conceal her inner turmoil without much success. She buried her face in a wad of tissues, alternating with fretting over her rucksack in a feeble disguise to hide her weeping.

Our valiant leader took charge and discretely triaged the situation. Once again, he decided on another's behalf, thereby removing the sense of utter failure of not *walking* the entire 300-kilometre pilgrimage.

I cannot remember how Ronelle got to our rest stop in the middle of an endless gravel road in the middle of what looked like no man's land. There did not seem to be any connecting roads or access onto our gravel road, but she appeared out of nowhere in the maroon Mitsubishi with perfect timing. I had not seen George call anyone on his mobile. How did she know where to find us? By now, she seemed to be an angel in disguise who mystically appeared to save the day when she was needed the most. Ronelle stepped out of the car and surveyed the casualties, each sitting on their little rock or pebble pile, petting and soothing his and her wounds. She walked towards George first, who was already standing up to advise her of the plan of action. Marcelle was adamant that she was physically fit to carry on. The trained psychologist knew that intentional walking could be an excellent remedy to aid an emotional torrent, so he let her be. Instead, he escorted Julie to the front passenger seat of the SUV. She would be hitching a ride next to Ronelle for the last stretch onto Enon.

There were no further incidences once we got going again. When we saw that George (and everyone else, for that matter) was managing a regular pace, we eased our tension somewhat. We tried to take the focus away from our fatigue and body aches onto other distractions and diversions. Counting the minutes in an 'are we there yet' manner was not helpful, so Elize suggested we call out names of books and movies that we have read or watched and why we enjoyed them. That had us going for a little while. Then Christy began the game where one person starts a sentence and the next person adds on another sentence, and the next another, until we have a short story. That had us in giggles, providing some welcome relief. An hour had passed.

Needing some time out again, I was happy to lag a little behind to find further entertainment solace with my iPod. This time, the music was soothing and gentle. Somehow a few love songs came through on shuffle mode from a playlist I did not know I had downloaded. Well, I did not know how to download music onto my iPod. These were things that my husband always did for me. He was the tech-savvy one and always sorted out the computers, TV, DVD, cellphones and anything else I was clueless at, which amounted to quite a lot when I think about it.

That bittersweet feeling settled into my neurons once more. My husband was not the flowers-and-chocolates kind of a romantic. He was an accountant; he liked budgets, forecasts, certainties, black or white, and definitely no grey. He liked knowing where he stood, what his place and duties were and planning the next course of action. This was yet another occasion where I had thrown him another blind curveball and sent him flying out the park. How was it possible that after 28 years of living with a wild card, he still stuck around? He had no idea how to plan his next move or what the outcome of this insane escape of mine would be, yet he had downloaded a handful of love songs just for me that I didn't even know were there. If this was supposed to make me feel better, it didn't.

Just when I thought there were no further pit stops, we were allowed another ten-minute break. The heat, the endless trails and the physical and mental exhaustion seemed incessant. It was 4 p.m., and in an hour or so, the setting sun would be signalling that our time was also up for the day. And we still had quite a stretch to go.

Eleven weary travellers gathered what residual inner strength they had and resumed the trek. I am not sure why I ended up taking the lead, but my legs set their own pace without a specific intention. We marched onto one of the dustiest main gravel roads I had ever encountered, and we soon figured out why.

Enon is a small-sized rural township 60 kilometres northeast of Uitenhage in the southern Eastern Cape. In 2011, it had a population of 2160 souls, and to date, a large percentage of its adult inhabitants are employed in the surrounding citrus, dairy and sheep farms. The other portion of working adults is either unemployed or employed in various shops and industries in the neighbouring commercial town of Kirkwood, 13 kilometres to the West. There are only two dirt roads leading into the town of Enon. And we were on one of them. At the end of every weekday, a procession of overflowing trucks, buses and bursting-at-the-seam taxis carried loads of people back to their homes after a long day's work on the farms. Each vehicle proved its resilience by repetitively carrying back and forth, triple the capacity of its passengers. However, they should be advertising the infamous back bumper sticker "Eat my Dust" instead because that is precisely what we were doing. With every truckload that passed, we were powdered with layer upon layer of a fine dusting that would have any respectable baker or pastry chef green with envy. And with every taxi that passed, the waving and whistling got louder and more encouraging. At least, that's what I initially thought. But then I realized we were the ones providing great entertainment for these folk. They were bemused at the sight of eleven crazy *umlungus* ('white' people) looking like giant-sized meat croquettes, voluntarily walking for miles (with perfectly good cars parked in their garages). They saw us loaded with random back-burdens that were not firewood bails or 20-litre water vats (because no normal person does this voluntarily in the middle of the day, or ever). Even the local police car and ambulance came past; their lights and sirens were not blaring, so I am sure they too came for the show.

However, the taxi-loads of folk arriving from Kirkwood seemed to be less amused with our parade. Their faces were a little more apathetic and drained, resembling the same blunted look of the hoards that travel the London underground every day. Regardless of what stare I received, I could not help but smile back both in appreciation of every amused greeting and in sympathy of every soul that had had a long, arduous day, albeit through my gritty eyes and sandy lips.

These scenes played out for another hour, and most of my fellow pilgrims had long lost their sense of humour. Their grey talcum-powdered faces could not hide the exasperation. We could see the town's single-story resident skyline in the seemingly near distance. However, it persistently remained far from reach. It was possible we could be hallucinating by now. We had been in the sun for over ten hours, and a few wayfarers had straggled far behind. When George thought we were just within the boundaries of the town, he waited for his herd to catch up, so we could walk in a group and not get lost amongst the alleyways that had no demarcated street names.

Hypocratic Oaths

We were sure that Enon was not an apparition when Livia slowed her grey sedan down to a halt next to the waiting crew and rolled down her window to salute us with a broad smile and a sunny, *"Hullo julle!"*

What a wonderful sight! Livia looked at us with a tinge of pity, a hint of amusement and a whole lot of kindness and adoration. It was the same look we got from Boetie earlier on that day. Our hostess was indeed worried that we had gotten lost, and when we had not knocked on her door by 5 p.m., she had come looking for us. She was well aware that walking after dark was never a good idea, regardless of which part of the country you were travelling in. Julie and Ronelle had already found Livia's place and were equally expectant of our arrival. We reassured her we were alright and would be at her place before dinnertime. She did not doubt that and drove off to finish up our supper, leaving us in another puff of dust, waving and wishing us a speedy arrival.

This time, the Green mile was significantly different from the one that walked into Alicedale. The muscle aches, sore hips, knee discomfort and painful blisters were ever-present, but I no longer expected death to await me at the end of the final stretch. There was a homely supper on standby, there was a haven to rest and wash my tired body, and there was evident hope. It was a green mile indeed, a lush contrast to the bleak brown and dry veld that surrounded Alicedale. Surprisingly, the verdant pastures and fields leading into Enon were not powder-coated but echoed the promise of new life and better things to come. This town was cushioned in a beautiful green valley, now basking in the residual golden rays of a setting sun and reflecting the sparkles of all the rainbow colours.

I have never lived in a township. I have driven in and out of townships for a day at a time to work at the local clinics as a medical student, and I have stayed for a month in a small village hostel near Tintswalo Hospital in Limpopo province during a community service block, where I celebrated my 21ˢᵗ birthday. But I cannot possibly know the challenges of living amongst an excess of extreme and limiting conditions.

However, there is something unique and nostalgic about its vibe, the music, the energy, and the pulsating of this particular piece of earth that resonates with Africa's magic and beauty. There is a captivating magnetism within the sound of kwaito, the smell of burning firewood, the sight of chickens on the *stoep* and goats in the backyard, of children playing bare-footed on the iconic make-shift dusty soccer field, that remind me this is where I belong. This is where my roots are. Africa is in every cell of my being, and it feels good to be here, on this day, at this time, and where I can just be me. Without conditions.

The smile within me got secretly broader. It was not appropriate to skip and dance into town, considering the others were virtually deflated and demoralized, nor did I have the physical strength to be merry. But I felt my heart opening a tiny bit, enough to allow a quiet satisfaction and peace that I had not had in a long while. I took it all in.

The welcoming committees of free-roaming cows staring back at us whilst nonchalantly chewing on fresh grass, wondering what took us so long. They were oblivious to the rush hour traffic and occasionally added some mooing to the hooting and whistling. People hustled and rushed to get home, skinny stray dogs barked at the bicycles whizzing past, TV soapies and boom-box music faded in and out of households as we walked on by, and children laughed, played and ran up and down the streets. Scattered piles of litter decorated the side paths, and a myriad of neglected potholes had left the road severely poxed. But there was nothing that looked or smelt out of sorts to me. The purple dusk brought with it a brilliant rising moon. The truck headlights highlighted a billion dust particles that danced and whirled in the previous vehicle's slipstream, and teenagers giggled and greeted us with curious grins. The scent of hearth fires and simmering stews had this unfitting strange white woman believe she was home again.

Hypocratic Oaths

The sight of Livia's modest home had us all celebrating in quiet jubilation. We happily greeted her once again as she introduced us to her husband and his sister, who had been helping Livia for the past two days in preparation for our arrival. I am not sure that they could remember all of our names, as we hardly had the strength to breathe them out after 35 kilometres of hard slog. Still, they just smiled with genuine acceptance and simply stood to one side, allowing us unlimited access to their house, amenities and hospitality. I politely shook their hands, but I really wanted to have given them each a giant heart-warming hug. I was in awe and humbled by these people welcoming strangers into their private safe space without caring for the apparent disruption to their daily routine.

Livia and Tyrone had built an add-on backyard cottage to accommodate their growing family. Twice a year, they sent their children to sleep over at relatives' houses and then moved heaven and earth in their own home to board and feed twelve strangers for one night in their little cottage. Furniture, boxes, and books were piled against the walls of the main house corridor to make room for George, Hank, and the only couple, Lenny and Iris. The remaining eight ladies were to sleep in the one-bedroom, one-bathroom cottage where a children's bookcase, a fridge, several cupboards, and plastic containers were equally stacked against the two walls of the entrance lounge. A mattress and sleeper couch had been laid out in this open area, as was a ladies' high tea and biscuit buffet set on top of a covered chest of drawers. Never before had I tasted such sublime home-baked butter cookies, and the pre-dinner cup of coffee far exceeded any appetizer I have ever enjoyed.

But before I could walk into this precious sanctuary, Livia had a large plastic wash-basin filled with warm water and salt at the entrance of the cottage, for whomever first wished to soak their mutilated feet. I got first dibs and sat on the *stoep* with my feet bathing in the healing salve, watching the first stars appear in the night sky, wondering how it was possible to feel such contentment when my entire body was weakened by muscle and joint pains. The Claasen's friendly Jack Russel came to take full advantage of a belly rub and happily settled next to me. How extraordinary that besides food, water, and shelter, love and affection are the only other things a dog seeks or yearns for. Everything else is irrelevant.

My gratitude was beyond measure at this point, only that it felt different this time. I usually gave thanks for my health but subconsciously felt bad that others didn't have theirs, or I would give thanks for the roof over my head and food on my table, but felt guilty that others were hungry or homeless. My gratitude had always come with conditions, and so it had not felt entirely liberating or rewarding. I was not sure who had made me responsible for the wellbeing of the rest of the world's population. Still, it seemed a hefty price to pay for my happiness, considering everyone is born with free will, and I have no control over other people's choices or soul's journeys. Perhaps I had inadvertently taken on this role when I accepted that medical scroll into my hands.

I did not appreciate it at the time, but this is what it can feel like to be *happy*; when unconditional thankfulness soaks through the skin and deep into the soul, it can leave a sense of complete satisfaction without the need to seek more.

I felt bathed in the miracle of just being.

As hungry as we were, there was no rush. We all seemed to gravitate to the lack of motion and action, just as one would try to ground oneself when stepping off a chronically swaying boat. There was no bell signalling that dinner was served. Our hosts simply waited for us to slowly gather around their long table set in an open-plan dining room and lounge area. It was a far cry from the sombre feeling of a Last Supper. This felt like a celebration, a rejoicing, and a promise of a brighter day to come. Was that not what the Last Supper was all about? The promise of Resurrection, with the understanding that new beginnings are only possible with the death of something else, including the death of old beliefs. And the only way to beat death is to live with renewed trust and faith.

Dinner was a feast filled with the goodness of the earth. It was an array of mixed vegetables, rice, pumpkin, green salad, and baked potato with chicken, followed on from a starter veggie soup. Maeve was at the table head and got the short straw when the pot of soup was placed in front of her. She dished out everyone's bowl of deliciousness. While Livia and her sister-in-law darted in and out of the kitchen, Tyrone stood in his lounge during the entire culinary affair, chatting non-stop and preaching historical musings to no one in particular. The term 'verbal diarrhoea' came to mind, but I sensed that he was only too happy to have new faces to impart all the knowledge he had acquired throughout the years in the space of just one hour. He was a teacher by profession and a devoted church follower, so it came naturally to him to share his passions. We graciously indulged him and were amused by his delightful company. I was looking at everyone with new eyes, a secret smile threatening to expose my Self.

We all ate to full satiety, and yet there was a great deal of food left over. I was sure a good portion of the neighbours would also be suitably fed by tomorrow. Our hostesses insisted on clearing the table to make way for pudding and coffee. Our reflection time tonight was unanimously postponed to the following evening, as the day's fatigue and post-prandial drowsiness had set in. We still had bags and food to pack for the next day, blisters to tend to, a shower queue to endure, and some journaling to do. I had taken ownership of the bottom bunk bed in the single room with three other ladies. Thus I could not linger on indefinitely, as I am sure once everyone had settled into their sleeping bags, the lights would be turned off.

During supper, I had quietly reminisced the day's events in my head. It had turned out to be a good day for me, even though it began with great heaviness and immense pressure to find the answer to this wretched question: "What am I looking for?"

Everyone evidently wants happiness, but are we not looking for it in the wrong place? We seem to be looking for it out there, outside of ourselves, chasing attainment that is forever out of reach. We seem to be forever climbing to get to the top of the mountain, but who sets the standard, and how do we know we have reached the top? There is no such thing because the journey is not about the destination. It is about the journey! How many times have I heard this and not understood its true meaning? We all seem to be chasing and struggling, expecting something or someone outside of ourselves to gratify us. We will be searching forever in that case. Perhaps it is true that happiness is indeed a personal state of mind and attitude that brings peace within a grateful heart. Happiness does lie within. Maybe I was getting another sneak peek into this reality when I became unfazed by the dust, the noise, the bustle, the trucks, and the taxis. Perhaps happiness is when I feel simple appreciation and gratitude, unattached to anything else happening around me or when I do not have to pretend. Here, in this internal place, I find the freedom just to be. Once I reach this holy inner summit of happiness, I am only required to keep on walking.

My dilemma was how to return to my normal daily routine without being bothered by everyone else's noises, opinions, actions, and drama. It seemed I was required to follow pre-conceived rules and requirements set by a faltering society, religion and old-fashioned culture. George had echoed these concerns during the evening, but he could also not offer an answer. But all answers do lie within each of us.

I later learned that Enon was named after the biblical place mentioned in John 3:23. Two thousand and something years ago, Aenon was a place near Salim, known to be resplendent with an abundance of water, and where John the Baptist repeatedly baptized crowds of people that sought Divine salvation and rebirth.

I could not see my miracle at the time when my feet were being christened in Livia's plastic wash-basin.

Someone called Vishal Raina once quoted that miracles happen when you have gotten your full dosage of pain and suffering. And Mike Dooley says that miracles are invisible until you arrive.

I now understand both definitions four years later.

8
RESURRECTION

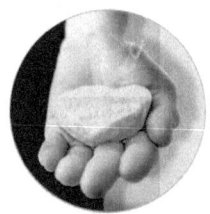

We are all vulnerable like infants.
We must look after each other, or else we shall suffer
- St Francis of Assis

I am not sure how I ended up in the bottom bunk-bed of a crammed tiny room that slept four grown adults. I suppose I was considered one of the lucky ones that did not sleep on a floor mattress, but I would have much preferred it. My night was spent in restless tossing, accompanied by the tune of a random dog barking. I felt claustrophobic with the first-floor bunk bed just twenty centimetres from my face, and every time the upstairs neighbour moved, I tried not to imagine the bedboard cracking and getting suffocated by a slumbering fellow pilgrim.

As a young child, I had slept in the bottom bed bunk of our shared bedroom when my sister got first pick of the upstairs bunk. Yet, at that time, I remember feeling snug and cosy, far from confined, and comforted by the fact that I had my one and only sibling close by for company. I guess everything is relative. I was probably a third of the size then and now clearly outgrown the space allowed for easy manoeuvrability. The semi-restriction of a sleeping bag was not helpful, but I did acknowledge that at least I had slept warm.

Last night, I developed an inkling of understanding why my mother has always insisted on being cremated. Her biggest dread in life is to be buried alive, to later wake up in the confines of a coffin six feet underground. This bottom bunk bed surely had the same burial measurements. Whenever the rare subject of funerals came up, my mom would ensure that both her children promised to have her cremated after I had personally certified her dead, one hundred times over, just in case. At least she trusted me in this regard. At this stage, I had no concrete belief or disbelief in reincarnation or what exactly waited for us on the other side after our physical death. Still, now I have no doubt that my mother was most likely buried alive in a previous lifetime.

The entire township was dead quiet for all of the night, except for the dogs. I would have expected to hear *shebeen* music until all hours, or even a distant drunken brawl or domestic discord. But alas, the canines were the only ones that decided this was the only time when they could hear themselves 'talk', as the human daytime commotion clearly does not allow for much socializing. So they make the most of the attention-seeking at night. They became so spent from all the nocturnal yapping that by the time we left the Claasens' residence in the early morning, they were completely silent.

Homely medicinal breakfasts can generally remedy grumpy insomniacs. By the time my plate of eggs, tomato, cheese and hot toast was finished, I had already forgotten the twilight serenade. A hot cup of coffee had quickly restored some sense of humour. Or maybe it was as a result of the habitual morning pill cocktail. Either way, when we finally gathered outside on the street for a farewell group photo and the daily ritual prayer, I was in a good disposition.

This was the first time that our hosts joined us for our morning reflections. Livia, Tyrone and Emmarentia made our circle bigger and joined hands with eyes closed and heads bowed to hear Julie's blessings for the day ahead.

These wonderful, kind and honest people without pretence were not only school teachers but community developers who sought out ways to uplift social standards and community wellbeing. They may not have realised the immense impact they had on these weary travellers, but they uplifted their spirits too. They were teaching healers, not only amongst their neighbours but towards every single stranger they met.

Again, I cannot imagine the challenges they face amidst poverty and neglect, but all I saw in their smiles was joy, sincerity, compassion and proud humility. All it takes is for them to look after each other.

It was another cold morning with iced fingers and toes, but my heart was filled with admiration and warm appreciation for such kindness and open-handed hospitality. And it was slowly filling up with hope for humanity and a new-found faith that humans were perhaps friends and not always foe.

The town of Enon was unrushed to wake up in the morning. A stark contrast from yesterday's afternoon flurry. The sun's rays were just peeping above the mountain peaks and shining through household windows, slowly raising town-folk eyelids to make them see another day. Our silent procession out of town was followed by a few taxis taking early risers to their workplace, and handfuls of children were walking to school. They were equally quiet and not overly excited about heading off to their destinations. Most of the surround-sound came from tyre-wheels kicking up dust again. The fine powder was already hanging in the air, but the morning dew kept it from coating our nostrils and eyelashes. Initially, anyway.

The walk out of town was up a gradual incline, and by the time I looked back at Enon, the sun had risen upon the entire valley, making it look like one of the most celestial city landscapes I have ever gazed upon.

This biblical town was soon out of sight, which left the mind to intermittently wander through the possible obstacles that today's trail could have in store and wonder whether the body aches, painful feet, ankles and knees would ever get used to the daily onslaught. My frozen left hand struggled to keep a grip on Colin, and my equally frozen right hand kept wiping the clear mucous that ran down my nose. More and more vehicles drove past as we were on the only exit route to the next town of Kirkwood.

Before coming onto the tar road, we persisted beyond two hours of treading on the hard gravel road. It etched through endemic bushveld and passed alongside mile-long rows of lemon and orange trees. When we came to the T-junction that levelled out the road onto tar, we turned right into it but first had a quick 'comfort break' behind the trees.

Not among the citrus ones, though. The ablution facility was behind a massive bluegum tree, which has provided many a traveller and passerby with cool shade and resting refuge for hundreds of years. We ventured behind this evergreen landmark two by two so as not to accidentally surprise someone with their pants down or in the middle of a naked butt-squat. If this tree could talk, it would tell us of the countless bums it has stood guard over.

Then came four kilometres of straight slogging along the tar road to Kirkwood. We walked in the 'emergency lanes', which just happened to be more gravel track passing by acres and acres of citrus orchards on our right, and towering pine trees, palm trees and bluegums to our left. A deep straight trench carrying fresh irrigating water from the Gariep

Dam ran for kilometres parallel to the road. It made the rows of palm trees not feel so out of place in this less-than-tropical setting. We drank from the fresh water, and I filled my water bottle, trusting that I would not develop bloody dysentery by nightfall.

Lenny met up with a local fellow, who was also walking into town, and the two of them kept each other company for the better part of an hour. The rest of us passed the time with light chatter in groups of two or three. Traffic had picked up again, with the locals hooting and waving, this time in definite encouragement. Several more people were walking alongside the orchards than we had encountered thus far. They may have wondered why we were walking for 'pleasure', as their long trekking seemed to be under duress or without another choice. At some point, I stopped to pat a gorgeous Great Dane and friendly Border Collie. A donkey cart with three passengers sitting at the back of the wagon rode by in the opposite direction, seemingly reassured that their two donkeys knew their way out of town. The usual pitiful and expressionless faces of the donkeys had me wishing I could relieve them of their harnesses and assist their escape into the wild mountains. I have this feeling every time I see donkeys, horses and cows attached to loaded tack and straps. But I guess there are times when a creature cannot escape what they were born for, albeit as a forgotten pre-conceptual contract.

Our arrival into Kirkwood changed my ignorant perspective of a small one-horse town to a busy metropolis, where commerce and shops of all kinds and a complete array of facilities were available to us. We walked past ATMs, the infamous PEP clothing store, several *spazas*, furniture and cellphone accessory shops, and a big Spar supermarket. It was rare for me to have an opportunity to physically walk the pavements of any town instead of just driving through on the way to a designated destination.

I have had the good fortune of travelling to various magnificent holiday places. But it always seemed such a rush to get there and such a rush to get back home. I often complained to myself that we never stop 'to smell the roses'. There is usually some or other excuse for not stopping at a *padstal* or side-street vendor. There is usually no time to stop at the Kirkwoods of the world; such is the desperation to escape civilization and get lost amidst wildlife and nature.

Even then, there is a significant difference between taking a game drive and going on a bush walk. Of course, game drives are wonderful and bring the exciting expectation of what lies around every bend. They also allow the opportunity to explore vast and magnificent areas of a wildlife reserve or park in a short space of time. But there is something utterly magical about a walk through wild bushveld, surrounded by the intimate mystery and beauty of mother earth, without the constant humming of a diesel motor and the squeaky mutterings of a 4x4 in the background. Walking allows the unusual smells, sounds and nature's touch to filter through your every sense and permeate into the soul, leaving you mystified in the middle of a place of peace.

Walking the streets of Kirkwood brought a similar satisfaction. Something I did not expect, as I don't usually see traffic, concrete and commerce as particularly revitalizing or exciting. But my senses were appreciating the sights of a city not in a hurry to see the end of the day. The smells of new leather from the furniture shop, baked pastries from the corner café, and the sounds of the Cape-coloured Afrikaans coming from curious and friendly locals invariably ignites a smile on any South African's face who values their humour and bittersweet heritage. As if being in direct contact with the pavements, the buildings and everything seen and unseen within the vicinity imparted their story and meaningful essence.

Most of all, I think it was the slowing down of time that enchanted me the most. It was a feeling that only ever graced me a handful of times, as everything around me always seems to be rushed or urgent or destined for some ultimate purpose that forever remains elusive. I rush to work. I rush through grocery shopping, I rush through cooking and cleaning (I do not particularly enjoy any of these), I am rushed by the next patient if I take too long with the previous one; I can't wait for the weekends to come, always planning ahead, running late or counting days for the next holiday.

For years, I bought into the illusion of not enough time. I even became obsessed with my wrinkles and forehead frown, that age was catching up with me, and I was somehow running out of time. But every time I rush, I am simply speeding closer toward the day that I am meant to die.

Our dashing through to each holiday destination also makes the return date seem closer. I had loved our first visit to the Kgalagadi Transfrontier Park in 2001, our stay in Moremi and Xakanaka in the Okavango Delta, our adventure to Mana Pools in Zimbabwe, and several other wild and memorable experiences.

But even our visit to the long-awaited bucket-list destination of the Serengeti left me a tad despondent. The rush and pressure were put upon our tour group to zoom over the Mara river and shoot through the vast plains packed with thousands of lulling wildebeest. This was all under the time constraints of an hour, as we needed to make our way out of the park before a designated time. Here I was, surrounded by an ancient natural miracle, amidst one of the Seven New Wonders of the World, and I was being forced to make haste, curb my incredible awe of this marvel, take quick snapshots, and get the heck out. I was so upset that I remember sulking for the remainder of the day.

Retrospectively, I am aware I missed out on the enjoyment and magic of what was.

Having specific expectations in any situation and attaching to their supposed exact outcomes can often bring disappointment. Lack of adaptability and flexibility when circumstances change will inevitably work in our disfavour. One of Lao Tzu's teachings in the Tao Te Ching says: "Be open to everything and attached to nothing."

Where have such masters been all these years, and why had I not heard of any of them before?

It is true that when the student is ready, the teacher will appear. At this point, I had not yet entered nursery school.

Today was shopping and restock day. But first, we had been given the street directions to meet at The Chameleon coffee shop upon our individual arrival in Kirkwood. A mid-morning brunch and coffee were just what the doctor ordered. Cliché, I know, but it really was. This lovely quaint café served delicious bacon on French toast and the frothiest and largest cappuccino I have ever relished. It also provided me with the freedom to sit in a quiet corner to catch up on my journaling without the concern of being unsociable. By now, everyone had probably become accustomed to my sullen silence and desire to be left to my own devices.

Today was also the day we said goodbye to Ronelle. She was to travel back home after enjoying a celebratory cup of tea with us, and George would be taking over the responsibility of the rescue vehicle. We were introduced to Lilly, an Indlela tour leader in the making, who George had taken under his wing, to train and share the practical management and operational responsibilities of these pilgrimages. Lilly was petit and soft-spoken and didn't come across as an authoritative persona. We would all give her a chance, but she had not walked these back-trails as George had, so I secretly hoped we would not get lost in the days ahead. Any extra mileage walked around in circles would no doubt be torture that nobody wished to endure.

We were given an hour to each do our necessary shopping. Our rendezvous time was noon in front of the Spar supermarket. I headed straight to the pharmacy. I was desperate for a handguard or a cushioning of sorts. My left hand was starting to blister, being continuously chaffed by Colin's *knobkerrie* handle. I also wanted to get my own knee guard so that I could return Maeve's precious possession. The tricky part was to convince the chemist to issue me with a long list of painkillers, anti-inflammatories, stomach protectors, and more cortisone, all self-prescribed and without presentation of any valid credentials. I had not thought to bring proof of doctorship, nor did I expect to have run out of all the medication I had brought along within four days of over-consumption. I also needed plasters, micropore tape, rubbing salve and energy bars. I suppose the sight of my traveller's attire (perhaps my dilapidated sun hat), the load on my back, and my flushed desperate plea for first aid relief, convinced the elderly pharmacist to dispense whatever I needed. Even if it was for the fact that I spent a small fortune at his shop (thank goodness I remembered the credit card), he did show genuine pitiful sympathy. I was very grateful for his help and made a mental note to add him to my prayers whenever I decided to start that affair again.

Apparently, I did not need anyone to get me lost. I could do a fine job of that myself. When I did not show up at the designated hour, Hank was sent out to look for me. He did eventually find me wandering close to the Spar but not quite there. Before the advent of GPS google maps, I had gotten lost on several occasions in my life just going from Johannesburg to Pretoria or from my house to a shopping centre I had never been to before. I have ended up at a very dodgy taxi rank on my way to High Court in the city centre and screamed and cried my way out of there in a total panicked state. On one occasion, I literally threw one of the first Garmin models into the trash in sheer frustration. I cannot stand getting lost on my own. I don't mind getting in a car with my hubby and going on a road trip without a specific destination, but I cannot get lost. I don't care to know where that phobia comes from, and I don't care to focus on the fact that losing my child is one of my biggest fears. Not in the sense of her death but in her disappearance that would leave me forever wondering in terror her possible whereabouts or unknown outcome.

Of course, no one likes to lose at anything or lose anyone that is dear, full stop.

So, it was no surprise that having lost the desire for living had made me tremendously uncomfortable.

Once we had regrouped after my feeble apology for the delay, we proceeded to walk out of Kirkwood back onto the tar road, to once again become immersed between rows and rows of lemon and orange trees. For the remainder of the afternoon, we walked amidst an abundance of lovely citrus orchards. The tar road merged into a singled-lane minor road, with spacious sandy boundaries on either side to allow oncoming traffic to diverge from whatever was opposing it on the narrow road. There were rows of neatly planted pine and eucalyptus trees that bordered the plethora of orange trees beyond the horizon. I imagined there is a symbiotic relationship that allows for better growth of all varieties, or perhaps the pine trees serve as windbreaks for their citrus friends to have a better chance of flourishing. Regardless of the reason, it was just lovely to be able to sit under their magnificent shade by mid-afternoon when we unanimously sat down for a tea break.

When we got going again, I reached for the iPod for added assistance to get through the last stretch of the afternoon. The sole under my left foot was in agony. I had taken another handful of tablets as soon as I walked out of the pharmacy, and their effect was wearing off too quickly. I hoped it was the accelerated metabolism from all the cardio I was forcing upon my body after years of inactivity, not because my liver was going into failure.

What was it with pain which insisted on repeatedly keeping you sidetracked from attaining any kind of bliss? I tried to concentrate on Enrique Iglesias taking back his love. His woman was running and hiding, but she could not escape his love.

Hypocratic Oaths

At some point, I noticed that only some of the citrus farms were fenced. When we eventually got closer to Broadlands Citrus Farm, there did not appear to be much in the way of fencing off of their property or produce. Nicky and Nicole Whyte were the current owners of Broadlands Estate. We were to board there for the night, even though they were out of town. The Estate had been in their family for almost one hundred years, and the management of the property and their citrus farms had been passed down from generation to generation. Someone later asked George if people don't make a habit of stealing the oranges from the unfenced trees that are accessible to everyone from the road. George had wondered the same thing when he first met Nicky. Their philosophy is that you simply plant enough for everyone.

From the moment we stepped onto their property, the result of this ethos was evident everywhere we looked. The two-kilometre gravel road leading up to the main house was longer and more charming than the entrance to Southfork in Dallas. Only there was no air of pretence here. Plentiful lush orange trees continued to line our path to the main house. They seemed to be taller and overloaded with bigger fruit. The pine and eucalyptus trees, the fever trees, the acacias, and every other ancient tree on their grounds were grander and seemingly the true custodians of this fruitful haven since its inception. Several tractors passed by with carriages filled to the brim of plump juicy oranges, their hand-pickers in tow, waving at us and cheering our arrival. They were all dressed in neat blue overalls, women included, and I sensed that Broadlands staff were well taken care of. The storage and packing warehouse was enormous and did not seem to lack any of the latest sorting and packaging equipment. Each worker seemed to know their valuable function in a team of over a hundred employees. The camaraderie and collaboration were tangible and reflected on a single ochre garden ceramic feature at the property entrance, where six human figures were hugging each other in a circle.

The main house was, in fact, a mansion. I cannot put into words the humble opulence that radiated from every detail, every item, and every room. Much attention and care had been given to comfort, space, beauty, tranquillity, heritage, and hospitality. No expense was spared. But this kind of priceless grandiosity was a rare find. It held no envy, no spite, and no greed. It was simply a bountiful oasis filled with every possible comfort and beautiful creation, ready to receive any visitor and welcome any stranger with the same endearing kindness and doting we had received at Livia and Tyrone's home.

I was fascinated by the fact that this morning I woke up amidst humble socio-economic limitations and was now going to sleep in a king-sized bed amidst abundant wealth. Yet, the feeling of open-hearted welcome, genuine kindness and homely affection was exactly the same.

It finally sank in. I know how to *feel* 'home is where the heart is'. For a long time, I knew that it was never about the size of the house, the price of the tableware, or the Egyptian cotton linen. Not that these luxuries cannot be enjoyed, but I always thought I was biased when I felt the loving care at my parents' house and later at my parents-in-law's modest home. They always received every friend, relative, and visitor with the same devotion and attention they gave their children. No matter the financial restrictions witnessed in my younger years, my parents always managed to squeeze twenty-five people around a small table in a small kitchen to sing happy birthday to the lucky recipient of a delicious home-baked birthday cake. It did not matter that my sister and I received school stationery as Christmas gifts or a pair of closed shoes for the coming winter as our Easter present since our feet did not fit into last year's pair. Instead, it was that little chocolate slab that usually got snuck in as a special treat, with a hand-written card and mom and dad's hugs and kisses that made me feel super special and held their worth greater than gold.

I realised this feeling is available in any place or in any circumstance where another human being gifts you with their love and kindness, regardless of their social status or bank account; the appreciation and value just need my recognition.

I removed my shoes before walking into the manor. Perhaps as a sign of respect, or maybe the new left foot blister needed the relieving coolness of the tiled floor. I would like to think that subconsciously I needed my feet to absorb the spellbinding heavenliness of the place, as I had yet to learn what *grounding* oneself was all about. Two very friendly manageresses guided us onto a massive back veranda overlooking colour-filled utopian gardens, where a welcoming sign and two large jugs filled with freshly squeezed orange juice awaited our indulgence. They also showed us the luxurious guestrooms connected to the main house for those who wished to unpack and shower before settling down for afternoon tea.

Despite the sweat, dust, and dirt that coated my body, I chose to first delight in two glasses of sweet home-grown orange juice, then took the third glass onto a wooden deck that overlooked a pristine dam. This estate even had its own little lake. With no one else around, I sat on a recliner chair in sheer admiration of this peaceful place with my bare plastered feet stretched out in front of me, listening to the lamenting geese and cooing doves. The air had cooled but was not yet chilly. The overhanging trees swooshed and swayed in a synchronized rhythmic dance that urged the senses into a trance. Puffs of white clouds shape-shifted across a blue sky dotted with a V-shaped gliding flock of geese. Perhaps the ones in the water were calling out to their friends in flight. A frog croaked out a mono-toned solo and a flurry of birds accompanied in background choir fashion. A peculiar insect hovered above a bed of daisies with its violin version of a song. That unfamiliar calmness settled in again and I found myself surrounded by blissful beauty and bitter-sweet quietude. I had stepped into a piece of paradise, and had no one to share it with.

Whenever I experience something really good or have learnt of any exciting news, one of the first people I usually wish to share it with is my husband. As much as I adore my parents, my sister, and my family, and I have wonderful caring friends, my husband is usually the one that catches the first winds of my enthusiasm. He has also been the sole witness of my dark opposite. But he too has a deep appreciation of magnificent landscapes, a desire for any escape into the untamed natural world, and lives for times of serenity amidst his divine place of worship – Nature.

He would have loved this spot. And I was torn between calling him and not saying a word. Another tidal wave of guilt threatened to inundate this moment of peace. Even though my body was taking a beating, how could I be enjoying such wonder and satisfaction when I had abandoned all responsibilities six days ago in a state of inexplicable despair?

Before the torrent opened up once again, I opted to send him a message hoping that he could not read my tone of voice. I simply said that I had arrived safely at a lovely guesthouse. I was unsure what awaited me at the end of this road but I was glad I had the opportunity to come and thanked him for his allowance. I can't remember what the reply was, if any, but the most important people in my life were suddenly a world away. And I was not yet ready to reach Cockscomb. This mountain peak shaped in the resemblance of a cock's comb was part of the Groot Winterhoek range in the Baviaanskloof area and the official destination of "The Crossing" Indlela expedition.

Once we climb over this final landmark, I am supposed to have all the answers, considering the day after, I will be heading home, apparently transformed into the new version of myself. I had no idea what that looked like, and the pressure to have all of life's mysteries acutely figured out was once more weighing on my mind.

Out of nowhere, a bouncy ball of a chocolate Labrador found my secret spot and demanded all of my attention for belly rubs and ear massages.

Hypocratic Oaths

The smile on my face was instant. This cutie pie was the photocopy of my Bruno and Bailey back home. We had a black and yellow Labrador, and this cocoa bean boy would complete a trio combo. How do these angels in canine disguise just know the right time to embellish you with slobbery kisses and pantings of love and reassurance?

Milo went on to greet the others, and I made my way back to the oversized back porch to admire the tasteful decorative art and furniture that donned each wall and every corner of the house. Nicole Whyte was an artist herself. Amongst classical, modern, and heirloom art paintings, her home was adorned with many of her beautiful creations. This extended throughout the entire property, from the large enclosed *braai* area to the pool deck, the kitchen, and even their massive laundry. This latest discovery, by the way, had us all relieved and rather excited that we could wash all our dust-covered and sweaty clothing in their industrial-sized laundromat. This was a treat, indeed. Marcelle once again made the communal wardrobe collection and made sure all of our items were washed in lavender blossom washing powder.

Back in my palatial room, I completely unpacked my entire purple tog bag onto the fluffy carpet and could not believe how many things I had compressed into it only a week ago. Now I could not seem to find any order with what I had and became irritated that I could not find my snacks. For goodness sake, it was not like I had brought along a large trousseau-chest to lose protein bars amongst poofy dresses, but then I remembered that I had packed very diligently and secretively. I was carrying thirteen individual small clear plastic packets of electrolyte powder and thirteen equal packets of meal replacement shake powder, one for each day of the hike. All of them white, and all looked like I was smuggling cocaine parcels across the Eastern Cape. So I had to look for them in every pocket and hidden ziplock bag because that would undoubtedly outwit every clever police Alsatian dog at O.R. Tambo airport. I gave up packing in frustration and went for an appeasing hot shower instead.

At 17.00, we met in the enclosed *braai* area to reflect on very comfy cushioned chairs and recliners. There was two days' worth of unravelling to get through, as we had not had the mental strength for contemplation at Enon. Reflection time always brought a tiny bit of anxiety, as it appeared to me to simulate catholic confession time. For years, I so disliked being forced to sit alone in front of a priest and confess to him how many times I lied or cheated or swore, only to wait for this well-meaning third party to tell me when and how I would be worthy of living again. I never felt better when I left the cubicle. In fact, I always felt worse even after the penance had been completed.

Fortunately, these pilgrim strangers were far from judgemental, and the sharing of my truths fell on non-condemnatory ears. As usual, everyone had a turn to speak their thoughts and process the day's events.

Maeve spoke of her sister's death seventeen years ago. She had become deeply emotional sitting in Boy and Boetie's kitchen. The mug with which she was served her tea had an angel picture on it and the word 'Joy' imprinted below the image. She had savoured every sip and had sat silently, keeping her tears and goose-bumps at bay. Her sister's name was Joy.

Elize later made the conversation lighter when her highlight of the day was watching the game I taught some of the others to play. I learned the game of the '*Poopdrolspoegkompetisie*' (scat pellet spitting competition) from my brother-in-law. The Afrikaans word alone was a mouthful. Whenever he and his family went camping, they would gather dry antelope poop pellets and stand in a row, only to spit these out of their mouths one by one to see who could spit the furthest. Kudu scat is usually the best, as it reaches the farthest range. But I had only found impala pellets. I can't imagine why, but I only had two brave pilgrims that joined me for this activity. I believed the others missed out. Spitting with fervour at nothing, in particular, can be so therapeutic.

. . .

Hypocratic Oaths

When my turn came to divulge my deep dark thoughts, I said something along these lines: "Yesterday was one of my longest and most difficult on this journey, but surprisingly the best one I have had so far. It started with my daughter's unintentional pressure for me to find what I am looking for. I realise that this miraculous epiphany will perhaps not come as a sudden divine explosion of enlightenment into my body system in a split second of revelation. Instead, I am satisfied to appreciate my newfound hope for humanity and the people of South Africa. I have enjoyed sitting with each and everyone one of you and our respective hosts at tea-times and at supper times. I've listened to your stories and challenges, observing kindness, compassion, consideration, and gratitude, and being thankful that you have all left me to my own devices while still asking if I need help. This Indlela is not about the kilometres, the distance travelled, and not even so much about the places visited. It is all about the people that endure this journey and the ones that offer us reprieve; their shared experiences, their cooperation, and their wisdom or counsel and most of all, the care and compassion that is shown along the way."

One can usually resonate and learn a lot from what other people have been through and why they behave in the way they do if you have the patience and the will to understand their unspoken language.

Then, I openly expressed my dislike for the job that I do, thereby hating waking up to that prospect every day. Julie had asked me the day before, "Why do you hate something that you are clearly good at?" Perhaps she had seen how I behaved when George fell, and we all thought he was severely injured. I did not have that answer.

The truth is that patients often do tell me what a 'good' doctor I am. That has different meanings for different people. Some believe a good doctor has all the up-to-date knowledge on all recent medical and scientific advancements. Or one that is at their beck and call and never says no to their unreasonable demands. Some believe a good doctor is one with an excellent bedside manner, even if they have no idea how poorly the doctor behaves during their anaesthetized procedures. Some professionals believe a good doctor has excellent surgical recovery rates and the lowest complication rates, despite being poor communicators and never smiling or caring for your opinion.

I was none of these and a bit of it all. I was a jack-of-all-trades and a master of none. And this had me in a downward spiral of low self-esteem and lack of confidence for many years because I was not very good at any one thing in particular.

Everyone always talks about finding your passion and do that so it can make you happy. I have been trying to find my passion for forty-odd years, and it was still as elusive as my epiphany.

In the years that I had worked in the trauma and emergency units, I still felt somewhat productive and an essential part of the medical world and team of doctors. I did see my worth on the occasions when I did manage to save a life or safely deliver a baby into the world or correctly diagnose a pulmonary embolism, stop a near-fatal bleed or even suture closed a huge gaping laceration.

But when I became a general practitioner in an isolated office, I believed I had joined the bottom-feeders of the profession. I was in such resentment of my fate seeing the same chronic conditions day after day, without the satisfaction of seeing instant results or recovery. Whenever someone asked me if I was 'just a GP,' I wanted to strangle them after screaming in their ears, "YES! And what the fuck is your superpower?!"

GPs are often disregarded by their specialist colleagues as inferior performers or not academic enough, not appreciating the multitude of different medical, gynaecological, surgical, and mental conditions of all age groups that we have to treat. GPs are often expected to be the middlemen or women plebs that have to liaise and obtain some order or continuum between patient care, hospitals, medical aids, specialists, and pharmacies. We become private investigators trying to source CT scans or blood results from 2 years ago, figure out which one of the "little white tablets" is for which of the seven chronic conditions they have. The number of people who don't know the names of the multiple drugs they put into their bodies daily baffles me (at least carry a piece of paper on you with the list). If an allied medical professional (and occasionally some specialists) do not know what is going on with a patient, the patient gets turfed back to the GP so they can figure it out. When patients want a fifth opinion after seeing several experts, they turn to their GP once more for a miracle, just in case we withheld the cure the first time around. When patients have depleted their own Google research and become desperate after trying a dozen remedies or get sick from incorrect management, the GP is left to pick up the pieces. We are required to be the good Samaritans, and some people believe we should work for free because the government clearly pays for our home loans, office rent, petrol, food, expenses, and kids' education - not! And let's mention the fact that GPs have to be proficient entomologists and reptilian experts to know about every single worm, fly, spider, critter, snake, or scorpion venom or toxin from every province and country. If you get bitten by any one of these, you must go straight to your GP with the offender in a glass jar or container for identification, as there is no chance that doctors have snake phobias either. Last but not least, GPs must be dedicated nutritionists and herbologists to know about every diet and fad (like they don't change on a monthly basis) and know every homoeopathic remedy, root, potion, powder, cream, supplement, and CBD oil concoction made by every Tom, Dick, and Harry (no offence). Not to mention every culture's homemade solutions (the Sunlight soap rectal enemas are my favourite) that have us adding to our medical education on a daily basis.

My low self-esteem had created a deep defensiveness that was the basis of this synopsis. It was no one else's.

Despite all of this, I suppose the reason why I seem to be a 'good' doctor is that I give people my time. Time to listen to their complaints, time to empathize, time to explain their diagnosis and treatments, time to make light of a dire situation, time to liaise with their families, their other doctors, the pharmacy, their medical aids, their employers. Time to make sure they leave my office satisfied with the answers and advice I give them because I don't like any unhappy customers with my services rendered. I have to make time for everyone that calls, messages or emails me and wants my attention in the same instant. This is all very consuming, but I have almost always smiled and attempted to understand and help. Little did I know that it is impossible to please every single person I encounter, no matter how hard I may try. And in the process of this constant attempt to give of my time, my energy got spent, and life in any pleasant form became unsustainable.

I now understand that being a good doctor has very little to do with my medical knowledge (I have never read a randomized double-blinded study in my life). It has nothing to do with being up-to-date with the latest information on how to treat Lyme disease (in my defence, not even the expert physicians can agree) and nothing to do with which medical societies I frequent (none).

But for years, I never saw that I had a 'gift.' This so-called time that I give to people, the attention, always wanting to make them smile or laugh, or make them feel better in whichever way; that is a gift. I never appreciated this. Perhaps I was blinded by the functionality of the role and responsible title of being a doctor, that I could not envisage my gift is *who* I am and what makes me Gisela, the human.

It was then odd that when George fell yesterday, I did not hate being a doctor and was quite okay with just sitting next to him. Perhaps I sensed he did not need any of my time or expertise. He just needed my *presence*.

George confirmed this fact when he finally spoke. Eight months ago, he went under the knife and had an operation on his right knee. He had just gotten to the point of full recovery when he slipped and felt he had injured the same knee again. Even though he is a leader and an esteemed health professional, there are times such as these when you can feel like just "a little boy" also in need of comfort and reassurance. So, he was very grateful that I was by his side, encouraging him to wear Maeve's knee brace and offering him two anti-inflammatories, which he did take after all.

He then admitted that he had said a very formal farewell to Livia and Tyrone in a leader's capacity, not as George, the person. Something he regretted. He advised that we all still need to *be* ourselves while fulfilling our roles.

The impact of that statement only hit me many months later. I had plastered on layer upon layer of artificial masks that I wore day in and day out in the face of the public, in front of friends, and sometimes family. The bitch in me was hidden behind many smiles, and the sarcasm was rife in my head. The compliant and always agreeable doctor, mother, wife, daughter, and sister was functional on the outer surface side of much dysfunctional and hidden resentment, anger, frustration, and desperation. But the thicker the mask gets, the harder it is to breathe.

I had gotten lost in my professional role. Most patients are under the assumption that doctors are able to diagnose and treat all human medical and mental conditions. They are respectable, prim, proper, wise, and competent. They don't get sick, don't swear, don't take medication or drugs, don't abuse alcohol nor smoke, and have no other life beyond their workplace, thus expecting them to be on call 24/7.

They could not be more mistaken. The problem was that I had bought into that illusion too and had been trying to keep up with the same pretence for over twenty years.

On top of this and simultaneously pretending to be Superwoman, I also suffered from a condition called the 'Pleasing Syndrome.' Please everyone, every time in every way, until emotional and mental death sees you part from this joy of life. Not only was this mask the biggest, but it was also the heaviest of them all.

I am not suggesting that I immediately start telling everyone that really pisses me off to sod off, but at the same time that I learn to receive from others (even if just graciously accepting a compliment), I also need to restructure my boundaries. I need to learn to say NO, graciously. On the same note, I need to learn to say YES to the things that I want more of, even if it is not in line with others' expectations or opinions of what is ideal for me. No matter how well-meaning their intentions may be.

What I do know for sure is that I have no problem saying yes to delectable food. Supper was served on another long dinner table, and the disciples gladly feasted on pasta bake, chicken lasagna, and an array of salads. An orange-baked pudding followed, fresh from the estate trees. It was, again, doctor's orders and a pleasure to receive this gift from beautiful people.

Evening tea was served in the grand communal lounge, where a warm fire promised to burn some of our old dogmas and where we comfortably sat to discuss the following day's route. I half-listened as I knew I would be following someone else and not trusting my no-sense of direction. My thoughts floated upwards like the rising smoke in the fireplace. There was something unique about George's admission of being afraid when he fell. But fear was not what captured my interest. We all fear things, and on many occasions, our fight and flight response is actually working in our favour, designed to keep us safe from harm. No, it was George's open confession to feeling vulnerable that had gained him further respect from me.

When we start taking the masks off and learn not to be so rigid in our roles, we risk becoming exposed. That vulnerability requires a deeper level of self-acceptance, wisdom, and bravery. It is one of the most valiant admissions and another vital key that naturally and indiscriminately allows a human being to care and show compassion for another.

To resurrect from a life of hidden and deadly thoughts and behaviours, one needs to abandon all burdening and prejudiced robes, to become authentically vulnerable and fully exposed.

This is far from a weakness.

It is courageous and liberating.

9
LIFELINES

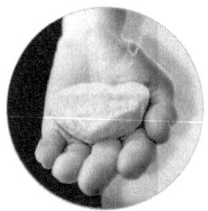

Who will you become when you stop fighting?

I woke up next to Lilly. I was grateful to be in a large king-sized bed where there was not much opportunity for close contact. Not because I am homophobic, but because there was something about her that unsettled and infuriated me, and I could not put my finger on it. I became aware of it last night when I tried to ram all my belongings back into my purple tog bag after finally finding my snacks. At least I had found *something*. But during that time, Lilly pottered around the room aimlessly, muttering under her breath so that I had to keep asking, "I beg your pardon?" Then she would mumble the same thing at the same decibel, thinking it was more audible. She was thin, pale, almost gaunt, petit in stature and persona. Her face was primarily void of expression, but her blue-grey eyes darted fleetingly with anxiousness on occasion. Her voice was so soft-spoken that her words almost cowered out her mouth, and her smile was so sweet that it was sickening to my stomach. She was a very dear lady who had suffered several traumas in her life, but in that process, she became so modest and so excessively humble that her confidence was all gone. Her opinions were meek, and she was a sheep following the masses. I wanted to strangle her.

She was almost a replica of my receptionist that I had just fired before coming on this pilgrimage. When I returned back to Johannesburg, there would be another personal office assistant in her place.

But I could not fire Lilly. George had taken her under his wing. Instead, I completed the morning's routine as fast as possible, plastering blisters, dressing, and donning the same pair of pants for the 7th day in a row. Only now, they smelt better than they had all week. I went to find some calm-down medicine in a large cup of caffeine, freshly-baked banana loaf, toast with boiled eggs, and of course, fresh orange juice. I packed a pecan nut muffin and peanut butter bread for *padkos*.

Reluctantly, I let go of the seventeen-year-old silver cat that had settled on my lap for breakfast and joined the rest of the team for a group photo at the entrance of the mansion's front garden. There, we circled together for morning prayers, and Marcelle ended our gathering with the question: "Who will you become when you stop fighting?"

I would write to her one day and let her know when I had figured that one out too.

In the meantime, I was just going to enjoy this beautiful crisp morning with the faraway gaggling of geese and doves cooing overhead in the tall swaying trees of Broadlands Estate and forget about my very painful right foot arch and super-swollen angry toes. My left knee was so much better, though, and I took Boetie's teacup advice and merrily rejoiced while watching the sun rays filter through the branches, leaving a quiet and peaceful farm behind. It was Saturday today, and it seemed their workers had the weekend off.

Soon enough, we were surrounded by more and more orchards of orange and lemon trees. Several other farms ran their own show, fence to fence with the same produce. Here and there, we waved to farmers' wives and some employees who did have to work on the weekend, dependent on their bosses' regulations.

My father would have loved to walk this mile. He is a multi-talented man, who from a young age, learnt to tailor suits, barber men's beards and cut hair, repair shoes, service, and fix simple car troubles, all the while being an accountant by trade. He repairs electrical wiring, paints and creates models from wood, shells, and stones. He does all the home DIY and is an avid gardener with a flourishing vegetable patch in his backyard. In fact, all my portable vases and pot plants go to his house for rehabilitation (and sometimes resuscitation) every few months. They always get returned alive, green, and blossoming. He has ten green fingers, and he would have been in heaven walking along these citrus forests.

The smell of fresh lemon brought back fond childhood memories of biscuits and cakes baked in mom's kitchen, making lemonade with plenty of sugar, and cutting slices of lemon for dad's gin and tonic while he would *braai* our lunch every Sunday afternoon.

I hoped they would not be too distraught by my sudden disappearance. I hadn't spoken to them since I left home a week ago.

George rode his bicycle alongside us for the first hour and a half. The bike had been strapped to the back of the maroon SUV all this time, and he finally put it to use. He directed us for the first part of today's route, as these forests were trickier than the "Amazing Mazes" of Zandspruit in Joburg. He would then back-track to collect and drive the SUV to the next overnight stop.

The orchards abruptly ended and gave way to various landscapes, from thorny bushveld to dry gullies, grassy flatlands, to lush hills again. We climbed significantly for another hour and jumped our first fence for the day before coming to our morning tea break and pit stop. Some of us sat on scattered rocks, others on abandoned tractor tyres. Munching on my peanut butter sandwich, "Miss Maeve" interrupted my mastication with the good news just received via SMS that her domestic employee's grandson has been accepted into college. She was his sponsor and was smiling from ear to ear with jubilation. I congratulated her and the grandson, trying not to spit bits of pecan nut muffin onto her shoes. Ahead of us lay a gorgeous green valley alive with bush, trees, sunshine, and water boreholes. It was a good day indeed.

From the top of the hill, the valley seemed decently fair-sized within the borders of its surrounding mounds, but it took us another eleven kilometres of slogging through those fields to get to a main National tar road. Here, we stopped for lunch at a very well-stocked and pleasant *padstal* along the N2 highway. It was a quaint roadside shop with delightful curios, fresh produce, jam jars, cold drinks, and homemade pies. I bought a bracelet for Lara and enjoyed the best *droëwors* and Coke Zero ever. I then peeled layers of clothing off and removed my shoes to rub my aching foot arch. We sat outside the "Padkafee" patio on picnic-style benches while two French bulldogs toyed and chewed on a dead *dassie*'s skull. I hoped it was not an ominous sign.

I noticed a sign that advertised the presence of cheetah in an enclosed 'sanctuary' behind the *padstal*; always a tourist attraction to make cars come to a halt at this spot. I went round the back of the property to use the restrooms and could not see any cheetah. I wished they were no longer there, as any small enclosure designed for a cheetah is certainly not a sanctuary. Perhaps, a temporary rehabilitation place, but nothing more. Although they are being shot and killed at a fast rate by ever-growing and encroaching game farms and poachers, I am not sure what is better. A dead cheetah or an imprisoned one.

To take my mind off the world's human overpopulation, I followed Lenny and Iris on another treasure hunt. They had cellphone reception here and had logged onto another Geocache location at the entrance gate of this pit-stop shop. This one was easy to spot, but it was a bit of a poor man's find with very few items in it for fair trade.

We were soon encouraged to pull up our big-people panties and stop playing, as we had another very long afternoon ahead to complete the 32 kilometres to Palmietrivier Co-op. Squeezing my feet back into the Salomon twins while trying not to wince, I was grateful for Christy's chatter and company for the first bit of the afternoon. I opened up a little bit more and told her this was my free-to-be-me venture where I had temporarily escaped from everyone's expectations and my deadly routine. She asked me why I still lived in Johannesburg, and it seemed like a silly question because my whole life was based there. But she elaborated by saying, "If you had all the money you could wish for and didn't have to work, and your family was not in the equation, what would you be doing?" I had no idea. I would be a rich lonely woman, I thought.

But it was a crucial and valid question. The same question was asked of me by a very respectable Theta-healer teacher when I attended one of her workshops eighteen months later. I hadn't given Christy's dialogue much thought because it was inconceivable to think about a life without my family. But I had missed the point completely. So Sonia asked again: "Gisela, if you had all the money you could need, didn't have to work, had all the resources at your disposal, and your family didn't need anything from you, what would you do for fun?"

Again, I had no idea. I had never considered it. I thought to myself, "I do have fun."

I laugh when I watch comedy movies and funny entertainment (she said that's only an escape). I enjoy myself when I go to weddings or big birthday celebrations where there is music and dance (she said that's only once in a blue moon). I enjoy joking with my husband, daughter, family, or friends when we get together at functions (but what about when you are alone or have all the time in the world just for *yourself?*)

Essentially, she asked me what I did that was fun, pleasant, or enjoyable from Monday to Friday. It dawned on me that the answer was *nothing*. Everything I did was either a duty, a responsibility, or a requirement.

Christy moved off on her own when she saw I was too hopeless to talk to. Julie took over and enquired about my left knee. She did not know about the right foot. I was not ready for another personal massage. Baby steps. She too moved on, and from then onwards, I either walked alone or had very little idle chat with one or another pilgrim.

The scene had changed dramatically, and we were walking on game farm territory again, and the evidence of drought, overgrazing, and disappointment was clearly visible. Springbok and steenbok plains stretched on for miles, dry, barren, and exposed. Several scattered bones lay strewn across the fields, and very old carcasses dotted the brown earth here and there, desiccated and forgotten. Plenty of buck scat peppered the thirsty ground, but I only saw a weary impala ram, a female eland in the distance, and a blesbok hiding behind a shrub as the only bearers of life.

We walked past two dead antelope whose hooves had long ago been caught on the game fence wiring on separate incidences, and they had both died slow, painful, and lonely deaths, hanging upside down in the blazing sun.

At 15.00, we stopped for a break. We saw bird tracks on the sand and soon saw two Kori Bustards moving rather speedily away from us. These large flightless birds were not happy with our intrusion. It might be obvious that animals will be skittish and untrusting when we make a point of repeatedly hunting them down. We quickly took our weighted bags off our backs when Christy picked a tick off her pants before taking her shoes off. A series of individual self-body checks followed, looking for invisible parasites before we all settled down on the hard-baked flat ground. George had now back-tracked by foot from the farmer's Co-op to find us at our rest spot. He had long gone ahead of us and had already met with tonight's hosts. Even though he had left Lilly in charge, he still worried about his brood and decided to come looking for us.

As he approached, I saw him pick up a pebble from the ground and with a secret smile, put it in his pocket. I had observed him sporadically scouting the dry river beds for the last few days now. I had asked him what he kept looking for and he told me that there are heart-shaped pebbles that he searches for whenever he is away from home. Some stones are millions of years old and uniquely shaped into hearts by natural erosion. He always found one and he always brought it back home for his wife. I thought of my husband. I did not deserve his good heart.

George's presence seemed to fuel our legs for only a short burst. We continued to trespass abandoned small homesteads that could not survive the drought. We saw other equally modest farms that had been overgrazed and sold to larger enterprises to turn into game and hunting farms. Here and there, we saw a few sheep and again passed abandoned sheering houses, storehouses, and abattoir buildings.

The sights of the afternoon and the relentless midday heat were wearing down our minds and bodies. Soon enough, our legs and spirits were just as deflated.

The last six kilometres were simply the hardest to endure. Everyone was feeling it, the silence amongst us was audible, and we were all fading. I have no idea how I kept one foot in front of the other, but I wondered if this is what old age is like. I felt ancient with aching bones, a hunched back, swollen joints, and a beaten spirit. I struggled to stay within the healthy boundaries of reasonable consciousness.

Perhaps my time has indeed run out. At what point do I start seeing the white light or having premonitions of my final hour? My bowels aren't giving me any sign of wanting to go out, so I resort to the saving grace of music and switch on the iPod, but I find it difficult to get a tune to help get my legs in sync with any marching rhythm. I keep fiddling with the select button, getting ever more frustrated.

Just as I was about to pack the iPod away, the song 'Iris' by the Goo-Goo Dolls streams into my ears. In a flash of a moment, I am back in the driver's seat of my green Fiat Uno parked at a random service station, playing this song to J.P. in the middle of one odd night in 2002. My heart virtually stopped and then took off at a gallop. "Jesus Christ, help me, please! I don't know that I can continue with this anymore. This is it. I am throwing in the towel! I beg you to take me now once and for all!"

No one answered my mental shout-out. My body froze into an ice sculpture, but the others passed me by without question, thinking I was changing my tunes. They were not wrong. The unspeakable shame that followed, the ever-present guilt that gnawed at my soul every moment of every day, was still very raw, hidden for years behind an enormous ugly mask that could no longer cover up the secret. And it had me paralysed in a state of shock.

Hot blood pulsated in my head, my tachycardia was out of control, short, shallow breaths struggled past pursed lips, and numbness found my hands. I recognized an impending panic attack and tried to slow down my breathing to process what was happening. It was as clear as daylight.

I thought we had dealt with this shit and had come to peace with it already. My husband had already forgiven me, soon after I had confessed my sin. My daughter was only three years old when, out of nowhere on a random Friday night, I had divulged to him what I could no longer hide. The shattered look that stared back at me broke my soul and spirit, just as I had destroyed his. Months and years of turbulent trials and attempts at rescuing our marriage had followed. I thought we had succeeded in saving our relationship, and he had proven it to be true, considering he has never left my side. Not for a single day. Throughout all our years together, he has remained loyal and slowly learnt to trust me

Hypocratic Oaths

again. I could not believe this subject was coming up now at this very unwelcome moment.

Strangely enough, no tears came this time. The song played to the end. Then I replayed it again and again and again; it slowed my heart rate to a bearable rhythm, then my feet found their grounding, taking one step in front of another until I had a regular pace to try to catch up to the others.

We had reached a very narrow single track that cut through very dense thornbush. Having to dodge several sharp acacia thorns to avoid being scratched, we did not always succeed. Large thorns kept tugging at our rucksacks, pulling us back and, on several occasions, getting caught in our hair and clothes. We lost track of the horizon as the top branches of bushveld towered above our heads, concealing our view and way forward. George told us to follow the waterpipe that ran along the confined track we were treading on.

Only then did I notice a long length of black piping that ran parallel to our path for the last five kilometres of the day. We followed this pipeline through dry river beds, through a long steep edge of a cliff, through high precipices of looming rock-face where we couldn't bear to look down below, and along riverines with large loose boulders where a foot could easily slip and result in a broken leg. We continued to follow this life-giving pipe that supplied much-needed and precious water to the Palmi-etrivier community. We saw there was no other source of water for miles around.

By the twentieth replay of 'Iris' (I wasn't counting), it had finally dawned on me.

A tingling sensation gently swirled around my heart.

J.P. had been a lifeline.

GISELA DE OLIVEIRA ESTEVES, MD

For a while, the world had lost all sanity to me, and I was in a meaningless, hopeless frame of mind myself. I had found some solace in the company of this person. He was an emergency service medic and was in the same mental state. Together, we escaped into Never Never Land fantasy conversations, dreams of what another world would look like. We laughed through sick stories and held each other's hearts while we wadded daily through violence, trauma, rape, misery, social abandonment, and the dying.

When we lost a patient, no words were necessary to read each other's minds, and the silence or music that followed the admission of failure kept us afloat, surviving, preventing us from sinking into utter despair.

But on the day that I took it too far, the lifeline suddenly ran dry. I could not look at him or myself in the same way ever again, and I soon changed jobs so I would never have to see him in the false hope that this would erase my memory of him and so I could pretend to run away from my shame and guilt.

For a while, I did hide behind a wall of deep resentment. I found many reasons to point fingers and blame people for this sequence of events.

I secretly blamed my father. When I wanted to quit medical school in 3rd year, he was so distraught that I persisted. It was the first time I had seen him cry. At the time, he was enduring an enormous sacrifice of his life working in dreadful conditions in rural Mozambique post-civil war, away from his wife and family, to afford my university fees. My parents almost got divorced during this time. I hated carrying that guilt too.

I secretly blamed my mother; I could never share anything dramatic with her, as she would worry terribly and I thought she could not possibly have any valuable advice to comfort me. She also turned the other cheek whenever life threw her a beating, so I suspected I needed to do the same, and just suck it all up.

I secretly blamed my sister; she got engaged on my wedding day and immigrated with her fiancé to Portugal soon after. My parents packed up everything they had in South Africa and followed her there. She was then caught up in the challenge of raising her first child, and I had no other relatives left here.

Newly married, albeit into a lovely family, I simply felt very much alone.

So, then I blamed my husband for the longest time. He was all I had, and I could not share a single thing with him. He did not want to hear my stories of blood, puke, and gore or of children dying daily of HIV, of decapitated car accident victims, axes chopping baby body parts for *muti*, or patients walking into ER with sliced abdomens holding onto their bowels with dirty rags. He hated the smell of hospitals, clinics, and medicines, so he never visited me when I was on call when other husbands did. He did not understand EMS lingo or know any of my work friends, so he would refuse to accompany me to colleagues' weddings or work functions. He did not like my moonlight working hours, and as a defence mechanism, he only did what he wanted to do. It was his way of coping with his bridal wildcard.

My colleagues had the same shit to deal with. My family and friends had other kinds of shit to deal with, and reaching out for psychological help was unheard of because admitting you need help erroneously means you are weak or have failed as a human being.

Plus, being a doctor, you are supposed to know everything and fix everything, right? People get shocked when doctors come down with flu or get cancer. It is like we are made to feel incompetent for failing to preserve our own wellbeing, because we have all the answers to life's riddles and are supposed to have a magical shield that protects us from all ailments. We also have cures that we don't share with patients so that we can stay in business.

So, feeling like I had no one else to turn to during those early 'grown-up' years, my husband and I began to live our separate lives under one roof.

This was by no means an excuse or reason for breaking marriage vows. This was no one else's fault but mine. I had chosen all of it, even though I was oblivious to it and thought I was the victim that succumbed to sin, thereby instantly becoming the perpetrator.

Retrospectively, I would not have wished my husband, or anyone else for that matter, to have also gotten lost in my mad macabre world.

The painful and soul-destroying emotional guilt that followed had me subconsciously punishing myself long after being forgiven by the person that mattered most in my life.

But, I thought all this drama was water under a bridge as we had not spoken about it in years. And here, now, following a simple water pipe through miles of challenging terrain, I breathed in the ultimate peace, the final consolation, and the deepest of gratitude.

With this divine revelation and realization that J.P. had been my lifeline at a time when I needed it most, I understood that he was a friend that heard me, a colleague that saw me, and a soul that kept me from drowning for a while. I was finally able to say THANK YOU. Thank you. Thank you. And I was finally in a place to forgive *myself*. Something that no man, priest, or God could do for me.

The black water pipe and the narrow path ended at a T-junction, where we turned left onto a wide sandy road and under which the water pipe continued to run unseen beneath the ground. The whole group was waiting for me to catch up so that I knew which way to turn. They could have drawn an arrow on the sand, but George waited to count every head. I told them I would follow their tracks. There was just something I needed to do first. They didn't hesitate as they must have seen a broad smile on my face and an invisible spring in my step. I would be just fine.

Hypocratic Oaths

At the T-junction, I noticed a landmark in the form of a massive pile of rocks strategically placed, with smaller pebbles on top of bigger rocks and stones.

I had been carrying my own stone that I had brought from home, and I couldn't think of why I had packed it. Years ago, it was given to me by a chaplain I worked with in one of the E.R. units. He always carried a series of polished oval flat stones with words or verses or Psalms printed on them. He would randomly give them to trauma victims that he was called upon to counsel. Out of the blue, he had once given me this particular stone with the wording 'Stone of Truth' written on it. I had given this stone to my husband soon after we had reconciled. He didn't wish to keep it and had given it back to me.

This was the last time this particular stone would ever weigh me down again. I took it out of my rucksack pocket and added it gently to the pile of pebbles. If I had a candle, I would have lit it too. But I settled for a short prayer of thanks to J.P. I wished him well, and I hoped the weight on his shoulders was also lighter and that he had found some peace in his heart. I thanked whatever God was out there for the sincere love I had for my husband. I wished for it to grow deeper, stronger, and unbreakable with every passing year. And this chapter of our lives was now officially closed.

By the time I had the others in sight again, the pain in my legs and feet was gone. A numbing sensation down my limbs was all that remained. My body vibrated with tiny tingles that had the hair on my neck rise in salute. At this point, I had my moment of celebration. Only this time, it was with tears of joy and relief. The sun had the consideration to stay a little longer behind cloud cover, to allow my fervent body to cool down, for my arteries to slowly and steadily pump revitalized blood through every fibre of my being. When the music finally stopped on its own accord, true peace had settled in a long-forgotten corner of my heart.

When an informal primary school and a yellow *N.G. Kerk* building blossomed out of the horizon, I knew I was close to the Palmietrivier Farmer's Co-operative. The sun then burst out into full view, sending bright rays of exhilaration to light up the centre of my core, and I felt like I was floating into the entrance hall of the community centre where we were to stay over tonight. It was extraordinary that I did not have the physical energy to hop and skip as my brain wanted. I did not have the interest in speaking the miracle that had just happened, nor did I care who took the first pick of the only six beds available. My soul simply levitated past every person until I was in the centre of another community oasis that welcomed me now. I had to take my shoes and socks off so my feet could touch the cool ground and so that I knew I was not dreaming. Not only from what had happened in the last hour, but for the fact that I could not believe I had just walked another 32 kilometres in nine hours.

A simple definition of a Co-operative would be to say it is a registered business where a group of people get together voluntarily to address their common needs. It provides specific services to its members and sometimes the local community. I was not sure what this Co-op offered when it was not hosting exhausted pilgrims, but I know it had something to do with children and farming. We were in a massive white school hall building with dozens of plastic chairs stacked up against walls. Scattered old velvet sofas from 1970 were arranged in a U-shaped configuration, and tables were covered in yellow-orange plastic cloths set in long lines ready for supper. One large table held stacks of dusty mattresses, another bore full bags of oranges and apples, and the best table of all served tea and coffee with a big hot-water urn at its centre.

A table-tennis and snooker table provided bedside surfaces, as the remaining half that did not get proper beds picked up one of the well-used mattresses and found a spot on the cement floor of the hall to roost for the night.

Hypocratic Oaths

Perhaps Palmietrivier Co-op hosted team-building events, farmers meetings, kids' *veldskool*, and even weddings. But today, Bertus Vos and his wife were allowing a strange bunch of very bittersweet people to squat on their premises. Lelanie and Teresa were already in the communal kitchen preparing a delicious chicken pasta and *pap 'n wors*.

I wandered aimlessly for the first ten minutes, taking it all in, and loving the simplicity, the reprieve, and even the fact I may sleep with a mouse or two.

When five super excited Jack Russells ran my way, I left my rucksack on the dusty floor next to one of the sofas, bent down to give them some belly rubs, and then escaped bare-footed to the outside back yard to enjoy the sweetest cigarette of my life.

I was smug in appreciation of those TV cigarette adverts where the man or woman light up straight after sex. It is the ultimate post-orgasmic satisfaction. And I was having one.

I sat alone on the grass with my back against the school hall, entirely spent and smiling to myself like an idiot, in a state of wonder and disbelief (much later, I recognized this is what true self-love feels like). My skin prickled and all the subcutaneous tissues reverberated in a pleasing frenzy. Even if it was the result of the nicotine influx, it did not deter me from my bliss. The last time I was near to an out-of-body experience, I nearly shat my pants. This was incomparable.

As dusk approached, bringing a slight chill with it, I went back inside for a cup of tea, joining George and Lenny at the coffee table. I waited for everyone to shower first. I was in no hurry. Time had suspended in space for a while.

However, when I did get my turn in the public bathroom, there was no water left in the plumbing system. Once again, I stood butt-naked without a towel staring at a small mirror above the basin, laughing to myself. The déjà vu and the symbolism of the moment totally escaped me. Plan B was just to grab the dog's water bowl outside the toilet and use that with a face cloth to wipe me down.

It felt better than a cleansing from John the Baptist.

Our dinner was well catered for the hungry adventurers. Lelanie had placed plates of brown bread with butter and golden syrup on the table. I last had this treat when I was a child. This was the main course on many occasions when we were left with our family friends' children at home without supervision for the holidays, while our parents were at work all day long. Before the era of cellphones and social media, we played properly with board games, music, cards, art painting, and charades. We used cheque books, bank stamps, and deposit slips to imaginatively build our fortunes (our parents were accountants at the bank). It was a carefree time in my life.

Someone said a thanksgiving prayer before we tucked into our food. I remember eating in silent appreciation and in recognition that I do love children. For their simplicity, unfiltered honesty, unlimited imagination, playfulness, and innocence. For the fact that they always see the glass completely full and the beauty and magic of life, that eventually escapes us when we enter adolescence. I was also pleased with knowing that the regret of bailing out of my Paediatric speciality when I gave up my allocated registrar post in 1999 was long gone.

Lenny and Iris had created a fortress of plastic chairs around two mattresses on the floor in the middle of the hall. That is where we sat for tonight's short reflection time, around their private boudoir.

Everyone was exhausted. It had been an incredibly taxing day on the mind and the heart. Elize was gravely affected by the two buck that had been caught on the fences and succumbed to excruciating deaths. Generally, the more upbeat and happy-go-lucky hiker of the group, tonight, she was physically and emotionally finished. When she stepped into a cold shower a little while ago, she had just burst into tears.

Almost all had a similar grim and tiring day.

I admitted that the day was physically draining. Still, I had generally felt better in spirit with fond childhood memories coming up and the sensation of youth wanting to make a sneaky playful appearance again. I had been silent all day about Marcelle's distressing mystery of how all our laundry had come out of the Broadlands' laundromat covered in bits of short dry grass. I confessed then that I had forgotten to take the unused *poopdrols* out of my pocket before joining my trousers with everyone else's shirts, pants, and underwear in the wash. Their fresh clothing had been laundered at a 5-star lodge in lavender blossom and buck shit.

The general gaping of mouths followed by wide-eyed surprise and muffled giggles told me I was forgiven.

I then concluded by saying that I had also let go of a dear old friend for good, and I had found some freedom within.

12 January 2021

Dear Marcelle,
When I stop fighting, I become free.
Love, Gisela

10

CLEANSE AND CROSS

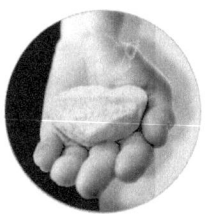

The more you wash, the more the others will smell

There was still no water in the plumbing system in the morning. I dry-brushed my teeth and cleaned my sleepy face with a wet wipe. George was amusingly distressed at not being able to go to the 'hair salon,' as he had no means to tame his wild grey hair. For the rest of the day, his wisdom-highlights would stand freely on his crown, swinging side to side in the mountain air. Fortunately, no one needed a number two this morning, or at least they held it in because we politely only left behind piles of toilet paper floating in gold-yellow liquid.

I had woken up long before my alarm clock was due to shake me out of deep sleep. I lay still for a while, thinking of fences. I empathized with Elsie's despair last night at witnessing such grim accounts of our wildlife. These fences that we build around ourselves can provide some sort of self-defence. We all need boundaries to protect us from things that threaten to harm us mentally, emotionally, and physically. But when these fences and walls are no longer healthy, when they separate us so distantly from one another and completely cut us off from the natural flow and joy of living, then death traps are all that await us.

But mostly, I marvelled at how last night had provided my best rest so far; snug in my sleeping bag, on top of a dusty mattress on a concrete floor, surrounded by old sofas, plastic chairs, and mice poop in the middle of a cold community hall. Not even the king-size bed at Broadlands Estate had provided such surreal comfort. I meant it.

I was fascinated by the energy and child-like determination that Lenny and Iris still had to go Geocaching last night. Despite Lenny's feet being in a blistering disastrous state, the two of them were inseparable sweethearts that had already weathered many storms and remained steadfast, looking forward to celebrating life in its simplest form with fun-filled opportunities that awaited enjoyment. To enjoy is to be *in joy*.

Maeve's morning prayer echoed this sentiment. She reminded us that this is the day the Lord has made. Be glad and rejoice in it. I was sure her sister Joy was talking and walking with her every step of the way. Then, she provided our intention or reflection for the day. I am continually amazed when reading these journal pages, four years after they were written, by how much wisdom they contained and how much of it did not sink into my soul until much later. The more I clean up my shit, the more aware I am of how other people are still so lost in their own mess.

I was very lost when writing the events unfolding on this Indlela, oblivious to the many seeds that were being planted for later fruition. It is up to me to lovingly feed and water these seeds. No one else can do it for me. If I don't, they will remain hidden underground, waiting for another season, another era, another generation to decide or choose differently. What we sow, our children will reap. What we don't sow, our children will reap.

Hypocratic Oaths

Before our group of pilgrims set off in silent ponder, I received a photo of my husband (dressed in my polka dot winter gown) and my precious smiling daughter, hunched over a large pot of rice they were cooking over our camping Cadac gas stove.

It is Sunday, and the Johannesburg Mini Counsellors are celebrating Mandela Day with 300 elderly folk from various old age homes. They are to entertain and provide lunch for them, and my daughter was responsible for bringing the rice to this event. They looked happy in the photo, and a stab of regret threatened to kill me once more. I was not there to help them. I would have probably added some peas or corn to the rice, or made way more quantity than was necessary, or just complicated the whole affair by bringing a pot of pasta as well, that would most likely not be eaten. Then, I would fret about how busy I always seemed to be and make my family feel bad that I worked so hard.

No, it was good they were alone to figure it out on their own. I have underestimated and disempowered them for long enough. They were quite capable of managing this on their own. I just don't give them that chance often enough. I have always disliked the 'helicopter mothers' that hover over their children every moment of every day, managing their actions and altering their choices to suit their beliefs. The intention is generally a good one, but they inadvertently disable their children from experiencing all of life's necessary seasons. I recognized at that moment that I might be one of those mothers, albeit it a small Curti one and not a C5 Galaxy monster. I promptly sent them a good luck wish for an enjoyable day and then messaged my mother. Thankfully, I considered her lovingly protective of us but never felt like she hovered over me.

If anything, she had been too busy and tirelessly working hard all of her life for our benefit, so I let her know that I was alright and wished her a happy, restful day.

We embarked on a calm, slow Sunday stroll. The clouds hung thick overhead but without the usual chill of the morning. We were all comfortable to walk together and alone, each in our thoughts, with only the crunching of boots on gravel and birdsong for company once more. Mountain faces lit up in the sun from either side of the road, and for a while, we drifted past a few sheep, carpets of knee-high olive-brown shrubs, and some road signs alerting us of kudu crossings and speed limits. We were now well into extensive hunting farm territory. The first *bakkie* to drive past us, kicking up the first of many dust clouds for the day, sported several men in the back of an open vehicle with their Jack Russells and a young boy holding a rifle. A few minutes later, *Oom* Frik also drove past us faster than the signalled speed limit, with his three Border Collies in tow, tongues hanging and panting in anticipation. I tried to remain neutral and side-tracked my mind into stocking up on my *poopdrol* supply, just in case of fun and games later on, but these were evidently not going to happen.

George had walked on ahead of us and later returned to find us once again (we were not lost because there was only one road we could be on). His knee seemed not to be bothering him at all. We had ended up creating a fair walking distance between each other, but after an hour and a half of quiet time, we gathered again for the first tea break of the morning. I enjoyed another dose of brown bread with butter and syrup, thanks to the farmers of Palmietrivier. Sitting next to Julie, I was satisfied enough to initiate some conversation and asked her how she was doing. I did not expect her to tell me that she had just found out her mother had terminal cancer the day before she was due to depart on this Indlela pilgrimage. Shocked and disappointed, she wanted to have cancelled this trip, but her mother refused point blank and insisted she still come. Julie had lost her father seven years ago to a debilitating stroke, and she was not ready for another impending loss. Her divorce had been just as traumatic. However, her mother had done all the reassuring. Even though she could not do chemotherapy, she would follow doctors' orders. For years, she had avoided medicines, preferring natural remedies, and had always been careful with her diet and lifestyle. She would now eat all the chocolate she desired, take all the morphine the doctor provided and would be very happy if Julie could just accept this as it is. Julie was given her mother's hymn book to bring along on this journey, as all she wanted for her daughter was just to *be* with her, regardless of her geographic location.

Good Lord! What a difference compared to Mimi's last dying days. I don't think she was ever given a chance to express her final thoughts. Perhaps she was at peace without anything left to say. Perhaps the day that she was rushed, as an emergency, into theatre for life-saving open-heart surgery, she rambled to her daughter what she thought were to be her last words, "I am sorry if I offended anyone, and please look after your father." My sister-in-law will remember all of her exact words.

Mimi did survive the surgery, even though the cardiothoracic surgeon opened her chest, and realizing there was nothing he could do, he closed it again in the shortest time of open-chest operations. The subject of death was taboo in our family like it is one of the most unheard of things in the world when it is one of the only things that is 100% certain in this physical life. Life AND death are inevitable. The life of one thing can only begin with the death of another.

I am sorry I never got to tell her I was sorry. I regret not having the courage to broach the subject with her or informing my husband and his family that this was the end. I entertained their false hope. When the SMS from the surgeon came through informing me that they had found a bizarre 140-gram tumour wrapped around her heart, which was infiltrating the heart muscle, thus preventing its removal, and when they promptly closed her up again, I knew. And I didn't tell anyone. I robbed them all of the opportunity to express their feelings, to thank her, to lovingly say goodbye. Grieving feels really bad, but grieving with guilt and regret feels like you are slowly dying from a mental and emotional cancer and leaves no room for any hope to ever return to life.

Doctors suck at giving patients and their families bad news. There are exceptions, of course, but we suck at announcing someone's death. We always seem to cower behind the infamous "we did everything we could" as if it will absolve us of any responsibility. But I made the worst of all omissions; I didn't even try.

Julie broke my chain of thought and told me about the farm she had lived at for the past twenty-five years, which now belonged to her ex-husband. For years she had refused for any of her neighbouring hunter-farmers to access her farm on their hunting sprees. She never wanted any part of that sport and was scoffed at by every surrounding resident. In spite, they would purposefully chase and inadequately shoot bushbuck into her property, leaving them screeching in pain to frazzle her nerves and her soul beyond any sensible tolerance. She was no longer there for that specific kind of anguish. She had found another one; loneliness.

I accept that certain cultural groups are still hunter-gatherers and only hunt or fish for survival, but I cannot understand hunting for sport or recreation. Nor can I fathom how anyone has the heart to look at another animal directly past their innocent eyes and pull a deadly trigger.

Yet, the biggest hypocrite of them all had just enjoyed a meal of beef *boerewors*, scrambled eggs, and kudu biltong for breakfast. If someone else pulls the trigger for me, am I absolved from partaking in the murder of that animal? I think not.

Our second tea break was outside Mannetjie Farm, where a bold sign marked "NO ENTRY – Beware of Lions" greeted us at the gate. The air was instantly different and eerie. It was as if the lions could smell death, both their own and of their prey. The fences here were much higher, with coils of barbed wire crowning the top of the electric gate. I only managed to drink my Rehydrate but could not stomach food. Canned lion hunting was just on another sick level.

Hypocratic Oaths

I pretended to remain impartial and wanted so much to stay in the bubble of hope that had surrounded me last night. But out of nowhere, and like big red shotgun bullets that suddenly pierced through my eyes, a trail of fresh crimson blood lay stretched out before my line of vision. I came to a dead halt while the right side of my brain conjured up some creative idea that perhaps this was made by two male impala rams fighting for territory and female harems. But the logical left brain instantly screamed in horror and rage that an animal had just been shot and killed, and a bloody trail was left on the ground, as a *bakkie* had minutes before carried away the dead animal (pray God, it was not alive and injured). It is one thing thinking about dying animals, but it is entirely something else seeing evidence of the deed. No wonder advertising companies place cute caricature cows on the front of dairy bottles and graphically designed sheep on lamb chops' supermarket packaging. The gruesome reality of how these animals succumb to their death is too dreadful to digest.

My rejoicing had just come to an end today.

That all-familiar menacing black cloud suddenly enveloped my every sinew and took possession of my every atom. Just when I felt smug that I had it almost all figured out, I fell hard and backwards into the pit of hatred and resentment I had for humanity. And no one could lift me up for the rest of the day.

Once again, George sensed my disdain and came to walk alongside me, trying to keep up with my stomping, angry steps. He asked, "Is it okay with you if we walk in silent company?" I allowed him into my space without the warning: "Beware - this bitch bites." For a while, we walked past more abandoned farmsteads, graveyards, houses with vicious-looking Alsatians at the gate, and past overgrazed eye-sore landscapes. I knew he would not keep quiet for too long. He tentatively opened the conversation by pointing out the beautiful colours of the aloes and the bright green bushveld. When I did not seem to appreciate the same wonder, he cautiously mentioned my daughter's question: "Have you found what you are looking for?" He offered, that for him, his biggest challenge is living with doubt. Doubting what is deemed good and what is not good because the definition of 'good' keeps changing as his perceptions change. I did not have a clue what he meant. I was too deep in my abyss and asked him how he managed to prevent hatred and anger towards others from seeping in and festering? He did not answer my question. In his mind, he simply asks himself, "How can I live with myself knowing someone else is sleeping out in the cold? Am I doing enough to prevent that? How else can I help others?" And with that, he left me to continue seething on my own. Once again, I missed his point entirely. I thought I had done more than my share for people. If I have to help another soul, I will drown alongside them too.

The water restrictions had gotten so bad in this area that every inch of soil, every blade of grass, and leaf of a tree was bone dry - desiccated and dying. Even the hardiest of cactuses (or cacti, I never know which) were falling over by the dozens, the porcupines eating their roots in desperation.

Christy made the second attempt at perking me up. She offered me some of her nuts and raisins, which she mixed herself to get the correct ratio of peanuts to dried fruit. I had never thought of doing that. I usually just buy what already comes pre-packed. Just like I do of most external opinions that come my way. I accept her offer and pick out the dried goji berries I don't like. She then offered me Wine-gum jelly sweets, and I wished she had the real Pinotage deal.

I asked her, "What is the wildest thing you have ever done?"

"Everything, short of heroin." She replied without hesitation. She suggested that I should do whatever I wanted and anything I pleased, at least once in my life. It usually works in your favour if you have a strong sense of control. Did I have this strength? I didn't think so. Besides, I had not contemplated what wild thing I would do given half the chance.

Skydiving? Shark-cage diving? Bungee jumping? This hike was as wild as it would get. I still had a young daughter to raise and could not think of indulging these kinds of dangerous whims.

Soon enough, Christy tired of my sulky mugshot and joined the other fellow ladies in their discussion about book clubs, including the latest and best reads. They then moved onto their favourite TV series and classics. When I could no longer stand their laughter and good disposition, I stuck my earphones in my ears and allowed the iPod genius to shuffle the songs for me. A few pacifying tunes later, Johnny Clegg's 'The Crossing' resounded in my head. I recall an interview on the radio where Johnny retold the story behind this track. He wrote the lyrics and dedicated this song to his friend and band dancer Dudu Zulu, who was murdered in the political unrest of the early 90s. It was a reminder that we can stay connected to loved ones who have crossed over to the other side and that we will all cross from the dark mountains and earth to the green fields of grace.

I played his words over and over again. I listened to this melody for the remainder of the two hours it took to reach Tygerhoek House, the home of Walter and Rose Middleton.

I truly wanted to believe that I could surpass my state of manic depression. Elated one day, I was despairing on another. I had tried several mood-stabilizing medications in the past, but they had not been helpful.

During our afternoon tea break, I did not eat or drink. I simply lay flat on the dusted gravel road with my head resting on my rucksack, wondering if I had finally reached a dead end. I dreaded thinking that I had come all this way and nothing would change by the time I got back home.

On the last stretch of road to Tygerhoek, I saw several dogs tied up in tiny cages on another farmer's property. The depression sunk to the very bottom of the bottomless pit. I despised the hurt and violence that man inflicted upon man, but I hated the cruelty that man inflicted upon the animals of this planet even more. I am no longer ashamed to admit that I love the animals of this earth more than I like humans. Humans are meant to be *custodians* of this planet and not take ownership or dominion over it.

This debilitating attitude of mine did not shift for the rest of the day, the entire night, and not even the following day. The reasons behind this hatred were a few. But it was only when I later began to voice the truth and acknowledge my true feelings openly, and I began to shamefully reveal what lay hidden behind the masks, the false smiles and the false confidence, did I know what my hatred was mostly about. I was shown in time that our world is simply a reflection or a hologram of our thoughts, words, and actions. What we think, do, and speak about our life is what is reflected back to us. The law of Cause and Effect is a Universal law. You can't change it any more than you can change the law of gravity, but you can choose to make it work for you or against you. What the universe was trying to tell me, in all its divine intelligence, was that I really did hate *myself* the most.

Bit by bit, month by month, I remembered all the times that I had been the cruel one, the one that did the neglecting, the one that abused my power and my title, the one that was too tired to care, the one that left another human to die. My list was long, and it could have any priest forbid any further absolution and perhaps even condemn me to hell himself.

For years, I worked at the Chris Hani Baragwanath hospital's surgical and emergency unit. It was called The Pit for a reason. It was a pit of the worst kind. It was a cesspool of diseases, blood, misery, and pity. It was the end result of senseless violence, abuse, neglect, and drunken behaviour. It smelt of vomit, urine, alcohol, and pus. It moaned, and it wailed, and it screamed all day and all night. And it was a train station of human abandonment.

Hypocratic Oaths

The consultants were doing whatever consultants do and so were hardly spotted. The registrars were too busy operating all day long and left the junior doctors to do unsupervised dangerous procedures. The nurses ignored the doctors' call for help and would triage patients according to how hard they felt like working, not according to how life-threatening their conditions were. The medical students and overseas exchange students tried their best to wade through the onslaught and hoards of patients that lay strewn in the corridors and overflowing benches, but they became more of a hindrance with incessant questions for answers we did not have. Essentially, it felt like the whole world had abandoned us all. By the time I reached my trauma rotation at the Joburg General hospital as a medical officer, my sense of humour and faith had also left the building. If a seriously inebriated patient threatened to assault my colleague at 2 a.m. while she was trying to plaster his broken bone, I would voluntarily sit on the patient's torso until he could hardly breathe and until she was finished with the casting. If his equally inebriated friend vomited on my shoes and swore obscenities at me at 3 a.m., and I had not slept in 24 hours, he would get stitched with his hands and feet firmly tied to the bed without a single drop of local anaesthetic on board. When sarcasm threatened to be the only thing keeping us sane during those weekend warzones, the EMS personal would tie bows of barricade tape onto a stuporous client's head and serve him or her to us in a wheelchair as a Christmas or New Years' gift to tend to. I had also laughed.

Some would get their raw road 'roasties' or abrasions cleaned up with pure alcohol, and I would secretly think they deserved it for drinking and driving or for beating up their wives and children. When I could not stand the smell of another burnt or charred body that had unsuccessfully tried to steal copper cables, I would put the ones with no prognosis in the corner of the E.R. and close the curtains. I could then continue tending to the others without having them in sight or smelling their charred stench. When I remembered hours later that I had forgotten to give them morphine and found them dead in their already half-cremated state, the guilt I felt was piled heavier than a ton of that copper they died in vain for. Needless to say, after fourteen years of working in the ugly world of public and private E.R.s, Trauma Units, and Emergency Medicine, I hated the calibre of my own actions the most.

After crawling under the last fence through a ditch already made by a warthog into the Middletons' property, the first scent of salvation this afternoon was the pleasant smell of peppermint. The sight of their cream-painted farmhouse and the enclosed porch was an equal blessing. These sorry-assed pilgrims were greeted by the delightful Helga, her bright blue painted nails, and her plastic frog earrings. She was like an energized colourful hummingbird making sure we were all led to our respective rooms and had a cup of honey-sweetened tea in hand because there was no sugar allowed in the house. Rosemarie Middleton did not believe in sugar nor ruining perfectly good food with salt. Helga was also Swiss German and had been in South Africa for seven years working in the catering industry. She was now helping the Middletons manage their farm. Walter and Rosemarie, who are well into their 80s now, can no longer cope alone in such a large homestead. I cannot remember if they have children or not, but they have been living here for the last fifty-three years and don't know what to do next in their old age. The farming community has altered drastically in the past few years. Youngsters do not wish to stay on farms anymore. They leave in search of fortune and fame. Farming methods have become more sophisticated, relying more on technology than natural science. They are not as physically and mentally strong anymore to endure these isolated and extreme environmental conditions. Together alone, but with nowhere else to go and with no one else to talk to, they craved company more than anything else.

I dropped my bag in the room left over for the snorers and exited through the back door, finding a backyard hill that led onto untamed thorn bushveld. I found an old water reservoir and sat down on the grey cement cracked by weeds growing wild, watching the water slowly trickle out from a waterspout. This water flowed directly from a mountain spring and could not be any fresher. Today's Dunhill cigarette tasted sour.

I thought I was sitting in silence away from people, without the non-stop crunch of gravel and away from chatter, but a Robin insisted on talking to me. So I just listened, the feathered creature oblivious to the fact that I don't speak bird.

I have just returned from a one-month sabbatical after surviving the first year of the Covid-19 pandemic and learnt that Robins carry the energy of angels, and if you see one unexpectedly or randomly, an angel is near.

Of course, at the time, I was focused on my victim state of affairs, too ignorant to notice the miracles that abound if I had cared to look. With only my blind side in view, I returned to my room to examine my self-pitying blisters. As I was the last to have 'showered' last night (they did not know about the dog bowl cleanse), the others allowed me to shower first today.

I felt remotely better, and with a cup of unsweetened coffee, I went to sit on the veranda to dry my hair in the last rays of the sun and catch up on my journaling. My pen decided to retire, and I had to reluctantly borrow one from Marcelle. The subsequent entries were now purple and not in black ink. When Marcelle handed over her pen, she advised in a motherly tone that I should accept, with an open heart, the caring and nurturing that is offered to me. Hank added, whether I liked it or not. Christy elaborated by explaining that giving and receiving is like a river that needs to keep flowing. It needs to come in, and it needs to be let out. Stagnation either way can become toxic.

The sunset was pretty, and we only met the Middletons after nightfall. They had come to join us for supper, arriving in the middle of our reflection time, which was being conducted by LED light, as there was no electricity here either. And no way to charge my cellphone. So I would not know how Mandela Day had gone until tomorrow.

Julie had already shared a quote from "The Prophet" by Kahlil Gibran. It said that we need to find joy in everyone. If we appreciate the joy in others, we receive joy within us too. Why do I resist it? I was not sure if she was talking to me, herself, or everyone in general.

Lenny had quietly listened to everyone's troubled traumas and thoughts of the day and advised that we need to wrap these things like a gift and throw it up to God to deal with; otherwise, it becomes too unbearable.

At the time, I did not know he was referring to *surrendering* to blind faith and trust.

Christy did not get to finish her reflection. Walter waltzed in mid-sentence, elated to meet us all and shake our hands. Rosemarie followed his steps, then nestled herself on the sofa in between Iris and Julie, her thin arthritic hands folded on her lap, equally chuffed to be able to share her stories with us.

She recounted how she met Walter. He was originally from the Karoo, and during a seven-week tour through Europe, Walter and his friend Ivor met Rosemarie in London, where she was studying and learning to speak English. When Walter left Europe, he invited Rosemarie to come to South Africa to visit. A few months later, she did, and the rest is history. Their fifty-three years together were marked on the photos, simple decorations, and paintings on the walls; on the modest furniture and homestead that remained unaltered, in the wooden floors that have squeaked a million times with their footsteps. It was noted in the antique plates and crockery that were inherited from Walter's parents. It was evident in the love of their spoken words and in the way Rosemarie constantly straightened Walter's dinner plate that was precariously poised on his lap, threatening to tumble onto the floor with his excited chatter.

Even their food was made with love. Helga had been directed by the matriarch of the house on how to make the perfect goulash. The beef was so tender, the vegetables so fresh, and the rice cooked to perfection. I was sure my daughter's rice today was just as delicious. The cinnamon pumpkin and crunchy coleslaw completed the precious savoury buffet. We all had second helpings.

But when Helga brought out a tray of warm oven-baked apples for dessert, personally made by Rosemarie, I felt more threatening tears brimming on my eyelids. This was my parents' favourite dessert and one they often made in my early childhood when puddings and ice-cream were a luxury.

My folks were both in their 70's. They still held full-time jobs and had no big investments or significant financial backup after all these years. I dreaded seeing them frail and vulnerable, and I was so disappointed with myself for adding to their burden. My parents had also endured a few lifetimes of dejected hardships, but they have just kept swimming through the tsunamis. Not once have they taken a sabbatical or ditched their responsibilities to go on a soul-searching venture.

It was all so sad to me – ageing people growing older, feeling alone, coming to the end of a lifetime without perhaps achieving what they had hoped for, or worse, even, not having had any purpose. The loneliness would probably be the worst pain to bear.

I envied Lenny and Iris and George and Gwenda; they seemed to have figured it out.

I dreaded the prospect of living alone if I continued to annihilate the people I love most, and I dread dying with the thought that no one would care for me anymore.

I regret the elderly man I left to die, neglected and abandoned in a wheelchair in the middle of a sick hospital corridor one hectic Friday night in 1997. It was commonplace for relatives to dump their old parents in hospital for the weekend, so they could have the freedom to get drunk and misbehave. Many of these elderly were either malnourished or just in need of some TLC, a bath, their dry, cracked skin creamed, or overgrown toenails cut, none of which warranted an admission into a busy 3000-bed hospital because all were already occupied. But on this particular night, I had underestimated this elderly man's broken and failing heart.

He had died alone and unseen, sometime between two and five early Saturday morning, when I was too busy with knife and gunshot wounds to notice his severely swollen legs and water-filled lungs.

There was no one to call. Relatives often left incorrect details. There was no time to process what had happened. A drunk man with a smashed-up face from a flying brick was spitting blood and teeth onto my white sneakers. I quickly signed off the death certificate and left a nurse to dispose of the evidence.

Looking back now on this day that I visited with the Middletons, I realize I had also been in mourning; for the old, the weak, the frail, the voiceless, the forgotten, and for the part of me that had died with all my sins a long time ago.

It is heart-wrenching yet powerful to know that I can clean up my own stink. There is no one coming to save me. I am the only God that can save myself.

I had just forgotten who I really am, where I come from, and what I am a part of.

At the time, I hoped to have crossed over by the next morning.

Not into another lifetime, but into a better version of me.

11

OMISSIONS

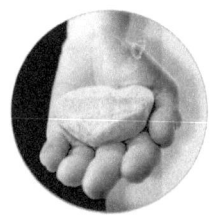

The answers are hidden in plain sight. It is the question that remains elusive

Somewhere between deep sleep and the awakened state, I saw myself setting up a ventilator machine and hooking it up to a patient in ICU who was struggling to breathe. The inspiratory snoring was laboured, but the expiratory struggle to push air out of the lungs asked for PEEP (positive end expiratory pressure). It meant keeping the small alveoli of the lungs open and oxygenated for longer. When I wanted to sedate and intubate the patient, my ears opened to the rhonchus of Maeve's breathing.

I found myself on a mattress on the floor of one of the rooms in the Middletons' house instead. The 'patient' was Maeve, and lucky for her, she did not need a tube stuck down her throat at 5 a.m. on a Monday morning. When Julie saw Maeve move into our room yesterday, she had promptly, and not so discreetly, moved out. In the morning, she apologized to Lilly and me for dumping us with the nocturnal snorting, but I told her it was not so bad. I had slept the whole night through. My brain had gone on strike from my ceaseless thinking.

It was the same vibe in the kitchen this morning – every man for himself, including the women.

I was desperate for a cup of coffee to down my usual cocktail of drugs, so I had gotten up early. I was relieved that I did not have to resuscitate anyone so early in the day. I would be the only one needing urgent attention. But considering I was not getting any sugar in my hot beverage, I added two extra paracetamol to initiate the revival. Whether it was to dim the pain in my legs or my heart, I did not care.

Boiled eggs and homemade tomato and ginger jam had been brought up from the main house for each of us to make cheese and egg sandwiches for *padkos*. Shortly after, Rosemarie walked in with a large bowl of cold oats with creamed milk and fresh apples. Loose *naartjies* and *piesangs* were also on offer as take-away treats. That is as much sugar as we would get from this dear lady, although her timeless smile and care were unlimited.

One of the proverbs printed and mounted on wooden frames lining the dining room shelves read: "HOME – the place where we grumble the most and are treated the best." I sat in this small dining room with my bowl of oats placed on top of an old large square table that filled most of the room space. Lenny and Rosemarie joined me. We chatted for a while as the others were still occupied in a frenzy of toilet turns, bathroom queues, finding knives, spoons, wrapping material, cracking eggs, and repeatedly boiling enough water for their thermoses and coffee.

> *"It is easy enough to be pleasant*
> *When life moves along with a song*
> *But the man worthwhile is the one that can smile*
> *When everything goes dead wrong."*

Hypocratic Oaths

This particular unsigned poem was printed behind a thick clear frame, leaning against several drinking water glasses, and it stared back at me throughout breakfast.

It was Lenny's turn to send us off with a prayer and the thought-provoking reflection for the day. George had hinted at the same thing when I had asked him yesterday how he managed to keep his anger towards others in check. He had left me in a confused cloud of dust by simply saying, "You just have to change the question if you don't have an answer to your dilemma."

With melancholic gratitude, I say goodbye to Rosemarie. She relished being part of another group photo opportunity but had the same sadness of a relative that bids farewell to a loved one for the last time. Walter met us on the way out of his property and drove behind us, waving and repeatedly wishing us well. The reluctance to let go was tangible. So was mine.

If I have to change the question to get an answer, then I ask why I am so reluctant to forgive myself once more. Have I not served enough penance? Do guilt and regret motivate me to be a better person? And who is judging how well I am serving, or when I will finally be deserving of some mercy?

The answer is hidden in plain sight.

Here is an elderly couple desperately clinging onto life, holding onto the residual livelihood of their farm, their memories, and to people, they don't even know. Here I am hoping the Middletons and my parents long outlast their ageing sell-by dates, yet wishing other younger people dead.

For longer than I care to admit, I have had the gall and insolence in my mind to decide who should live and who should die. I had gone beyond the act of the God-syndrome by conducting decisions of which rat-resembling premature neonate gets the only available ventilator in NICU. Or which gunshot victim gets first dibs into the next available theatre, or deciding which mother-to-be is the closest to delivering and gets access to the labour-ward and much begged for analgesia.

Far worse, I had decided in my mind that murderers, rapists, paedophiles, corrupt government officials, obscenely obese patients, end-stage AIDS patients, and severely disabled persons should all die. Like as soon as possible. Because most were a burden to the medical services and society in general and consumed precious resources like water, animals, and oxygen. Before anti-retrovirals were available, there came an era that had patients suffering the most gruesome deaths, and I could not bear to see their desperate sunken eyes pleading for miracles that I did not have. The morbidly obese forbid the success of most medical and surgical interventions, as it was almost impossible to insert any lifesaving tube or device into any orifice or vein, and EMS cannot even carry some out of their own houses. The despair on family's faces and the futile attempts at any kind of rescuing had me wishing they could be put out of their misery even before they arrived in my emergency room.

The night shifts at the Rand Clinic were the worst. Most convicted criminals injured during their crime or arrest were brought here in handcuffs and chains, escorted by policemen. To this day, I don't know how I kept a straight face and the bile from oozing out my nostrils. Written across each patient file was each perpetrator's offence: murder, rape, armed robbery, assault with rifle, high-jacking. Refusing to even ask the cops about the state of their victims (they were either taken to other hospitals or the morgue), I read no further than their names and kept my hands steady as I sutured them or treated their wounds. But my heart raced faster than Schumacher's joyride, my legs were jelly, and I had no guts to look in their eyes. I did not wish to betray my thoughts, and I was simply petrified they could identify me in the streets one day and take advantage of me too. I wished them dead before they had the opportunity.

The shameful and open admission of this despicable thinking that had long fueled a sick judgement in my head was the beginning of my redemption. Along with the awareness that my guilt and my self-proclaimed punishment for being responsible for patients' deaths, even if their disease or injuries were beyond saving, made me understand why I did not want to owe or need anything from anyone. I understood why I could not forgive myself. These thoughts and emotions pushed me to serve beyond the call of duty, hoping I would not die by my own sword. Nor anyone from my family, for that matter, as if I could control their fate.

These thoughts had me imprisoned in my own jail so that my repentance had been to sacrifice my livelihood to make up for all my indiscretions. But when these fear-filled beliefs can no longer sustain any form of redeemable existence, when they are close to choking me to death or pushing me over the cliff, it is time to let them go.

And *I* am the only judge in this mind-game, and *I* am the only one that can decide my fate. It is time to forgive myself once more and release the self-castigation.

The sight of Cockscomb came into view. That initial distant mirage was now becoming a reality, one that soon required overcoming. In two days, we would be crossing over its peak, and even though I was not quite ready yet, the ache of needing to be with my family again no longer made it a daunting mission. In fact, by the time we reached our first tea break for the day, that subtle sense of reprieve had started to show itself again. Even though my right foot arch was searing, the rest of my muscles were no longer knotted in an origami scramble.

I refrained from the self-diagnosis of Bipolar disorder, as I had been wrong on many occasions, and I chose to believe this was one of those times. How is it possible to feel consolation and peace one moment and complete turmoil the very next minute?

On the third day of our hike, I also thought this diagnosis belonged to Hank. He spoke in tongues sometimes (intellectual philosophies that made me feel like an uneducated cretin), occasionally with verbal diarrhoea, but then he shrunk into an introspective space so deep, no one could reach him. Today was one of those days. From the time we left Tygerhoek, he bolted ahead all of us, and we only saw him again at lunchtime when we had reached our next landmark of a very dried-up dam somewhere in these drought-stricken lands. How he found his way was miraculous, because George's well-intended thought-out handwritten maps were Egyptian hieroglyphic charts to me. I was rather amused eating Helga's lovely cheese and jam sandwich while attempting to read today's map that went something like: "On the slight uphill, turn left at the gate. At Paardehoek farm (unmarked), walk in the *veld* and around the yard and rejoin road. Stay in the valley and head west (it was cloudy, where was the sun?) At the dilapidated house, do not go north. Go through thorny *sloot* (a ditch) up to a fence. Keep to the jeep track on the other side and head west. If in doubt, stay in the valley." No offence George, but WTF?

This was the reason I walked somewhere in the middle of the group, with some of the ladies chattering in the front and with Lenny and Lilly trailing behind the lot of us. Two hours after our first break, we reached an uphill (there were many, so I was never sure if this was the one George meant). Tapping into cellphone reception frequencies, my phone began to vibrate in my pocket with messages pinging through frantically. Thinking something was wrong, I checked to find several uninteresting ones, and a surprising one sent by my husband giving me good news.

He had just come from his Cardiology appointment this morning, and the doctor was happy with his condition and did not feel the need to prescribe medication. This made me smile with relief. For months now, he had been suffering from an erratic and irregular heartbeat, with intermittent tachycardias (fast heart rate) and chest discomfort. This had unsettled him for a while, and it was his second visit to the specialist. We still did not know what caused these electrical miss-firings, but the doctor could not find any apparent abnormality. Secretly, I suspected my husband was still trying to mend his broken heart. I messaged back to say I was happy with the news and happy all was well with his heart.

It was not long after that that another miracle stopped me in my tracks and stared boldly back at me. I picked up a heart-shaped stone that was not even in a dry river bed, just incredulously there, in the middle of nowhere, waiting. Rose-pink, with a subtle shimmer, larger than the other round ones, and splendidly perfect. Words suddenly faltered, but a symphony flooded my brain, and my cardiac rhythm galloped in unexpected rejoice and wonder.

I had found a gift to return to my love and could not wait to give it to him. By the time we stopped for lunch at the dried-up dam, I could not wait any longer. Oscillating between hesitation and excitement, remorse and gratitude, sorrow and love, I took a photograph of this gemstone in the palm of my hand and sent the picture to *marido* with the inscription: "You have all of my heart and always will."

He replied, "Bring it home."

I sat on a cushion of thorns one last time. A bone-dry dam is just that. Flat, desiccated, and with sharp debris jutting out of its hardened surface. But I was thick-skinned and stubborn, and for that moment, I ate my other egg sandwich in surrendered serenity. The rest of the afternoon's walk, I set at a calmer pace. Despite the uncomfortable heat, I was comfortable walking alone, being at ease within my own skin, and more accepting, without the need for music to push me along. The morning scene from Clint Eastwood's western movies of brown sand, dusty wind-whirls, and overgrown cactuses, folded up behind me, giving way to green bushveld and hills that were alive with the sound of birds and crickets.

At some point, I ended up the last one on the trail. Without concern for following the map (I knew George would come to find me if I got lost), I decided to simply sit under a tree and take in the silence of the buzzing flies and the whisper of the swaying leaves. As much as walking out the demons deliver the soul to a higher divine frequency, stopping to take in nature's stillness and perfect cycles of life brings quietude and belonging that wraps my heart in a layer of peace that it has only felt on very few occasions these past few years.

I was aware that I was not entirely in the clear. When I finally arrived at the Rudman's Farm, the fatigue that settled in was fighting for first place with my newfound tranquillity. That was just it. I was truly tired of fighting. The battle of the brain these last two days (and years, in fact) had worn me out and depleted more life force. Even though today had been one of the shortest walks, my body felt like it had crossed a continent.

The first landmark of today's final destination that stood out to greet us was the Rudman and Thompson's family graveyard. Generations of elderly, couples, youngsters, relatives, ground staff, and even a stillborn's tombs lay side by side in neat rows of eternal rest. There was no social distinction or family hierarchy here. Every person that ever lived or worked on this heirloom farm was granted equal value. They even honoured strangers, regardless of their circumstances. Iris later enquired about the oldest grave on the property, which was dated 1789. Apparently, a hunter from Rhodesia by the name of George Rautenbach had been laid to rest here after being killed by an elephant. I stood solemnly in this cemetery with Iris for a while. I was not sure what was going through her mind. Perhaps she felt sensitive to her mortality at her current age, but I was very comfortable with mine. I was not bothered by my natural death, even if it happened tomorrow. I had prayed for it more times than I dared to remember. But the day I decided to embark on this journey and walk away from The Drop Off zone, I knew I was walking away from my emotional death to find a way back into the light again. Even if I had no clear direction or knew how to go about it, I would not wish for the easy way out anymore. No matter how long or dark the re-birthing tunnel would be, I was going to persevere and push through until I could breathe God's air again. So, for now, I merely sent

Hypocratic Oaths

out a silent wish that my long-standing human discrimination could finally be laid to rest at this very moment, in this sacred place.

The path leading up to our guest quarters seemed to be teasingly never-ending. The Rudman's property was enormous and pretty picturesque. George made himself at home as he led us past the main farmhouse, past gardens dotted with emus, ducks, turkeys, springbok, and chickens with fluffy hair on their feet. The territorial rooster crowed out our arrival in case the hosts had missed the twelve rugged pilgrims walking across their fields. George did not wait for the Rudmans to come outside. Perhaps he had prior instructions to head up straight to our lodgings, where we would stay for the next two nights. Tomorrow would be a rest day, with no walking to be done.

The larger guesthouse had a small kitchenette, sitting room, bathroom, and two rooms accommodating eight people. The other four were housed in a smaller log cabin further down the property next to a water reservoir. I did not wait for the others to take the first pick of their beds. My rucksack had been cutting into my shoulders for the last three hours, and I unabashedly took ownership of one of the top bunkbeds. There was no way I was going to sleep on the bottom coffin-bed again tonight. With all my possessions strewn on my bed, I sat on the floor, took my shoes off, and placed them on the cold tiled surface for soothing. My mother would have a fit if she saw me walking bare-foot on an ice-cold floor. I was sure to catch a cold or the flu, but the amount of chemical pharmacology on board would surely prevent the invasion of any rogue virus. It had already gotten rid of my tuberculosis. Feeling sunburnt and dehydrated, I slowly sipped on water and Rehydrate to prevent a far better chance of getting sick from heatstroke and kidney dysfunction.

I then gravitated to the kitchen for a cup of coffee before a late afternoon cleansing hot shower. Water is truly a life-giving force.

The sight and cuddle of a dog is a close second for me. There are some animals on this planet that have come as angels in disguise and are true healers. Happy puppy faces, wagging tails, furry cuddles, and panting smiles always have my defensive walls momentarily unguarded. They are an energy source for those that can appreciate their magic. George had noticed this every time I stopped at a gate or fence or *padstal* to pat a dog or rub a cat's head. It was probably the only time he saw me smile or my eyes light up to a midday glow. When we walked to the main farmhouse for dinner, I greeted a bouncy Border Collie behind a fence before meeting his owners, Charmaine and Hannes Rudman. Kneeling to eye level, I allowed the dog to sniff me and say hello. He was pleased with my clean bum because his tail wagged that much faster. George had walked behind me and agreed this was a friendly fellow and finally asked me why I had not become a vet instead of a doctor if I loved animals so much?

I replied, "Imagine my disdain for people who are cruel to animals if I am already hateful of people who are cruel to other humans?"

He looked at me incredulously, like I had just said the most stupid thing he had ever heard. "You can't have the good without the bad, Gisela. Pain is inevitable in everything and what makes the beauty of life so euphoric. They go hand in hand, and we have to embrace both, just like love. Love is a beautiful thing, but it is guaranteed that you will lose it in some way or another, either in death, divorce, or disappointment. But if you are never going to love anything for fear of getting hurt, then get yourself a pet rock and stay unloved for the rest of your life."

He abruptly turned away and walked on to greet Charmaine with open arms and lovingly pat Hannes on the back, leaving me gob-smacked and utterly dejected at the sight of an empathic psychologist that had just had about enough of my nonsense. I wished the earth would crack under my feet to swallow me whole once and for all.

I hated that he was right.

Hank had not been seen all day (a brief appearance at lunchtime let us know he was still alive). At some point, I thought he might have finally absconded from this whole charade. Initially, I thought he was just in one of his sullen moods. However, somewhere later in the day, I sensed that he was most likely annoyed with the intolerant bitching of some of the others who sarcastically and not so secretly complained about his early morning daily habits and incomprehensible musings. I thought cyclists were hard-core passionate sportsmen and women who inconsiderately bypassed anyone in the way of their record times, often clipping their rival's back wheel to ensure their own success. But hard-core hikers can be far more cut-throat. Rosemarie Middleton had told us a story about the Mountaineering Club she belonged to as a youngster. She participated in a challenging mountain hike when she was four months pregnant with her first child. Each person was responsible for their daily water rations. By the fourth day of the hike, Rose's water bottles ran dry, but she did not receive a single offering of a precious drop from any of her fellow hikers. She completed the trail the following day in a state of stuporous dehydration, while the others did not bat an eyelid. I wondered how many such razor-sharp-tongued ladies were amongst us for Hank to have disappeared for most of the day and only be seen at mealtimes.

Reflection time had me wondering if I was one of those mean bitches. A bit of cockiness had settled in my voice when I stated that I would spare the group my thoughts today, as it would be fairer to pay a professional to listen to all of my crap. I left it at that, as I did not trust the bile rising in my throat again. This time, it was Lilly's timid and unsure voice that triggered the raging bull bucking within.

She could not decide what kind of a day she had. She wanted to speak but didn't know what to say. She whispered three words and then took them back again. With her head submissively bowed and stooped body fearing judgement, she avoided any human or eye contact. Her uncertainty, meekness, and lack of personality had me wanting to wrap my hands around her throat and choke her until she could shout and scream what she actually wanted to say. The image of her sitting in martyrdom kept shape-shifting to the receptionist that I had just fired. The desire to kill fueled my guilt that I had employed Elizabeth only three months prior, ensuring she resigned from her previous job but would now find herself unemployed and with a tainted resume.

Writing these words years later, I am now in constant awe of what life is really about, the lessons presented to us to transform, evolve, stretch us beyond crumpled wings, to fly away from our confined and pre-conditioned cocoons. The world that we experience is a direct reflection or mirror of our thoughts and beliefs. If these thoughts and beliefs remain indoctrinated and programmed by other people's ideas, we are stuck living someone else's limiting ideas and life. If you question what no longer makes any sense to you, you stand a chance of awakening to the magic and wonder of this world and this magnificent life. This means, if you believe or focus on a world that is cruel, cruel experiences will reveal themselves to you either in real-time or on social media. If you think that the world is out to get you, you may miss out on opportunities or be subjected to credit card fraud. If you believe you are not worthy of abundance, health, or joy, you might only receive what you ask for – lack, dis-ease, or dissatisfaction. If the world you are experiencing is a reflection or hologram of you, then whatever you don't like about the reality of that world is a direct reflection of a part of you that you don't like about yourself.

The answer is hidden in plain sight.

Lilly and Elizabeth were a direct reflection of *me*. They were 'showing' me what I further disliked about myself. I did not stand up for myself. I did not have the guts to speak my truth. I was submissive to everyone else's opinions and expectations, and I was weak in character and a doormat for patients' many whims and demands. No wonder I coughed all the time…

Another self-loathing reflection.

I remember a death threat from a vicious-looking son that brought in his very obese and very blue puffing father, who was busy having a clinical heart attack on a hospital gurney. I could not find a vein to give him analgesia or medication. The now hypoxic and confused Michelin man kept pulling off his oxygen mask and rattling the cot-sides in distress. The ECG electrodes kept slipping off his sweaty body, and he refused for anyone to touch him or draw blood for analysis. He was a dead duck sitting when his son pointed his threatening finger in my face and spat, "If my father dies, so will you, bitch." I hated myself for not telling the fucker to get out of my sight and let me do my job, or else I would call security or, better yet, stand back and let him watch his father die. Instead, he watched me silently fumble in a pathetic attempt to save a man who had long ago given up on himself.

I despised myself more than I had hated the both of them put together.

There were countless other times when I did not speak up. I have watched doctors verbally and physically abuse patients. I have watched tiny premature fetuses gasp for air in filthy sluice rooms as they were discarded for not meeting ventilation criteria in overburdened, under-resourced hospitals. I have watched AIDS patients being denied blood transfusions because they were going to die someday soon anyway. Again, I could give a long morbid account of the times when I said nothing and of the times I did nothing.

Forgive me, Father, for what I have done and for what I have failed to do.

I can't remember which of the pilgrims mentioned today that their brother once noted: "The view is great if it wasn't for the mountain." Most of the time, we are the mountain in the way. But the view is great, inclusively, because the mountain is a necessary and mystical part of the view. And we are better fulfilled once we can appreciate both.

Following my reluctance to speak, George had then confessed that despite an uneventful day, he had felt "down and grim." He could not explain why. He only knew that he missed his family but did not have any other major reason for his melancholy feelings. Perhaps this was why he did not have the patience for my depressing statements today?

However, he knew better. When he is in this kind of mood, he simply "relishes" in it, without judging it, without berating himself, without asking a thousand questions why and not attaching to the dis-eased feeling of it. He just lets it be and is simply an observer of it without getting sucked into its centre turmoil.

He openly admitted that he seriously feels for people who suffer from major depression because he does not understand what that is like. I envied him too.

Elize was calmer today. She, too, agreed that no matter how disturbing the sights are that leave you rattled (she was again referring to the dead buck), you cannot keep the fences up so high that you are unable to connect with others and where others cannot reach you. You have to let your loved ones in, so you can experience the love that lies beyond the fences.

Lenny was in a quirky mood, despite his feet being abysmally injured. I had no idea how he was still walking or talking, for that matter. Maybe he was on better drugs than I imagined, but he began his sharing by quoting a Koan riddle. I did not know what these were but later discovered that they are questions posed to Zen Buddhists during meditation to help them unravel greater truths about the world and themselves. Zen masters have been testing their students with these stories, questions, or phrases for centuries, which may seem like paradoxes at first glance. It is up to the Zen student to tease out their meaning. Often, after a prolonged and exhausting intellectual struggle, the student realizes that the Koan is meant to be understood by the spirit and by intuition and not by the thinking brain. "What is the sound made by clapping with one hand only?"

Leaving us all baffled, he then quoted the first verse of the lyrics to "Blowing in the wind" by Bob Dylan:

> *How many roads must a man walk down*
> *Before you call him a man?*
> *How many seas must a white dove sail*
> *Before she sleeps in the sand?*
> *Yes, and how many times must the cannonballs fly*
> *Before they're forever banned?*
> *The answer, my friend, is blowin' in the wind*
> *The answer is blowin' in the wind*

I sank into my penthouse bed, exhausted, confused, and with more questions than I had answers to. My belly was stuffed with liberal portions of chicken soup, chicken stew, macaroni and cheese, vegetables, and bread. My brain was void of harmony.

After Hannes and Charmaine's very gracious supper, I had stood under a spectacular sky of bright stars and constellations and phoned my family to personally hear their voices. My parents gave nothing away. They wished me well for the rest of the journey. My sister asked me if my pants were falling off my butt with all this walking. I told her I had actually gained weight! Or my pants had shrunk in the Broadlands buck-poop enriched laundromat wash-cycle. Every hospitable host had been feeding us so generously; I had retained more calories than were being used. My daughter told me her dad makes a good mother; he can also wash clothes and cook rice. And *marido* told me that my daughter makes for a good housewife; she can make her own food and clean up the dishes.

I suppose this was a journey for them too. By choice or by force, they were being made to see another side of life, of what was possible when the reflections of their worlds have suddenly changed.

Perhaps my family can begin to see a window of unlimited potential in themselves when, like me, they stop asking the wrong questions, find the answers blowing in the wind, or in plain sight if they choose to visualize and dream a better reality.

12

BREATHE

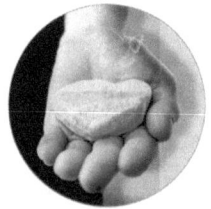

When the going gets tough, take the day off

I slept all night long except for the one time I needed to pee. The dead quiet of the farm valley had allowed for either a restful sleep or my mind was so tired that I could not even wake to the noise of silence. My full bladder was far more strong-willed, though. In my attempt to descend from the top bunk bed in sleek stealth mode so as not to awake Marcelle sleeping on the bottom bunk, I proceeded to walk in the pitch dark straight into her purple tog bag on the floor, crashing over it with a rather loud scuffle. "Bummer," I thought. A vast improvement from the F-word, I realized with glee.

Not even the feet blisters complained. Relieved of toxic fluid that my body no longer needed, I climbed back into bed and saw the night sky was clouded over by grey cotton candy. I lay innocently gazing out the window, hoping that I was not responsible for those slowly waking up to the dark of a new morning, perhaps too early for a day that was allocated for rest.

This was the only day of the entire pilgrimage when we were not going to hike. Any walking performed would be absolutely voluntary. This was maybe why the other five ladies in the room giggled under their covers like mischievous school girls in a school dormitory looking forward to a treat of a day. One of them said the other should wake up Iris in the adjacent bedroom to watch the sunrise, one of her favourite hobbies.

I was still lying quietly in my safety tower, pretending to be asleep because I was busy sending out one wish into the heavens of this dawn. Never again do I want to wake up dreading the day ahead, wishing to wake up dead. What a stupid thing to say!

I had 'prayed' for so long to wake up dead (I wanted just to have died in my sleep so I would not be accountable or responsible for my cowardly premature departure), but did not realize then that the Universe always answers YES. If you wish to wake up dead every morning, the Universe, in all its divinity and unwavering Law of Attraction, can only say YES. And you will wake up devoid of any emotion, desire, or sign of wanting to live.

At this point, I did not know that you have to intentionally substitute the stupid wish for a better one. It is not sufficient to simply say, "I don't want this, I don't want that", and just leave it there. Not wanting something keeps you thinking about what you don't want. Miracles happen when you state, think or write down what it is you DO want. Repeatedly, habitually, forever.

Knowing what you do want changes the direction in which your life is heading. It is the gear-lever that shifts the circumstances from the dead-end track onto the one that heads off into the mountains and valleys full of infinite potential and new life.

But the moment you make a conscious decision that you no longer wish to travel down a particular dead-end track is the moment when the pause button is pressed on the speed train. Then, the WILL to seek another way is the first step in changing the direction in which your life is heading.

It may be imperceptible at first. The scenery may look the same, but it will slowly begin to change as you gain momentum. Momentum requires the action to move (make a phone call, join that dance class, declutter your house). You may not have a clue what lies along the new trail, and that is perfectly acceptable and expected, but then comes step two, when the trust or blind faith is at its grandest test.

Do I even know what it is that I *do* want for myself? I had long ago stopped dreaming or envisioning for something other than believing my days were limited to being stuck behind four white walls seeing one ill person after the next. I felt like a postmaster on auto-pilot stamping a script into someone's hand as they leave my office one by one, day after day, year after year.

It is interesting that when young children are at nursery school and in the full presence of their imagination, adults will ask them, "So Johnny, what do you want to *be* when you grow up?"

But when teenagers are about to finish high school and take the next step into adulthood, they are asked, "So Jane, what are you going to *do*?"

Perhaps, that is when things get a bit twisted. We are trained to *do* and so have forgotten how to *be*. We are human *beings*, after all, but have been programmed to become human *doers*. When we become so preoccupied with what we (and others) are doing, we forget how to be, how to feel, and how to exist in the moment.

Not knowing what else I wanted out of my life, all I could feel for today was to do nothing in particular. Whilst the others got so busy packing, organizing and washing laundry before breakfast time (not sure why you would want to do that on a rest day), I grabbed a cup of coffee and wandered around the outside of our guesthouse to sit on a pelvis bone. I had found a very dried out cow carcass lying in the exact position it had succumbed to outside of the Rudman's property yesterday and brought it up to the house to serve as an improvised stool. There was nothing I could do about the cow, whose spirit had long since left its skeleton, but I was very grateful for the comfort it now provided to my backside. I had previously seen Beverly and Derek Joubert, the famous photographers and movie-makers living in Botswana's Okavango Delta, use an elephant's pelvis as the perfect toilet seat to crown the top of their long drop pit latrine.

I paused between sips of caffeine to listen to a farm awaken to a new day. The air was serene, fresh and sweet-smelling, but the sounds of the ducks, geese, turkeys, sheep, doves and a rooster at the bottom of the fields were loud and vibrant. I noticed we were levelled on a high rise, surrounded by eloquently chiselled mountains, insisting on keeping the sun hidden for a bit longer in anticipation of their best-kept secret.

I reflected on the events of the past few days and wondered about the last stretch of this pilgrimage. Tomorrow, we would cross over Cockscomb. I did not know what awaited me on the other side, and I worried I would forget the newfound insights, teachings and experiences I had shared with strangers, who were now evolving into friends. As if to secure these into the conscious and subconscious recesses of my mind, I began planning what my family and I could do the following weekend after I returned home.

We sometimes went camping or fishing at a dam on the weekend or visited a nearby game park on a school holiday, but I wanted to get out there into nature far more often with my newly acquired appreciation so that it would be engraved into every neuron and fibre of my body before it faded out of existence again. And before I got caught up in the death-trap routine of my current way of living.

Hypocratic Oaths

Breakfast was served at 8 a.m. in the Rudmans' main farmhouse. We walked together down the hill, and again I greeted their friendly dog before being welcomed by our hosts. Everything seemed brighter in broad daylight. We had entered their house the same way last night for dinner, but this morning, the dog's coat was shinier, his lolling tongue more cerise and their small garden appeared greener and more optimistic. Only a tiny section of their lawn was tended to and watered. Their pool was empty, with the remainder of the property covered with sand and pebbles, feathers and sheep fur. But despite the heavy drought upon their land, Charmaine and Hannes managed to keep their home alive and gracious.

This morning's reception committee were four stuffed animal heads hanging from the top walls of their entrance hall - a mounted quartet of kudu, wildebeest, warthog, and springbok. Their cold glass eyes staring back at me and stern expressions forever frozen in time had them begging for an answer as to why the hell they were hanging up there. I apologetically walked past, ashamed at something I was not responsible for. Or was I?

I proceeded to pacify my discomfort with a plate of scrambled eggs and meat sausage. I wondered which animal's muscle the meat belonged to that I was eating. Was I not participating in the general orchestration of the demise of these animals? Even though I may not be pulling the trigger, am I not as guilty of murder, or worse yet, a cowardly accomplice that prefers to point fingers at another person doing the dirty work for me?

Many cultures had hunted meat for the pot to ensure their survival when there was no grain, vegetable patch, flowering trees or shopping centre available just around the corner. I can accept that without a problem. But the majority of the world's Eastern culture is vegetarian, and they have managed to thrive into a population of a billion without slaughtering millions of animals for consumption.

I am in the fortunate position to have a wide selection of plant-based foods at my immediate disposal and click of an online shopping button, which can surely keep me as healthy as any Buddhist monk. How can I justify taking another animal's life for the sake of my enjoyment and pleasure and just because I can afford it?

As soon as we finished our share of Weetbix, yoghurt, cheese and animals on toast, Charmaine brought out a bowl of freshly cut kudu *biltong*. Not only did we all enjoy a fair portion of the meat, but both the vegetarians amongst us had a taste of it too. Maybe some things in life are just too irresistible? Or perhaps we should not be too strict in defining who we are according to the A team or the B team?

I suppose we often think we are justified in our behaviours by acting from behind the high fences of false protective groups – democrats or republicans, feminists or patriarchal societies, western or eastern medicine, gay, straight, rich, poor, black, white, omnivores, vegans, us or them. This human habit we have of separating ourselves from others who are not of the same split image, ideals or opinions, can leave us feeling more isolated and lonely. We have been led to believe we have to defend ourselves against an invisible enemy by discriminating against a multitude of colour, diversity and offensive people, thereby relinquishing our free will and choice, which is part of the magnificence of this planet and our birthright. The higher the fence we hide behind, the more we allow it to define us, or the bigger our set judgement of something else is, the less likely we are of ever escaping the overbearing and stifling dominion of these false groups.

Little did I know that a few months from this day, I would become a self-righteous hardcore vegan (with an attitude that would put Rosemarie's mountaineering club members to shame). I was trying to find a loophole in a tangled steel fence of disdain for meat-eaters whilst attempting to eat at a table with carnivores. That journey was another pilgrimage of its own.

Hypocratic Oaths

The seed was probably planted on this day in a random farm in the Eastern Cape. When everyone else went off to do their rest-day-thing after breakfast, I hung around the homestead. I ventured behind the small green garden to the side of the main farmhouse, where two tiny calves mooed longingly behind a wooden fence enclosure. I did not see a mommy cow, only three little lambs in a neighbouring pen equally bleating for attention. I knelt by these cutie babies and tried to pat them, but they were not interested in cuddles. The two calves instantly grabbed hold of my fingers and began to suckle with strength and determination I did not know was possible from such tiny creatures. They were hungry, and I wondered where their mother was. When they realized there was no milk coming out of my digits, they bleated even louder with desperation. A little kid goat suckled with a vengeance on his goat mommy's teats, and I had no idea how I could share that milk with the calves. I was so fixed by their cuteness overload, the precious suckling sounds and their trusting interaction that I did not know what to do with their heartbreaking plea for food.

I looked around, but the chickens continued to lay their eggs underneath an old retired tractor, the Border Collie had run off to chase the rooster, and the only human farm workers in sight were taking a tea break under a tree, oblivious or uninterested in my dilemma.

Soon enough, Charmaine came marching out of the house, looking for one of her employees to tend to something in the garden. She was also ignored. It must be difficult as a woman to lay the law in a perceived man's world. When she saw me standing next to the calves, she walked over and, without realizing it, took a bit of a rest-break herself as she chatted to me for a while. She admitted openly that the ground workers don't like gardening as she is very specific about what she wants and likes.

Fascinating, I thought. If you are steadfast with your own wishes, you can't please everyone. If you comply with everyone else's wishes, you still can't please everyone (I have several patients for whom I have been to the moon and back, and they are still disgruntled). Where is the middle ground?

I was far more entranced by these mooing babies to ponder that any further. My instinct was set on wishing to protect and save them from any further distress. My helplessness was not evident to Charmaine. She was a practical woman by nature and fierce by force due to her circumstances. She was also a mother, but her children had long grown up and moved off with lives of their own. It can be a very harsh and lonely existence, as most of the farmers' children nowadays want an easier lifestyle, whatever that is. She wished she could also just get up and go from her life and venture off on a wild hike like we were doing. Little did she know how challenging this adventure had been for all of us.

She confessed that she had no real friends and her husband was her only companion and everything else she needed from another human being.

This drought had taken its toll on all the farmers in the area, and they had to sell or cull all of their cattle. The cows were dying of starvation, as there was nothing to graze on, and the lucerne was just too expensive to afford. They had kept some sheep on their farm but had no source of income since January of this year and were living on a very large bank overdraft. When that overdraft was finished, so they would be too.

Last Friday, they had paid R15000 towards staff salaries and general expenses. All of the property's fencing had to be re-done, as they had a huge problem with jackals and caracals crawling under their fences and eating their lambs. It was lambing season now, but this drought had caused the birthing ewes to abandon their babies. For most of the day, Hannes' job was to scout the hectares of dry land, picking up the sick or starving lambs and bringing them back to the house to be hand-reared, as their significant death toll was further indebting the farm's income. The milk used for the calves and lambs was also costing them an arm and a leg. They paid R900 for 25 kilograms of milk, and each baby calf drank one litre of milk at a time, several times a day.

After losing all their cattle, Charmaine had been distraught for months after that. Thinking he was doing his mother a favour, Charmaine's son had gifted 'ma' with these two calves a week ago for her to hand-rear, not realizing the cost of it was more than she could afford. But she was an animal lover and had already grown so fond of these forever-hungry babies.

It also broke her heart that they paid R1000 for every jackal and R550 for every *rooikat* caught and killed on their property. They could not afford the loss of stock any more than they could afford the milk and lucerne, but they were fighting for their survival, just as the jackal and caracal were fighting for their livelihood. She, too, had no answer to this dilemma.

What you lose on the one hand, you gain on another. It is a natural cycle of life if the hands keep alternating between the losing and the gaining. But when the one hand loses all the time, living can become very difficult with the incapacitated use of only one hand or one paw.

She then concluded, "These are hard times for all, but when it gets good, it gets very good!" With that said, she turned on her heels and went to find Simon so that he could help her transplant the clivias to a shadier spot.

I retrieved a breakfast apple from my pocket and wondered where this one had come from. How could such a juicy sweet apple be grown in a valley that was so water-stricken? I also wondered if I could sustain my body on fruit and vegetables alone. I would never be able to eat veal again. Staring into the opal crystal eyes of those precious creatures, whilst they feebly tried to suckle and nurture from my hands, I could not bear the thought that on many occasions, I had sliced into tender strips of pepper-flavoured meat that once belonged to these darling sentient creatures.

Wishing to clean out more of "those damn spots" that tainted my hands, this Lady Macbeth promptly walked up the hill to fill a pail of water and proceed to wash her dirty laundry. I emptied the kitchen dustbin and used it to soak my filthy pants and fishy underwear. Iris was amused at the sight of me squatting with arms dipped into a lime-green dustbin that scrubbed my laundry and insisted on taking a photo so that I could show my family what I was doing. Not only did my family not need further evidence of my guilt-ridden attempts, but they had also already seen me wash dishes in a plastic bowl whilst sitting on the desert sand of a wild bush camp, then take a dump into the same plastic container that same evening, when I dared not encounter lions outside our tent.

I made an added attempt to erase the swirling of thoughts that plagued me on a day that I should be at ease and rest. I voluntarily walked up a portion of Pinnacle Gorge's southern façade to escape further conversations. Every time someone spoke, it conjured up more confusion and unanswered questions.

But the serenity and the contrasting beauty of the farm and the landscape kept pulling me back to ground level, insisting on anchoring me onto a steady and secure place, where I was sure to find my footing. Sitting on a ragged rock overlooking the guesthouse and farmhouse below, I wanted to cry. Again.

I lied when I said I had stopped dreaming. I don't know if I would call it dreaming, but I did have one residual desire buried deep in the confines of my heart. I didn't entertain it much, simply because I believed it was an impossible wish that would forever be out of reach. When I grew up one day, I hoped to own or live on a farm just like this one. I had the fairytale idea of waking up to the crowing of a rooster, sitting on a grand porch with ten dogs at my side whilst I sipped my early morning coffee, deciding on which cow I would milk first and which pot-belly pig would get belly rubs first. I dreamt of rescuing animals, providing them with a forever safe home and of never having to see disease, violence or suffering ever again.

Today, that dream had evaporated into thin air the moment Charmaine ended her tea break with me. The realistic idea of running a farm such as this was just too daunting. It was as if someone just cancelled the children's Christmas forever.

Somewhere between the orange juice and the biltong at breakfast, Charmaine spoke about her daughter-in-law, who was currently frequenting a hotel school in Cape Town. Because of their recent challenges, the family needed to diversify their income potential. They built the guesthouse for mountain clubs, hikers, cyclists and visiting groups like us to use. But for that, they had to spend money on water pipes, reservoir tanks, septic tanks for sewerage, gas for heating and general infrastructure equipment and furniture. I wondered if it was even worth their while. I had no idea how much I was paying them for the night, as all our B & B costs were included in one single pilgrimage price. But with the lavish bountiful amounts of food on offer and copious amounts of tea, coffee, and milk consumed, I doubted they were making any decent kind of profit.

This all seemed too much effort just to stay afloat and survive.

With that thought, the last ray of hope for a different lifestyle of my own in the country was sliced to bits, just as the earth was ploughed and torn open by the tractors churning in the distant fields.

The baboons teased me from the treetops above with their 'ooh-ahh' yakking. They are hardly ever seen, as they too get shot for raiding farmers' crops despite their natural territory dwindling due to human encroachment. I watched the same waning of the lit cigarette in my hand and wished for some clarity to come to me hidden in the wind that blew the tobacco ash away.

The tractors ceased their noise, indicating it was time for lunch. My disappearing acts were becoming a habit, so no one asked where I had been for so long. The kettle had boiled for the umpteenth time today, and I made instant tomato soup and ate it with crackers and cheese cubes, whilst Marcelle made a list of golden oldie movies to watch when she got back home. The post-prandial fatigue settled in, and not even the Da Vinci Code pages could keep me awake in the sitting room's rocking chair. It is the only time my brain stops with its unabated onslaught of thoughts. Note to self: when the going gets tough, take a break.

The first part of the afternoon siesta was divine. Then, I remember having a dream for the first time on this trip. I was back at work, frantically catching up on patients' blood results, but the receptionist kept interrupting and pestering me with silly questions and asking me for a job. At some point, I thought she was a secret agent spying on me on behalf of another doctor. George sensed my distress and took over my waiting area, calmly speaking to my patients and welcoming them into my office.

I can't say that I woke up rejuvenated after this nap, but it felt amazing to sleep in the middle of a weekday. I couldn't remember when last I had the opportunity. I wondered if my dream had something to do with a colleague that kept messaging me daily, wanting to know exactly what I was doing and how it was going. She did not understand that when I said I am coming here for some alone time and was going to disconnect from the outside world, I meant just that. I had not replied to the messages. I guess this was a good time to practice those healthy boundaries.

A hot shower improved my mood as always, so I packed my dry laundry and prepared the tog bag for the following day. It was time for reflecting again.

We assembled in the guesthouse's sitting room and were not given a break from this task on our rest day. I reclaimed the rocking chair.

Surprisingly, Lilly spoke first. This time I seemed more tolerant. Albeit softly, she fluently spoke about the more minor things in life that she noticed and appreciated today, from the magnificent mountain-view framed by the shower window to the croaking frog concerto, the water that filled the reservoir, and a sunbird that flirted with flower blossoms. I could not make the connection at the time, but Lilly spoke of a pretty Robin she had seen at Pinnacle Gorge by the water reservoir today when a few pilgrims had their feet dipped in the cool water. I had seen one yesterday at the Middleton's water reservoir, too; only it had been an empty one. I remember silently thanking her for the reminder to notice life's smaller miracles.

Julie was still devastated. Five years had passed since her divorce. Her children had also moved on with their lives, and she had been alone for long now. Even though she had been married for twenty years, she had tried to save that relationship on many occasions from a turbulent, high-riding and alcohol-infused lifestyle. On her last rescue attempt, her children had dissuaded her from returning to her already failed marriage, as they knew they would lose both their parents in the aftermath. For a long while, Julie could not conjure up any happy memories, not from her marriage and not when her children were growing up. To top it all off, she continued to be haunted by the memories of her ex-husband. He was on the same Indlela "Crossing" trail with another twelve pilgrims, just one day behind our team! He seemed to follow her every thought and every step in her struggle to break free from this bondage. I felt sorry for her.

Christy briefly counselled that only you can take charge of your own emotions, or else you allow others to control your feelings, thereby giving your power away.

In contrast, Lenny thanked his wife for being on this journey with him; even if it was just to bring him some tea, he joked.

I did not wish to give much detail of my day, so I merely mentioned my chat with Charmaine. I admired the farmers' resilience and determination for surviving despite all odds against them. I empathized with the tough decisions they were faced with on a daily basis, from killing jackal to when and how to nurture baby calves and lambs.

Retrospectively, I was in awe of their courage. I secretly harboured a little envy that they lived out in the country, amongst the beauty of nature, regardless of its seasonal limitations and management challenges.

Hank spoke philosophical jargon again, and I wish I had recorded his musings because perhaps they would have made more sense to me now that I had my head out of where the sun does not shine. He used the analogy of feeling like when someone makes you look at a beautiful flower, then suddenly they slap it, leaving you upset and shocked. That is how he felt today. But sometimes, you are the person that also slaps the flower, and then there are your loved ones that also slap that flower. He was finding it hard to accept himself and others. "Join the club, my friend." I did not say this out loud.

Brenda then read an inscription from a book left on the guesthouse coffee table. It was a composition about the prolonged drought and economic crash of this area in the 1800s. A certain Mr. Harry Middleton survived this disaster by breeding ostriches and selling sheep wool to foreigners. He later donated an ox-wagon and some oxen to a bankrupt farmer so that he and his family could start up their life again. We wondered if Mr. Harry was related to Walter Middleton's family in the Cape. It was a beautiful story of hope, and it had Marcelle and Elize in tears.

Elize said she is a very simple person, without any profound thoughts or any dramatic revelations. She was simply moved by everyone's stories and happy just being here.

Marcelle admitted that Cockscomb is a giant monster for her. She also wanted to leave many things behind her once she crossed over that peak. She thanked Julie for sharing her challenges; she could relate to Julie's pain as she was also finding it difficult to accept certain things in her own life. They must just make peace with it and move on.

Finally, George apologized for the sense of gloom yesterday. Having spent the day in the mountains, he felt much better and had a wonderful day today. He had been a psychotherapist for over ten years, trying to help people from all walks of life, including those that harm others and themselves. He has done numerous hikes and trails worldwide and spent time visiting many different cultures. He realised that everyone on this earth is trying to do the best they can, with what they have, from where they are, and trying to find their way around this big mystery called life. Personally, he had let go of the unknown a long time ago. All he could do was focus on the beautiful things and beautiful people that are part of this mystery.

He then talked us through tomorrow's route, excited for our milestone, but warned us to beware of the Puff Adder Valley.

Throughout our time together, I did not get to ask him which religion or specific belief system he followed, but it did not matter. His ethos had always been en pointe, and that is what is important. He did not need to belong to any false separation group.

Another buffet awaited us at supper time, and the disciples gathered once more around a long rectangular table. Hannes Rudman did not eat with us but kept us company whilst we tucked into a meatball *bobotie*, broccoli quiche, honey-sweetened carrots, a green salad and left-over mac 'n cheese. A chillied butternut soup was first served with bread and butter, and I had the first taste of menopausal hot flushes when the chilli pepper reached the back of my throat. We gratefully feasted like kings and queens, having still found gastric space for chocolate pudding and custard.

Hannes spoke whilst we chewed. He is a fifth-generation Rudman on this farm and chooses to live here for the love of it. He loves farming and loves the lifestyle. Some people enjoy chasing a golf ball around on a golf cart. He loves ploughing the land on his tractor. Even though the newer generations wish for city life, his son is one of the few youngsters that are just as passionate and runs one of their farmlands twelve kilometres from here.

He also loves the way their community comes together to assist and support one another. It has been their way of survival. The citrus farmers do make a good deal of money, but they cannot grow lucerne. In drought times, the prices of lucerne skyrocket for the demand. Whoever can harvest hay in the area sells it to their neighbour at a lower price than their commercial suppliers. One of the neighbouring farmers has fewer cattle and more grazing ground on his property, so he allows the Rudmans' sheep to graze there. In return, Hannes and his family help them to back-burn the *veld* and create firebreaks so fresh grass can grow when the rains come. One hand feeds the other, and that is how they survive out here; by looking out for one another. His satisfaction for life was visible in the jingling of his large midriff every time he laughed, and every time, he grinned a tired but happy smile.

We ambled late out the farmhouse, feeling utterly spoilt and thankful for this family's open-armed hospitality and kindness. George lagged behind to call his wife, making the most of the cellphone reception. It was a slow and quiet walk in the dark and up the hill, our torches swinging side to side to avoid any stumbling. I paused for a moment to allow fresh mountain air to fill my lungs and stop the sands of time. I breathed in the silence and peace of the night.

By the time we were halfway up the incline, George had already overtaken us. But without the use of a torch or a headlamp. He said he could see the way far better in the dark, just by the illumination of the moonlight and bright stars. He said you would only see the magic of the stars' light in the pitch black of the night, and ancient civilizations have navigated best in the darkest of the nights when the heavens' constellations shine the brightest. I doubted the moon was more brilliant than my LED, but I switched off my torch anyway and allowed my eyes to adjust to the newly and naturally enlightened path.

A smile spread across my face. By George, he was right again!

13

HEAVEN

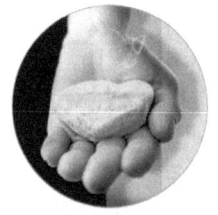

Nkosi Sikelel' iAfrika

The penthouse top bunk did not allow for a restful sleep this time. Same bed, different night experience. No apparent reason for my restlessness. Perhaps only that it was Cockscomb-peak-day today, and some trepidation had set in sometime between midnight and now, when Mr. Rooster was cock-a-doodling out of tune so early in the morning.

I was a little pleased, though, that my intermittent insomnia was not from the gastro trots. We had all filled our bottles and glasses with the tap water that drained from the water reservoir, oblivious to the fact that four of our pilgrims had taken an afternoon swim yesterday in the tank that supplied our drinking water. In their defence, they had not made the connection either. When Hannes overheard the culprits admitting to a refreshing dip in the reservoir, he gently reminded them that they had been swimming in the farm's only freshwater supply. Sheepishly, no one owned up if they had urinated, bathed or washed clothes in it or not. I would like to believe not. Any other thought was far too gross.

But I guess there will always be someone pissing in your backyard. You can only hope to have acquired the skills to dilute any offence, that you are not taunted nor adversely affected by them.

I was not the only one that dressed in silence. There seemed to be a collective hush to the morning ritual, not a foreboding one, just quiet contemplation and preparedness for the final climb and ultimate destination - the result of weeks of preparation (for some) and days of endless walking and pain of various thresholds for all.

Life was supposed to be different after today somehow, but I had no idea how to incorporate all that I had experienced into my habitual routine.

An ethereal cloud of mist slowly wisped across the top of the mountain escarpment, its orange-purple vapour bringing forth the first solar rays into the dawning sky. There was still a remnant of hope that a magical show-stopping revelation was waiting for me at the summit, like a trophy prize perched on a totem pole when I reached the finish line, having mercifully completed the gauntlet games. I dared not dream, and that was a mistake I would come to regret.

To this day, food continues to replenish my soul. Caffeine remains an addiction. But I am glad the opioids I was abusing at the time did not take a permanent grip on my self-control. A cup of coffee and a handful of pain-numbing tablets were the grand finales to a breakfast of fruit and yoghurt, eggs and sausage on toast, and peanut butter sandwiches. Hannes bid us a brief and nonchalant goodbye; he had farm matters to attend to. Charmaine loaded us all into the back of her farm *bakkie* and backtracked two kilometres beyond her property gate to the start of the trail that would lead us up to Cockscomb. She waited until we had finished our morning reflections and adage for the day, before giving us all a warm tight hug, and wishing us Godspeed and much good fortune.

Hypocratic Oaths

We gratefully waved back at her until she was a small figurine at the bottom of the hill, whereby she too had a kitchen full of dishes and food to sort out for tomorrow's pilgrim group arrival.

And now, I mentally sent out my first formal invocation in a very long time. I prayed that from henceforth, I set my intention on the future only to move forward, that the only time I looked back was to reminisce on the beautiful landscapes and people that I have been blessed to witness and enjoy. I prayed for God's light to shine upon this land, this earth, these farms and its people that are trying to survive from it. I prayed that His grace is ever-present in these wonderful folk's hearts and minds, that their every sinew be filled with strength, courage, hopeful thoughts, and the happy memories of fruitful times. I prayed for God to bless Africa. Amen.

The ascent to the top was underway, and a subtle hazy fog surrounded each walking pilgrim in a surreal layer of divinity. The air was chilly and humid but easy to breathe. The hills were rocky and the path tortuous, but the ground became covered in dew-dotted green blades of grass and leaves. Our feet were raw and blistered, but the climb was facilitated by accumulated gracious hospitalities and promising expectations.

The first song to play from the ever-loyal iPod was Johnny Clegg's 'Scatterlings of Africa'.

Before becoming a world-renowned musician, Johnny studied Social Anthropology and lectured at Wits University. During this time, he joined musician Sipho Mchunu and founded the band Juluka in the early 70s. Belonging to a forbidden multiracial band in the apartheid era, he was nevertheless spectacularly successful in setting the standard for the Afro-Anglo 'crossover' popular musical ensembles of the 1980s. This particular song references a scatterling as a person equivalent to a vagabond or drifter, whereby Johnny honours the uprooted and displaced people of Africa, including the victims of colonialism, specifically the impoverished Black South African victims of Apartheid.

However, this track was sung with a broader meaning also. Science believes that all human beings have originated from Africa, with the 'Olduvai' Gorge in Tanzania as the birthplace of humankind. Johnny too acknowledges the entire human race in this song by referencing the "scatterlings of Africa" as all equal. When he studied the remnants of bones found in archeologic excavations, they appeared to be from one race only. It does not matter what we look like on the outside; we are all the same on the inside.

I did not know this until I researched the lyrics much later. Still, he sang that each scatterling possesses a "burning desire" in their heart, symbolizing a refusal to give in to the harrowing circumstances which dictate their lives. And that we are all "on the road to Phelamanga". *Phelamanga* is an old Zulu word that refers to a metaphysical, ideological destination.

Perhaps he was right; we are all on the hunt for an everlasting Utopia. We will all know that place in time, even if in death only. At this moment on my own personal Mount Sinai, I saluted this brilliant artist and humanitarian and gave thanks that he reminded me to love one another as the Creator loves us all, precisely the same and exactly as we are.

Every time I looked back over my rucksack, the countryside repeatedly transformed into an ever-more mystical and extraordinary scenery until the slow-moving silhouette of our bodies penetrating further into verdant forests resembled Dian Fossey's "Gorillas in the Mist". As much as I had stopped dreaming before embarking on this trek, I did have a bucket list with a few items scribbled on it. At the time, it seemed more like an impossible fairytale inventory, but I now issued out my second wish for the day. When my daughter turned sixteen and was legally old enough to access the Bwindi Impenetrable Forest National Park, I hoped that both her and *marido* would be my companions as we walked side by side, tracking the mountain gorillas of Uganda. After all, they share 98% of our human DNA, so we are virtually related and surely look the same on the inside. Amen.

Hypocratic Oaths

An hour and a half later, Lenny climbed into a bathtub. I did not know whether to laugh or check my GCS (Glasgow Coma Score) conscious levels. In the middle of an Eden mountain without any sign of civilization (except for us, if we can be called civil) was an abandoned white enamel oval tub plonked on a flat rocky outcrop. It was void of any water and shelter, so it did not even provide adequate bird perching or field mice nesting. Lenny sunk fully clothed into an invisible bubble bath, legs straddled and drooped over the edges, his walking sticks resembling oars on either side of the tub. He looked like he was ready to row himself into the stratosphere and follow Aladdin on his magic carpet. The wide grin under his sun hat against a wild, untamed backdrop was priceless. But realizing he was not going to fly to the peak, he made an undignified attempt to get out of the tub and proceeded to tackle the remainder of the climb along with the rest of us.

It was a fair-paced tempo up the incline with several momentary stops to gaze over our shoulders, to appreciate the peaceful scenes and entrancing sierras. The energy had become animated at the prospect of reaching the summit, and it was not long before we were walking across a plateau that stood as close to Cockscomb peak as we would ever get.

There was no visible signboard or a stone-heap with flags and mementoes from previous conquerors to signal our arrival at the top. There was no welcoming committee this time or finish line to cut through, nor was there champagne or fireworks to celebrate our accomplishment. There was but a second white bathtub at the centre of a flat rocky platform that heralded our journey's pinnacle destination. And that was good enough for me. We knew this tub marked the spot, and we had all made it to the summit. The giant rooster comb mushroomed behind us, and it provided all the photographic evidence we needed to hallmark this day forever.

Julie, Marcelle and Christy flocked to the edge of the tub and dipped their feet inside the empty jacuzzi, singing Shosholoza at the top of their voices whilst waving their hands in the air. This song is South Africa's second national anthem, usually sung to express the hardships and heartache of working in the mines. But in Ndebele, it also means "go forward or make way for the next man". I would like to think that we had all progressed forward in our evolution as human souls through the hardships of this pilgrimage and burrowed through a ton of earth to sprout above the ground, to blossom and transform into our unique versions of a divine creation. Because once we are in full bloom and remember *who* we are rather than what defines us, we are then in a better position to provide shade and refuge to the next downtrodden traveller instead of remaining a seed buried underground for others to trample on.

We spent about an hour contemplating, staring out into the horizon, capturing the moment with cellphones and memory, each one to their own intentions and introspections. I presumed the peanut butter sandwiches would now set the stage for some magic, as food can often do, but the expected epiphany did not implode through my body. There was not even a tingle or a goose pimple. But I was not disappointed because not even the slow indulgence of a banana could conjure up unpleasant thoughts. There was simply an acceptance that, for now, all I wanted was to relish in one smile, one hug, one blessing, and one breath at a time. And that felt peaceful and good.

The descent began with trepid treading on loose gravel and soil. It was a long, winding and undulating single track that had us circumventing hill after hill on a path intended to have us sliding off our feet if we were not careful to place our boots on solid ground. The track was steep, and for the next three hours, it had me concentrating far more than I dedicated to any of my final varsity exams. It was taxing on the body, legs, and toenails that kept bumping against the hard caps of my Salomon shoes. But it did not deter me from spitting out the last of the *poopdrols* in my pocket in the final round of the *spoeg* competition. I achieved very good range, and I declared myself the winner of the game simply because there were no other contenders, just witnesses.

It was a good game.

We need to be cautious playing the game of life. We can easily get caught up in 'competitions' that often have us feeling left behind, not fast enough, good enough, clever enough, not pretty enough, not this enough, not that enough. We then allow others to place their opinions of our worth on a rating scale, and by doing so, we disqualify ourselves from the race.

After that, no amount of medals, money, materialism or consumerism can ever make up for the lack of our self-worth. We keep believing that happiness is somewhere out there, outside of ourselves, with a partner, with a career, with our children, with the amount of financial gain, when all that happiness is, is how you feel about yourself and what you believe you are worthy of.

As I said, the biggest bummer or blessing is that there is not even a damned race. We have forgotten that we are eternal souls having transient physical experiences. When we 'expire' through physical death from this particular body, our soul gets recycled into another vehicle, into another life to have another turn on another level. Much like the different levels of Jumanji or a round of chess because apparently, our souls think life is a lot of fun in this physical plane, and we can't wait to get back into the game after our umpteenth funeral!

I can't remember when we stopped for lunch, but somewhere along the way, I got chatting to Maeve and felt comfortable enough to share with her my many photographs of doggie biscuits and doggie birthday cakes that I had been making since the beginning of the year. I had endeavoured in a new hobby as a fundraiser for an animal shelter. The only other skill I had besides inserting chest drains and intravenous lines into people was to bake for my favourite creatures in the world. And I realized I was pretty good at it. I had already contemplated giving up my medical practice to start up a doggie bakery franchise. I had no idea how to fund it or how to go about it, but at some point of losing faith in humanity, I wished to serve the rest of my time here dedicated to the fortunate 4-legged beings to ultimately help the unfortunate ones that had no voice.

Maeve admired my new skill and was surprised that there were such things as bakeries for dogs in the USA and that I wished to bring the concept to South Africa. She was, however, horrified that I would give up a successful medical practice to do just that.

At this point, I did not tell her that I just did not have the balls or belief in myself to take that leap of faith.

Perhaps it is an excuse, but too often, we put our dreams on hold for the sake of our children. We worry that we won't have enough to provide, educate or give them the opportunities we didn't have. But denying ourselves for extended periods of time will either motivate us or, more likely, leave us secretly resentful. We think we may be doing them a favour by these sacrifices of self-negating, but our kids don't care if we are the CEO or the plumber. They simply want to know they are loved by us *unconditionally* and deserve the time we spend with them. I know my child could not care if I sold dog biscuits for a living, as long as I was happy. If she catches wind that I have ever sacrificed for her against my own free will, I will only have given her feelings of guilt. It would become a burden for her, and that would suck.

After a long time of not seeing any creatures other than the twelve bipedal hominids, two majestic klipspringers darted ahead of us and climbed up a rocky incline, then stopped to stare back at us to monitor our every move. The klipspringer is a small gregarious antelope known to be nocturnal but often spotted during the day. They are monogamous and well camouflaged against their mountainous habitat. The male is never further than ten metres away from his precious female, with whom he mates for life.

There were one or two females in our group that had picked up the pace, simply eager or in musk, but in a certain hurry to get the next 24 hours over and done with, so they could get home to their sweethearts. A baboon echoed in the distance and cheered them on, remaining once again out of sight.

We had descended the same distance on the other side of the mountain range, which we had climbed up during the morning. By now, we were venturing in a valley, following the flow of a stream and marvelling at the vegetation that had become greener and beckoned a myriad of birds to this source of life. Having skipped from one rocky outcrop butting out of the stream onto the next, we crossed over to the other side of this narrow river and continued to head west.

However, by 15.00, we suspected we had gotten a bit lost or veered astray. George had gone way ahead of us, leaving Lilly in charge of the flock and responsible for leading the way. The ladies in musk were far from happy and made no effort to disguise their displeasure at wandering aimlessly for a few extra kilometres. Or they may have gotten a bit agitated at the sight of leopard *spoor* recently imprinted on the river-side mud, and hence the urgency to get to our last overnight stop.

When we spotted the hermit's house in the distance, we sighed with relief and silently thanked George for his pre-departure directions and look-out beacons.

Hermit-man lived isolated from the human world in a single lopsided mud-stick hut, surrounded by alpine escarpment and a few cows, chicken and sheep. He was nowhere to be seen, probably hiding in terror inside his safe house at the sight of eleven strangers stopping and squatting down in his front yard for high tea. His female canine companion was far friendlier and came to greet each one of us. She wasn't just being polite; she was searching for food. She could have had an entire meal if she ate the ticks that fed off her body, but perhaps she had made friends with them already, considering they seemed to be well settled into her coat. Feeling like we were definitely trespassing this time, we ate our leftover fuel and Rehydrate in haste and moved on a further two kilometres to find the right gravel road onto Kammievlei.

Once we climbed over the last fence of this journey, we looked back at Cockscomb and observed the sun rays already caressing its peak with paint-brush streaks of liquid gold and orange. It is not only clouds that have silver linings. I suspect every one thing and circumstance does too.

I allowed the others to walk on ahead whilst I stayed behind to sit on the sandy curb and enjoy my last celebratory cigarette. Lilly did not venture too far as she was in charge of safely bringing the last sheep home. She was discrete enough to remain out of sight whilst I had a private moment with Johnny Clegg's moving verses of 'The Crossing'. I played the song repeatedly, and by the end of the third encore, the last of the grey Dunhill smoke had evaporated into thin air.

Johnny, I believe you, and I trust that I will always see the white light shining at the end of each dark tunnel. It felt magical and surreal already.

Our hosts were once again out of town (I was not taking this personally). I was not about to get perplexed at this stage, thinking quite a few of our hosts might have wished to evade us. Of course, there was no town or civilization for miles around here, but they were not at their farmhouse and had left their very trusted caretakers to welcome us into their home.

Noos was a short, robust and very amiable hostess. Her broad toothless smile and wrinkled laughing eyes had us doubting her words that it was a headache to run this place all by herself, ignoring the partner in crime standing next to her. Monica was the exact opposite; tall, lanky, serious and probably calling the shots. They looked like female versions of Laurel and Hardy.

But they seemed to be impeccable in setting out a welcoming buffet of biscuits, olives, rice cakes, paté and crackers, whilst simultaneously kneading that night's *roosterkoek* dough with fervent determination. Several juice cartons, tea, coffee and fruit had already been put on display. My eyes darted from one delectable item to the next. My stomach was more excited than a fat kid in a candy store, but I greeted Noos and Monica first, thanking them for the wonderful reception and only then sat down to partake in the cordial feast.

I showered and repacked my purple tog bag for the last time on this trip. I gave all my leftover protein bars, suspicious meal replacement powder packets and rehydration sachets to Hank. This was not his final day. Hank had undertaken to continue with the second leg of the Indlela pilgrimage, which involved hiking for a further 300 kilometres onto Knysna. He was to join a new group of pilgrims in two days to start the '*Kom Nader*' stretch with them from Patensie to end at The Heads of the Knysna lagoon. The terrain, climbs and passes were twice as challenging as this first leg we were about to complete. His feet had also taken a beating along with the rest of ours, and I had no idea how they would endure a double onslaught. This was the first time I suspected that Hank was possibly crazy after all. Needing all the help he could get, he graciously accepted my poor offerings. After which, he swaggered outside to the front yard to light up a fire in Rulo Beer's *braai* stand. The aureate sun had started its curtaining behind the dusky green hills, and the orange-purple fire flames pulsated a warm pyrotechnic display that filled the air with wonder, bliss and serenity.

Noos put together a 5-star three-course meal. I dared not think what she would serve if she had a team of cooks at her disposal. We lavished on tomato soup with freshly baked *roosterkoek* and butter, then enjoyed potatoes, peas, beans, *mielies*, homemade pickled beetroot, and chargrilled chicken made by Hank on the *braai*. It was more than any of us could finish. We sat together in quiet satisfaction at the long dining room table for our last supper, then spoke our final reflections over coffee and dessert. We were required to share the outcome of this pilgrimage and what it signified for each of us.

George initiated the ceremony by holding a heart-shaped stone in his hand. When he conceived of this Indlela idea, he wished to attribute an added meaningful significance to each of the four stages of the entire Indlela pilgrimage. The first stage he called "The Crossing," or the crossing over. Its unique significance was the Placing of Stones Journey, where each person brought along two stones, one to place on a cairn at the top of Cockscomb Mountain in celebration of someone dear to them. The other to represent something that each one would like to leave behind in their life, which they could leave or let go of anywhere on the route.

I had missed this memo. Was it pure coincidence that I had brought along the 'Stone of Truth' in my backpack? I had left it somewhere on the route on a pile of abandoned burdens from people who were equally ready to let go of what no longer served them. The other stone I had found along the way. A rose-coloured heart-shaped one, but one which was returning home with me for someone most dear to me.

George handed his stone to the person on his left and asked her to pass it around so that we could all hold it for a while before handing it back to him. He would then take a piece of each of us back home with him. He thanked us for our presence, courage to come along and wished us well with the rest of our life's journey.

Lilly then read a Vietnamese poem, and Julie read a poem about a Lotus flower. Hank was grateful for a renewed sense of calm and peace. He did not have many words, as his pilgrimage was only halfway complete. Elize quoted a portion of St Francis of Assisi's prayer: "Lord, make me an instrument of your peace; where there is hatred, let me sow love; where there is injury, pardon; where there is discord, union; where there is doubt, faith; where there is despair, hope; where there is darkness, light; and where there is sadness, joy." She had also prayed for our country and its people today. She prayed for rain and harmony amongst us all.

"Nkosi Sikelel' iAfrika," she said.

Brenda had been worried all along that she would not be able to complete the whole pilgrimage, so today, she was elated and thoroughly satisfied with her achievement, one she thought was inconceivable in her sixties.

Christy thanked our group and noted that it is the people that make all the difference in our journeys. She was reminded to keep pulling down the fences that keep us separated from one another and not wear the masks that society forces upon us to hide our magnificent selves.

Marcelle was equally thankful to all of us but did not have much else to add. She was desperate to get home. Her husband was meeting her at our final destination at Patensie tomorrow. When I saw how she greeted her bulldog first before she had the courage to look in her husband's eyes, I hoped for her sake she had also left a 'Stone of Truth' behind on Cockscomb.

Lenny felt joyful at having at least one day where his feet did not blossom with fresh blisters. I would like to think it was from the spare fluffy hiking socks I had given him, in addition to the notion that his feet had finally surrendered and succumbed to the flow and peace-seeking pace of his retired life. He referred to Hank's analogy of hitting the beautiful flower yesterday. He observed that people have certainly become indifferent in their endeavours – passive, aggressive and malicious indifferences. But when we encounter such attitudes, perhaps we are catching those people at a time in their lives when they are at their most hurt, injured or have been left uncared for. We can find further tolerance if we see it.

He did not look directly at Hank nor me, but I sensed those were words meant for both of us.

Iris begged us not to miss out on opportunities. She was also retired and, in her long life, had regretted several lost moments that she could never take back. We were all surprised to hear that her father's ashes are scattered on Cockscomb's peak. It had been an extraordinary but sorrowful day. She had never asked her father why he had loved the mountains so much. She did not know many things about her parents, and it was too late to ask now.

I was in greater awe of this elderly couple – their determination, newfound fun and zest for life, and the courage to never give up.

Maeve had already told me that she would be on an aeroplane to Tunisia in a week. She surprised me right after I had shocked her with my pink peanut butter iced dog cake picture. She had taken up a teaching post in remote North Africa and was excited but mostly nervous about moving alone into a far bigger unknown. This was a huge new chapter in her life, a transition she sought after, and I did not have the chance to ask her what had brought on such a drastic decision. She thanked us for supporting her by simply being present on an endeavour which she dislikes. She detests hiking and climbing hills even more so. The reason she took on this challenge was to push her faith to new heights, to see that there is indeed something much grander than her. She discovered a divine Creator that coordinates order and purpose, and for her to appreciate that fifty million years' worth of rock formation does not just happen by chance.

I was just as grateful for everyone's company (I had loathed their presence on the first day). To me, "The Crossing" was not just about reaching the summit of a mountain. I explained the meaning behind Johnny Clegg's namesake song, and I hoped that everyone present had in some way crossed over beyond a burden, a challenge, a broken heart, and onto a spiritual path or a place of deeper fulfilment, happiness and peace.

When I finally settled for the last night on a shared double bed, I placed my charging phone on the bedside table and turned off the screen light. Trying to slip quietly under the duvet so as not to wake my already sleeping bedmate, the corner of my left eye caught the phone screen switching on again. I turned my head a full 90 degrees to stare at a screensaver that spontaneously changed from a photograph of my daughter to a swirling purple default picture without me touching it or being anywhere near it. I reflexively turned to my partner to ask if she had just seen what happened, but I did not wish to disturb her. I turned back to the phone, blinked several times, but the purple swirl was still swirling on its own accord.

I had not taken any more drugs at dinner time; my last Myprodols had been at breakfast. I was not that tired to be dreaming and not crazed enough to be hallucinating. I continued staring for a long while until the screen light switched off automatically. I slunk into bed, pulled the sheets up to my chin, switched off the side-lamp and wondered what that was all about. I did not know whether to be freaked out or simply mystified. As I slowly slipped into unconsciousness, I was aware of a secret smile that was left spread across my face.

We are all destined to walk the road onto that one *Phelamanga*. The way back to heaven. It is not a GPS coordinate in the celestial cosmos. It is a space found in the being of the heart.

I felt that I was now en route.

14

THE LONG WALK HOME

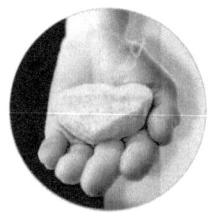

A pilgrimage is never complete

Just when you think you have it all figured out, you go to the toilet in the middle of the night, forgetting that you are *not* supposed to flush. At least in Kammievlei, that is. Doing so at 3 a.m. has the water pump cranking up in a rage, sending screeching fluid throughout the plumbing system, whilst waking up all of its household members in a nightmarish belief that aliens have suddenly uprooted the entire house.

I had secretly snuck back to bed in the hopeful expectation that I had not been spotted and that being the first to make a cup of coffee at 6 a.m. in a very nonchalant mannerism would not give me away. Part of being childlike is that there is still a naughty or innocent urge to pretend. It stimulates the imagination, or so I am told.

Yesterday, we had asked Noos and Monica if we could have breakfast by 7 a.m. to get an early start to our final stretch. However, I gathered that these ladies were indeed very friendly by nature, but they were also high on much more than just life itself. At 7 a.m., they walked into the kitchen with grins and goofy eyes to *start* making breakfast. They had missed the boat, as the men of the house had already taken over the kitchen and were whipping up an appetizing storm.

The ladies in musk had looked so grim this morning that the male A-team had deftly jumped into action. George scrambled the eggs. Hank fried the bacon, and Lenny gave them both moral support. Then, it was every man and woman for himself and herself. There followed a flurry of toasting bread, boiling kettle ten times over, finding the oats and pouring milk, packing fruit and making cheese *roosterkoek broodjies*. I added homemade fig jam to my sandwiches, and with a full tummy, I was already looking forward to this treat. I tasted homebrewed Honeybush tea and bought a packet of the same tea from Monica. It was their side-line business, and I was happy to support it. I supposed they were experts in all sorts of dried herbs and grass, but what else is there to do in Kammievlei when the guests are gone? I then filled my thermos flask with piping hot *moerkoffie*. It was bound to provide the last turbo boost down Gamtoos Valley onto Patensie. Or a bout of last-minute diarrhoea.

Oom Johan would have been horrified at our hasty and inattentive consumption of good food. I had met this dear man on our one month guided trip to the Serengeti in 2013. *Oom* Johan was a patient, diligent and kind man who paid attention to detail and no longer saw the point of rushing through life and certainly not speeding through any God-given meal. I guess that once you lose a child, you become more aware of the importance of the smaller things that life has to offer, and you never take anything else for granted, ever. Or else you end up numbing the pain with tranquillizers and sedatives, as his wife did on a daily basis.

This day, we left behind a generous tip and an impressive mess in the kitchen and dining room. But it did not deter Noos and Monica from joining our group photo and morning circle. The early dawn rays were just beginning to highlight the tips of the peaks in the distance, whilst

Hypocratic Oaths

Hank spoke of circles being one of the things that keep us connected by the hands and through the heart.

We broke the circle of friends for the last time and walked away in silence, each finding our own pace for the next five kilometres towards the cellphone tower, our first tea break and the last one of our trip.

We floated past beautiful views and hundreds of fluffy sheep. The dew-sprinkled grass glistened even without the illumination of the sun. The birds flew in slow motion, and it seemed to me that Alice had gone down the wrong hole and missed this particular Wonderland. Perhaps she was still lost in Alicedale because this part of the world was far more magical than any hasty rabbit or smoky caterpillar had ever encountered.

The sun slowly advanced towards me to kiss my cheeks when I was not focusing on anything in particular. I squinted and smiled, adjusting my hat ever so slightly so as not to appear rude but to protect my face from flushing.

I noticed Lilly straggling behind, saying she just needed some space. I had stopped trying to figure her out. Clearly, I did not know her hurt and so ceased to pass further judgement.

My thoughts veered off to my parents, family, and all that is good in my life. I thought of my daughter and recognized this is my greatest achievement thus far. Motherhood has given me a great sense of purpose, and my parenting skills leave me feeling proud that I have done an excellent job as her mother so far. If I ever did wrong by her, she can write her own book about it one day, and it would be an instant hit, as all she touches turns to gold. So even then, I would have succeeded.

The cellphone tower disconnected us from our tranquil silence, and my attention went straight into unfolding the foil wrapped around Noos' cheese and fig jam *broodjie*. It was delicious, and with the *moerkoffie* sips in between the sweet 'n savoury bites, it made it even more heavenly. As my father would say with a G 'n T in hand, it tasted like mother's milk. The coffee was starting to get a bit lukewarm, as the flask I carried was not of the greatest quality. It was given to me by my daughter's school principal, and I was the only mother that received a gift on Mother's Day this year. I offered some coffee to Hank, who was sitting next to me. As I was commenting on the beverage that he was so looking forward to, was getting cold because of a 'fong-kong' thermos, I stopped in mid-sentence. When I moved closer to pour into his mug, I looked down to see a heart-shaped stone that stared me boldly in the face. That shut me up instantly. We both drank our coffees gratefully, and I then proceeded to find several other beautifully shaped stones, including a large crème pebble in the shape of the African continent. *Marido* would be happy with this one too.

The following stretch had Lenny and Iris walk beside me in idle company. We chatted for the longest time in all the days that we had hiked together. I asked how he now occupied his time, and he spoke of his quest to restore the Palmietrivier catchment area in his suburb to its original pristine condition. It is a unique ecosystem under threat with polluted water and illegal rubble dumping, and he saw it as worthy of rescue and restoration. He had lived in this Durban area for over forty years and had managed to source five million Rand from various funders and donations. However, most of it had been 'lost' or gone to other projects at the last minute or used (abused) by other partnerships. It had been a long, frustrating and challenging process, but he was not completely giving up after so many years at it. However, now that he was retired, he had backed off a little from that venture and taken on several other smaller projects to keep him occupied and otherwise sane.

Lenny then asked me about my practice and the kind of patients and diseases I treated. I replied as objectively as I could. He knew I was not satisfied with the job I had, so he did not dig deeper.

Iris intervened with an account of her snake bite experience. They did not get to know which of the venomous snakes had jabbed her on a random coastal hike, but she required urgent airlifting to a hospital in Umhlanga, where she spent two weeks in ICU fighting for her life. Since then, they had developed a somewhat suspicious distaste for doctors. Iris had three treating doctors, all with varying opinions on how to manage her life-threatening condition. She had almost died and blamed the doctors for her near-fatal episode but could not fault the poisonous snake nor the fact that she was walking on their natural turf.

Lenny then added salt to my wounded ego (as if I had been Iris' doctor). When Lenny had called on their GP with several unanswered questions, he agreed to visit Iris in ICU (because GPs have those miracles not possessed by specialists who studied those extra few years). Lenny was later billed for the GP's visit, which left an even bigger sour taste in his mouth. How could his GP charge for a 'courtesy' visit? I understand that Lenny must have been in a state of complete fear and panic, and all rationale can fly out the window when you are watching your spouse fade. It has been years since that incident, and Iris is thankfully well and healthy, but Lenny has apparently not recovered from that insult.

It never ceases to amaze me how doctors are perceived as the ultimate pro-Deo Samaritans who must give their time, expertise, resources, counsel, and sell their soul if insisted upon, all for *mahala*; all for nothing.

People don't walk into a grocery store expecting to not pay for their groceries, so I can't see that it should be any different from other essential services. Just because patients don't walk out of a doctor's office with a bag of potatoes and sliced ham, it does not mean they don't have to pay for services rendered. It grinds me when someone asks me for a discount on my fees when they are sporting bright neon gel nails, strawberry hair highlights and the latest designer shoes. Or they profess they can't pay me until month-end because they need the money for the medication I have just prescribed. Yet, they buy a weekly supply of the *People* magazine, a carton of cigarettes, and half a dozen chocolate-coated doughnuts per day to support their 150-kilogram frame. If there are not enough Rands for private health care, we have public health care and services almost freely available. But the inconvenience of spending a whole day in a crowded clinic waiting for a grumpy nurse to attend to you means that you would prefer instead to put your trusted doctor out of pocket. Trust has clearly lost all value these days. I wish I had the guts to one day say: "I didn't know your life was worth shit to you."

Fortunately, I hardly see this kind of mindset nowadays - mine and patients. When I shifted from a belief that I was being taken advantage of, the world reflected back at me that my time is valued. My patient profile has since changed significantly. I am happy to accommodate many patients that have genuine financial struggles, and I do a fair share of pro Deo work, but it is at my sole discretion and no longer under duress. Patients are now mostly understanding and appreciative of what I do. And it is simply because I changed my own mindset and chose not to remain a whining victim, blaming the world for my self-inflicted martyrdom. It has made a world of difference to the enjoyment of my every day.

But at the time of thinking how unrealistic Lenny had been, I was impressed by how cool I behaved with where the conversation had gone. I felt like I had turned into one of the penguins from the Madagascar movie. I had a confident and professional grin on my face and thought, "Just smile and wave, boys. Just smile and wave." Definitely a step in the right direction.

I needed a break from shop-talk, so I was happy to stop a second time for a pee-break and some restoration on cheese, crackers and water. We still had another ten kilometres of steep climbs and precipitous descents to conquer, so we were still working out our bodies, minds and souls right to the very last minute of arriving at the *N.G. Kerk* of Patensie.

When we reached our third self-proclaimed tea break spot, George again returned from his advanced progress to find us and show us where to turn off the gravel road back onto farmland territory. We might have only reached Patensie at nightfall if he had not done so. As we trekked 90°west from where we were heading and peaked over one of the never-ending hills, we saw the destined town's church tower and church bell in the far distance. This unmistakable beacon is the primordial centre point of even the smallest of *dorpies*. We descended once more through a single track lined with wild cactuses, aloes and thorny bushveld on either side. Below on the trough of the valley lay rows and rows of the now-familiar citrus and fruit orchards of the Eastern Cape. I walked past these sweet-smelling forests with longing nostalgia, as if I had already been gone from them for several months. The orchards gave way to the small rustic homesteads of the labourers that worked these farms. Skinny dogs barked, and nonplused children watched us walk by. I did not give myself the time or chance to process whether I was happy to have completed this insurmountable deed or whether I was disappointed that it was over so soon.

The sight of our rendezvous point brought momentary inertia. We had all made it without the need for any helicopter evacuations. I was genuinely grateful to have been given the opportunity and freedom to just be me, not Dr Gisela. They are one and the same, but Integrity, or the integration of who I am and what I do, is a slow process.

We embraced each other with warm camaraderie and well wishes, and in my newfound admiration for these beautiful strangers that had transformed themselves into friends and had left only fondness and appreciation in my heart, I also took a piece of them with me to keep in my memory forever.

Years later, I found a quote that embodied my experience with these souls who held my hand and heart during one of the most difficult rites of passage I have ever endured.

If any of them ever happen to read this book at any stage, I wish to reiterate my gratitude: "To the few individuals in my life who have listened without judgement, spoken without prejudice, helped me without entitlement, understood without pretension and loved me without conditions - Thank you."

This is what it means to belong to a soul family. Even if we don't have any blood relatives or cannot co-exist with any of them for whatever reasons, we all have one or more of these. They exist in the like-minded people that speak our soul's language.

This pilgrimage had initially seemed like an eternal inferno of a painful body and a battered soul. Still, as we re-grouped for the final farewell in front of the church grounds, I oscillated between thankfulness, admiration, victory, remembrance and subtle angst for the unknown predictions that lay ahead. At least it was not Tunisia. But I was to take a return shuttle to Port Elizabeth this afternoon to catch my flight back home. And as much as I relished the beaming photograph taken of me sitting like a queen on the throne of the Padlangs Coffee Shop's oversized garden chair, I was not yet ready to return to work.

However, the longing to see my family was tangible, so George closed our ceremonial excursion with a final prayer and a reminder to all of us.

When he had set out to plan and plot out the Indlela pilgrimage and its 4-stage route, he had asked one of his very esteemed and wise colleagues at the University, "What if I can't complete this pilgrimage?"

She had promptly replied, "My dear friend, a pilgrimage is never complete…"

She was right.

15

SURRENDER

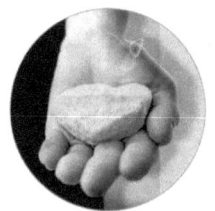

Old habits must die hard so that love is all that is left to revive - Gisela

I was desperate to remain in my giant Indlela bubble for a bit longer. I postponed my return to work for another few days. Perhaps I sensed in the depths of my subconscious mind that once I got stuck neck-high into the hustle and bustle of city life, work, family and home responsibilities and regressed to old thinking habits, I would be right back at The Drop Off zone in a short space of time. Perhaps that suspicion was a knowing or an intuition that we are all born with but have allowed to fade into a forgotten world where we got lost listening to other people's instructions and dictations instead. When we repeatedly ignore that intuition, gut feeling or higher-self signal, it will find many ways to abruptly remind us of who we really are.

On the 31st May 2018, just nine months after the Indlela pilgrimage planted the seed, I was forced to pass through the most painful, pitch black and shameful birthing canal imaginable. I had my Dark Night of the Soul on this day.

I had no idea this 'existential crisis' was even a thing. I may have bunked that particular lecture at medical school, but I know it is not even mentioned in this day and age of 'modern' medical teachings. How would the Anatomy Professor teach about the Understanding Amidst the Absence of Meaning? One clue lies in the pineal gland of the brain, but I would have most definitely been oblivious to this concept at the time, even if he had tried.

I was soon back in the rut of school runs, work demands, sickness, misery, mundane domestic responsibilities, and social expectations, and the freedom to be me had evaporated after the first month of being back in Johannesburg. To add to the pressure cooker, our family trio had made the unanimous ethical decision to adopt a vegan lifestyle after binge-watching a series of documentaries on the atrocious handling, cruel slaughtering and unhealthy breeding of en-masse commercially farmed animals. Growing up as a 'pork-'n-cheese' kind of girl, the Portuguese culture has one of the most carnivorous diets in the world, with every animal body part and blood used for some or other dishes.

From one day to the next, we decided we no longer wished to partake in that kind of unhealthy consumerism, but then I had no idea what to feed my family, including a thirteen-year-old daughter who did not eat fruit or vegetables. So, I devoured as much nutritional and culinary information as possible, and I experimented endlessly in the kitchen, often with many unpalatable creations that not even the dogs would eat (okay, so Labradors do eat everything). I was petrified that I would become known as the first 21st century doctor to admit her family to the hospital for severe malnourishment and nutritional deficiencies.

Of course, one can live a perfectly healthy life and often a far more nourished one on a plant-based diet (we are all still alive and well). But in my initial ignorance, I enrolled at the NY Cornell University for an online Nutritional Studies Course which added to my study and work-load for the subsequent twelve weeks.

Soon after that, I had regressed to feeling exhausted, drained, angry and hopeless all over again. All the fences and masks were up in full-thickness resistance, and the pressure cooker was ready to explode.

That fateful Thursday in May was the worst and best day of my life.

It poured with rain all day long. It was an ice-cold, grey and wet winter's day in the city. I was late in dropping off my daughter at school and so arrived even later for work, just as my phone rang, reminding me that I had forgotten to pick up Lara's friend this morning. I was meant to have given her a lift to school too, so I rushed back to collect her, drop her off at school and arrived again at work to a waiting room full of patients. It was a difficult day filled with the appeasing of a terminally ill patient, vomiting babies, obnoxious brats with equally undisciplined parents. I listened to complaining geriatrics, a phone that would not stop ringing, a doorbell that would not stop buzzing, a man with extremely offensive body odour I could not stand, and the overwhelming urge to tell the whole world to fuck off again.

I rushed through the afternoon without eating to be on time to pick up the two girls from school. Just as I turned off into the one-way street leading up to the school, I hit a massive pothole hidden under a pool of water, and an instant loud bang almost had me popping a haemorrhoid. Realizing I was not shot, I was more disappointed with the hissing of my right front tyre that had burst on impact. I brought the car to a stall on the side pavement. I looked for an umbrella in the back foot-well to venture outside for damage assessment, but there wasn't one. Lara had seen or heard my car and came asking for money to get a hot chocolate from the tuckshop. Her friend was nowhere to be seen, so I sent her back into the school grounds to look for her and forget the damned hot chocolate. She also wanted an umbrella, but I said there wasn't one in the car.

With no other option, I opened the boot of the car and hauled out the spare tyre and jack. I could not find the key that released the wheel mag. I climbed back into the car and phoned my husband. Having found the key to remove the wheel mag, I then proceeded to huff and puff with a ratchet in hand to loosen the wheel nuts in vain. They were screwed on tighter than my arse. I tried standing and jumping on the ratchet, a crazed woman putting on a show in front of the whole school at peak hour, where not one single person stopped to buy a circus ticket nor offer to help.

Lara had returned by now, drenched and cold, informing me that her friend already had another lift home. We weren't going anywhere if I could not change the tyre. I asked Lara to phone her dad again. He said he was too far away at work to come but would get a tow truck to come to help us. The two of them continued with the conversation. Drenched, frozen, manic, and trying to deter visions of my child and me in hospital with pneumonia, I made a last attempt to loosen the wheel nuts. I could not see through my water flecked glasses, and my hands were chilled beyond sensation. I crouched down with multiple jerking efforts as my jersey lifted and exposed my butt crack. Ice cold rain trickled down my underpants as the first nut began to turn. As I got up to catch my breath, I smacked my head up against the side mirror with such force that in one single moment of complete and utter exasperation, I lost all sense and sensibility.

The only thing my body and mind instinctively succumbed to was to clutch my head and grab my hair with both fists so tight I could rip the skin off my skull in a swift scalping motion. I began to scream, scream and scream some more until there was no air left in my lungs.

I remember climbing back into the car, dropping my face into my hands and sobbing uncontrollably in deep anguish until my body was left completely spent.

I am not sure at what point Lara slipped beside me into the passenger seat, her side profile tentative and shocked at finally seeing her mother cry.

She was still holding onto my phone. She whispered nervously, "Dad, I think mom is having a mental breakdown."

I don't know how I changed the tyre, nor how I drove home. I just remember feeling totally deflated, remorseful and destitute. I was so ashamed to have behaved in that manner in front of my daughter. That was the worst thing I thought I could do in her eyes – lose all self-restraint, and allow her to bear witness to my weaknesses.

And this was finally my WHY. The reason I decided to choose differently.

It is interesting that we humans have to touch the rock at the bottom of the ocean regardless of how out of breath we are before deciding to swim up for air. I do not know another animal that punishes itself in the same manner - a fascinating evolutionary trait. We only stop smoking after we nearly die from the first heart attack. We change eating habits or start exercising after recovering from a dreaded disease, or we only reconcile with estranged family members when one of them is terminally ill.

I thought the walk of shame at The Drop Off zone was my turning point or that time-out on a soul-searching hike would switch the rail tracks for me, but it wasn't then. It was, in fact, a complete mental breakdown in front of my precious child that had me phoning my sister for a new direction.

The following morning, I woke up with the one and only severe migraine I have ever had in my life. There was no life left in my muscles to get out of bed, and the pain behind my eyes was worse than any blister I had walked through. I called my receptionist and advised her I would not be coming in to work, this being the third time I have ever done so – once when I got Swine Flu, the other when my mother-in-law was on her deathbed.

I dialled my sister's number and finally surrendered, "Ok, I am ready. I need help."

This was my epiphany! The will and choice to surrender and accept that my ego is no longer in control and that my soul needs to get back into the driver's seat. Of course, it initially felt like I had failed or was giving up, but surrender is quite the opposite. It is indeed a strength and a learnt art of allowing my higher self or soul to take over the reins and point me towards the path of ultimate redemption, forgiveness and self-love. It is giving in to the part of me that is directly connected to the Divine Source and the perfect GPS to direct me towards the destination of my desires whilst guiding me through the necessary painful transfiguration. It is the acceptance that I did not know how this process would happen or where it would take me, or who would help me. But that I was *willing* to surrender to a blind trust in a Divine Universal Intelligence, to believe fervently in an unseen Faith that produces miracles, and to take the next step in the complete opposite direction to the one I had been on thus far.

One week later, I was sitting at the psychologist's office, feeling pathetic and at my most vulnerable and most desperate. I suppose that is how newborn babies feel the moment they are extruded from a warm, cramped and comfortable womb, only to bear their all and be at the mercy of those who will be nurturing their soul back to a new life. Crying and screaming is clearly a necessary part of the process. If not, the doctor will slap your back hard and repeatedly until you wail the breath-holding blue out of your body.

I did not appreciate this at the time. I could not fathom how I had come to this point of being in front of a therapist. Shit like this was not meant for me. It was meant for patients and other people who could not see the truth of their circumstances. How humiliating and humbling to now be in this position.

Hypocratic Oaths

When my daughter was born, I bought a book that became my bible in the rearing of my offspring. "How to Talk so Kids will Listen & How to Listen so Kids will Talk" was voted the winner of the Best Parenting book by UK's Mumsnet. I either got landed with the easiest kid in the world, or their formulas and advice were like magic. I secretly believed I was Supermom, with the cardinal rule being: "There will be no lying, ever". It worked most of the time. No matter what age she was, my child was always told the truth. If we did not want her to touch other people's kitchen cupboards, we would not tell her there were monsters in them. When the dog needed to be put down, she came with to hold her pet as the vet took Daisy out of her misery. When she wanted to know what an Adult Entertainment Shop was, we told her that is where adults go to buy things they use for mating (it was the best I could muster as she had been watching lions mate at the Kruger Park since she was two years old). I had the kind of child that if you explained the truth, the reasons why she could or couldn't do or have something or go somewhere, she graciously accepted them with complete trust in our guidance. That was the primary purpose of not lying to her so that she would trust us without question. Perhaps I needed her to trust me without any doubt. After failing my husband and losing his trust, I did not wish to ever fail my daughter. This was a great plan, and I thought I was in total control of it.

Yet, here I was, sheepishly confessing to another professional stranger that I did not know why I was here, I did not know what to do with my broken self, but I desperately needed his help. Near the end of the hour with him, and just when I thought this was a waste of time, Dr Carl asked me where I felt the darkness and the despair in my body.

I said, "In my chest". The tuberculous cough had returned, and I thought it was my usual winter bronchitis.

"Close your eyes, put both your hands on your chest and take three deep breaths," he encouraged.

Oh my God, really? I did as I was told.

"Now feel the darkness, feel the despair, focus on your pain and feel it deep in your chest, Gisela."

I started to cry, tears slowly streaming down my cheeks. I had no way of wiping them, as I was instructed to keep clutching at my chest. The quivering lips and runny nose added to my embarrassment, as I hated crying in front of other people. I started to hate him too, thinking, what kind of psychologist is this idiot making me marinate in my anguish and detest for myself? Did he want me to go home and slice my wrists?

He remained quiet for a while and simply allowed me to be. I am not sure for how long, but when I could no longer stand to feel any more torment, Dr Carl said, "What is the first thought that comes to you?"

"I want to kill you," was the immediate one.

Then he added, "Now say THANK YOU."

An Understanding slowly and steadily dawned upon me.

Another minor victory of an epiphany, only I was oblivious that it was one at that moment.

I was not required to inform him of my revelation. I only needed to sit in the awareness of my newfound realization and become even more disappointed at the one word that echoed in my head: *Dishonesty*.

It took another second to sink into the fact that I had been the biggest liar of all time. I had been lying to my daughter her whole life, without consciously meaning to and with supposed good intention.

By pretending to be Superwoman, I had lied to my child. By pretending that I was unaffected by poverty, injustice, hardships, and crime, I had lied to her. By trying so hard to look happy all the time, I had lied to her. By slaving away at work and home, I had lied to her about what we are worthy of. By never crying nor showing my true emotions in front of her,

I had lied to her. By not speaking my inner truth, by not standing up for what I believed in, by omitting to say and act upon what the heart was feeling, by unquestionably following social, cultural and religious indoctrinations, I had lied to my child. I had lied to myself, my family, and to every person I knew.

The 'Stone of Truth' had finally completed its whole purpose and journey, even though I thought I had already laid it to rest.

For someone who hates unfairness, dishonesty, injustice and corruption, the cognizance that I had been the biggest fraud of all felt worse than a knife through the back.

But it was also the beginning of the healing.

We are all connected to the Divine Source, through our higher-self, our soul. We are all miracle extensions of God. The truth lies plain to see when we put the ego to one side, quieten the noise of the mind and reach for that divine connection and guidance. When that happens, the fog clears, the veils lift one by one, and the awareness holds us through the transformation and brings us closer to deliverance.

This is the true meaning of Integrity – to integrate my outer self with my inner self so that I can live without the masks.

Becoming aware, choosing to shift, choosing to forgive me and forgive others once I have appreciated the lessons learnt is the new beginning. The middle is long and adventurous, and there is no end. When you think you have reached the end at the close of your physical life, you continue the journey in another lifetime.

So, the unveiling of my Truth continues to this day. It requires the constant unlearning of false pre-conditions to make space for new belief systems that are working for me and not against me. It is a never-ending journey that I have *chosen*. It has allowed me to meet extraordinary friends and healers, experience weightlessness, learn exponentially, feel inspired and creative, feel joy, and be cradled in a safe space whilst I painfully peel and expose each layer of false indoctrination amidst soul families supporting and encouraging me to spread my wings as I transform into better and more beautiful versions of myself.

I have read countless self-help books, including the long-awaited 'You Can Heal your Life' by Louise Hay. I have attended workshops and seminars, participated in Theta-healing courses, sound meditations, listened to hundreds of podcast and YouTube videos of great masters and sages, opened myself to alternate and holistic therapies and new habits, and have discovered a world that is alive with wonder, hope, peace and unconditional love.

The pilgrimage is never complete, but I have been gifted with the choice of walking it, and the walk becomes more magnificent and rewarding as my soles discover new ground and find new footing towards my inner soul.

My daughter was the reason I stayed and didn't jump off 'The Drop Off'. But she cannot be the reason that I live for. I cannot put that burden on her, nor is it her responsibility to ensure my livelihood or happiness. I am the sole provider of that joy and self-realization. I wish for her to find her own truth and not take on the role of rescuer. I wish for her to see that normal human emotion ranges from fear, anger, guilt and pain, all the way to the other spectrum of kindness, compassion, gratitude, joy and love. The feelings that don't feel good are as normal as the ones that do. We have just been taught to reject them or 'feel bad' when we feel bad. Those mislabeled 'negative' feelings are simply the contrast or reference points of where we are in our journey of becoming.

We get stuck or suffer mental and physical dis-ease when we cannot move beyond them. But when we acknowledge them and pause to reflect on what they are showing us, we can overcome and move through the hurt to a place of self-realization and an understanding that we are all deserving of all that is abundant, joyful and love-filled. It is our birth right.

I know I am heading in the right direction when my now seventeen-year-old teenager still randomly comes to sit on my lap (her weight and height equal to mine), when she places her arms around my neck and tries to snuggle her head into my chest, imagining to be a toddler again. I take in the smell of her hair and relish in the warmth of her body. I cannot help but smile and surrender every time to the miracle and magnificence of this Divine Creation that has blessed my life so completely.

I know I am doing right by her when she closes her eyes and whispers tenderly for no one else to hear but me, "I love you, *Mita*."

EPILOGUE

The Truth

Three years ago, I attended my first Theta-healing workshop. The dark clouds still weighed heavily upon me then, although I had already started psychotherapy.

As part of the introduction to the world of Energy and the understanding that *everything* visible and invisible is energy (just at different vibrations, frequencies and densities), the workshop teacher showed us a demonstration of what she meant. Our conscious and subconscious thoughts are energy too. Each thought triggers an emotion or sensation that travels as a vibration along neural pathways to communicate and command our cells into action. How our cells respond to that energetic vibration is how we perceive physical and mental wellbeing or dis-ease.

Also, not only do our thoughts create feelings and sensations, they can interfere with another person's energetic or electromagnetic field. That is how well connected we all are – people, animals, plants, the Earth.

A volunteer was required to stand in front of the whole class, with his one arm stretched out to shoulder height. His strength was tested as the teacher tried to push down on his arm, which he resisted upwards against her force. He was then asked to close his eyes and turn his back towards us, whilst the rest of the class was required to think of unhappy or unpleasant thoughts as a group effort and direct them silently towards the guinea pig. The victim did not know what we were doing, as it was intended not to influence his behavioural response. When his arm strength was tested again, his arm slumped to his side with very little force applied. His energy field had diminished.

The exercise was repeated, but this time the class was required to think happy, joyful thoughts and quietly direct them again at the volunteer. This lighter and higher vibrational frequency took longer to achieve, as the teacher is intuitive and clairaudient, so she could feel how long it took us all to think happy thoughts. When she was satisfied that we had sent the victim enough good vibes, his arm strength was tested again, and no amount of force she applied could get his arm to budge from a 90 degree outward salute. He stood firm and resilient. The student was oblivious and wanted to know what had just happened.

When I was required to think of happy thoughts, I searched every memory in every corner of my mind, and all I could come up with was the joy of the day in which you were born, my precious child. The instant I looked at your sweet, perfect face, baby browns, pitch-black hair and rosy pouty lips was the moment I fell in love with you and when my heart knew the feeling of unmeasurable elation.

Of course, I have been in love before, but this was new, different. This was indescribably magnetic, deeply soulful, and it held incomparable awe and adoration for the miracle that lay in my arms. It was inconceivable that such an angelic creature could gloriously come into existence and bless my life and that such a Light could now be mine.

Every time I am asked to do this exercise or when the grey clouds threaten to hover over again, this memory invigorates my soul with fresh air and illuminates the dim path ahead.

But, I am aware that you are not mine, sweet Lara.

I am simply your temporary custodian because you have been born with free will, as every other child and adult have been. You have come with your own soul contracts, and you have your journey to fulfil. All I am required to do is hold you within safe boundaries whilst you play, experiment, choose, decide and feast on the marrow of infinite possibilities that life has to offer. I cannot always prevent you from falling and scraping your knee, nor can I prevent you from feeling the pain of disappointment or a broken heart. But I can hold you, embrace you, comfort you and love you, irrespective of the choices you make. Because no choice you can make is 'bad', it is simply the only way to wander, to discover and climb to the summit of your greatest wishes and desires.

You will only know the sweetness of life if you can compare it to the bitter. You will only know the joy, exhilaration and wonder of life when sadness and apathy threaten to blow you over. May you always find a way to ground yourself safely and steadily, or ask for help and guidance until the storms pass and the sun shines upon you once more.

I do not have all the answers, and I often think I get it all 'wrong'. I now know there is no such thing as wrong, as all our experiences are simply opportunities to grow and move towards a life of our dreams, of our choosing and accord. I did not want you to make the same 'mistakes' as I did, but I am not in control of your personal journey. And I know you chose me – for my strengths and my weaknesses, for my virtues and my vices. So, I have come to believe that I am already the perfect mother for you, and all I can do is support your choices, help you lighten your load and carry your worries when you ask me to and love you without judgement.

I hope that my experiences show you a way of travelling through life with more simplicity, resilience, hope and the awareness that you are the master of your Creation called life and your own personal reality, regardless of other people's beliefs or critique. And when you are tired or at a loss for answers, I trust you will know to rest, press the pause button, reach out for assistance and get off the speed train for a while. Everything in life also has its seasons. There is no race, and you cannot get disqualified – you are an eternal being having a temporary physical experience, so you cannot get it all done and cannot get it all right. There is no such thing. The aim of the game is for you to find a way back into love. That is it. There is no one holding a stopwatch or a whistle. All that is required is for you to fall in love with yourself in the awareness that you are a divine miracle and part of the Oneness while remembering to have fun along the way. When you remember this, you will instinctively know to consider and care for others and the All That Is with the same acceptance. That is the only purpose of this life's game for which we all return to play over and over again.

I wish for our dreams to flow in parallel, for our journeys to criss-cross time and time again, so that we can evolve, live, love and laugh independently and together.

I am deeply thankful for you. That you have chosen me to be your mother has been the grandest and most precious gift I have ever received. I accept it willingly, and it is an honour, a privilege, and an absolute pleasure to have been joined with you on this *jol*.

Even though I now know that I am not responsible for your happiness and you are not responsible for mine, you are still my most outstanding teacher and wise master. Every day you live, you provide me with the opportunities to choose magical fascination and amazement, grace and excitement, and wholeness I did not know existed. You have made me feel like the most beautiful and priceless woman in the world. You have me imagining that I hold a secret treasure that no one else has access to.

You have me in awe of your perfect human imperfection and vibrant glow. You have me believing, hoping, smiling, and alive. Thank you, my angel.

You have shown me who God is.

God is unconditional love. We are all a spark of God and are born with that divinity, worthiness and incredible joy already. I pray for you to know a God that loves you just as **WHO** you are, and not for what you do; that you believe in a God that has created you perfectly from the moment you were conceived, no matter which gravel roads or glitter runways you take. May you experience a God that rejoices every valley you wade through and every peak that you conquer, One that celebrates your every blister and every crown. May you always see, feel and know that this Divine Cosmic Universe lives through you and IS you and cannot exist without you. And therein lies your power – it is already yours.

May you live a life entranced in mystery, wonder, magnificence and abundance.

For the few moments in your life when you forget who you are, and you will, I will be there - loving you wholeheartedly and unconditionally for as long as I live this life.

This is not just a promise. It is my Truth.

APPENDIX

bakkie - a pickup truck

biltong - lean meat which is salted and dried in strips

bobotie - a South African dish of curried minced meat baked with a rich, savoury custard

boerewors - a South African sausage containing spices, usually made of beef and pork

boma - (in eastern and southern Africa) an enclosure or stockade

braai - grill (meat) over an open fire

broodjies - sandwiches in Afrikaans

bundus - a largely uninhabited wild region far from towns

compos mentis - having complete control of one's mind

dagga boy - a large Buffalo bull

dassie - Rock Hyrax mammal

APPENDIX

dit was nou 'n lekker boskak - now that was a good bush-dump

dorpies - small villages

droëwors - traditional dry sausage

hullo julle - hello guys

jol - an occasion of celebration and enjoyment

julle – you (plural)

knobkerrie - a short, heavy wooden club with a knob on one end

Kom Nader - Come Closer

kombi - a minibus

mahala - for free in Zulu

mana - sister in Portuguese

marido - husband in Portuguese

mielies - sweetcorn

moerkoffie - strong ground-coffee

Muito obrigado - Portuguese for many thanks

muti - African herbal medicines

naartjies - tangerines

NG Kerk - Dutch Reformed Church

Oom - a title of respect used to refer to an older man (Uncle)

padkos - snacks and provisions for a journey

padstal - a road-side shop or stall

pap 'n wors - maize meal or porridge and traditional sausage

APPENDIX

piesangs - bananas

pomp 'n blaas - pump and blow

poopdrol - animal poop pellets

poopdrolspoegkompetisie - poop pellet spitting competition

rooikat - a Caracal (lynx)

roosterkoek - leavened or unleavened bread-rolls baked on a grid-iron over a fire

roulades - a sweet or savoury dish of filled rolled meat or pastry

shebeen - an informal licensed drinking place in a township

sloot - a ditch

spazas - small shops in a South African township that often operate from someone's house.

spoor - animal tracks or foot-prints

stoep - a partly enclosed patio or veranda

Tannie - a title of respect used to refer to an elderly woman (Auntie)

tissue – paper handkerchief

umlungu - Zulu word for white persons

veld - open, uncultivated country or grassland in southern Africa

veldskool - the equivalent of summer camp for young children

ACKNOWLEDGMENTS

This book would not be possible without my beautiful and precious parents. They were the first to love me into being, and so began my journey toward the ultimate enjoyment of this miracle called life. Thank you for your never-ending devotion. I am honoured to have you as my role models and my first superheroes. To my sister, who chose to come to play with me during this lifetime, you 'get me'. I adore you and thank you for being my wisest counsel. To my family and friends, I thank you for your love, comforting company and unfailing support. You are all priceless.

I am so grateful for Toast Coetzer's travel article in the April 2017 issue of the *Go!* Magazine; he turned the page for me and gave way to a new chapter in my life. I am privileged to have met George Euvrard; thank you for your guidance, wisdom and direction, and thank you for leading many-a-pilgrim towards the Light. Sincere gratitude to all my fellow Indlela pilgrims, their stories and their company. You have helped me more than you know, and I wish for your souls to always feel at peace.

To all the patients who have ever fallen under the care of my hands, I thank you all for the lessons that taught me to become a better version of myself, and I ask for your forgiveness for any offence or omission from my ego-self. I am honoured to be your doctor. To all the doctors, colleagues and front-line warriors that I have had the privilege of working with, thank you for all you do for others, for our camaraderie, your assistance and the crazy-sane sense of humour.

To every child I have ever met, I love your purity, your trust, your honesty and your wonderful sense of fun and imagination. You remind me every day of what needs to be unlearnt. To every teacher, preacher and healer that I have encountered, I am grateful for every piece of the puzzle that is shaping me back to my true self. This cocooning out of the real me is made possible with the divine guidance of a great many masters that have come before me. I am so pleased to have access to and read new truths from enlightened souls such as Louise Hay, Dr Brian Weiss, Anita Moorjani, Dr Wayne Dyer, Dr Joe Dispenza, Dr Bruce Lipton, Abraham Hicks, Neale Donald Walsch, Mike Dooley, Marianne Williamson, Dr Caroline Myss, Dr Thomas Campbell, Vianna Stibal, and many other spiritually awakened heroes whose books now line my shelves. I know there are countless others out there awaiting my discovery. I am deeply thankful to the enlightened souls whom I have personally met and allowed to reach deep into my core to restore my faith in humankind and life in general – Sonia Nel *aka* Nianell, Dr Ian Opperman, and Jan Gazzard. I receive your magical healing, wisdom and unique gifts with awe and gratitude. Layla Walters and Phoenix Walters, thank you for being the first to show me out of the dark and helping me to believe there is nothing to fear, ever.

To all the soul family members that I have met on self-improvement workshops, courses and seminars, I thank you for providing me with a safe space for my confessions and evolution. You are teaching me benevolence and trust.

To the editor of this manuscript, Louise Stokes, I am deeply thankful that you undertook this daunting task and perfected the essence of my words. I feel privileged to have been your first, and I feel honoured that you were mine. Robert Harris, a big thank you for the cover photographs, which came naturally to you but required resilience and dedication following an unexpected turn of events. To the very gifted Monique Bailey for the cover art design, I cannot express in words my emotion when I saw your magical creation and knew you were an angel in my head and heart; I am deeply grateful. Thank you Phillipa Mitchell for your free-spirited guidance, unwavering diligence, and relentless advice. Along with Gregg Davies' patience and earnest typesetting, you have launched this manuscript into cyberspace and unleashed a dream of mine into reality. Thank you to Michael White who was equally accommodating and helpful in printing the hardcopies, so I could hold this gift in my hands. There are a thousand and one other people out there who provide me with a considerable amount of support and entertainment, and facilitate my pleasure on this planet. Some know it, and others are oblivious to my existence – I thank every musician, artist, author, entrepreneur, innovator, scientist, designer and entertainer, hairdresser, beautician, chef, farmer, waiter, petrol attendant, municipal and utility worker, miner, teller, shop owner, public service staff member, my lawyer, accountant, gardener and domestic helper. To every receptionist that has endured my bipolarity, I am sincerely grateful for your support, tolerance and gatekeeping.

I thank every animal on this planet - they exist as angels in disguise. To every creature that has sacrificed their life in the name of science, technology, medicine and the advancement of civilization, I am humbly grateful.

Most of all, I am deeply grateful to the love of my life; *marido*. You are my lighthouse for the countless times I have been lost at sea, and you are my rock when I am anchoring others. Thank you for staying, for riding the waves with me, and thank you for a deep, sincere love that has no measure. I would not have it any other way, as we both take less for granted on our adventurous gypsy trails and can knowingly smile through all of life's wonder. To my precious daughter, your mere existence is my sun, moon, rainbow and every magical colour that illuminates my life. Thank you, angels.

To every lovely person reading this book, I thank you for your contribution. A portion of the proceeds of this book is donated to various animal welfares and charities. May I recommend that you don't loan out your book, but instead, gift your friends and family with a copy of their own. *Muito Obrigado.*

ABOUT THE AUTHOR

Dr Gisela de Oliveira Esteves graduated from the University of the Witwatersrand as a medical doctor in 1996. She completed her internship at the Chris Hani Baragwanath Hospital, followed by one year as a medical officer in the Department of Paediatrics at the Charlotte Maxeke Johannesburg Hospital. For years, she then worked as a casualty officer at various trauma and emergency departments. Her passion for flying, coupled with a favourable opportunity, allowed her to join the *STAR* helicopter rescue flight team. She later joined the *International SOS* group of flight doctors on rescue medical evacuations throughout sub-Saharan Africa. In 2008, she joined a general medical group practice and, in 2015, ventured on her own. She is currently working as a GP in private practice, taking time out to travel and write. She lives in Johannesburg with her husband, young daughter, and three Labradors.

www.ingramcontent.com/pod-product-compliance
Lightning Source LLC
Chambersburg PA
CBHW022042290426
44109CB00014B/953